IMPROVING HUMAN SETTLEMENTS

The authors of the articles in this volume are from both developed and developing nations and are all actively engaged in their respective countries in determining how best to cope with the problems of rapid population growth and widespread urbanization. The papers range from discussions of overcrowding in India and other areas of extremely dense population, of the effect of settlement on previously sparsely populated areas such as Canada's north and the tendency even in such environments for the population to concentrate in urban centres rather than remain scattered in smaller communities, to a discussion of the ethical and moral principles that must govern our response to accelerating population growth in order that mankind survive.

Among the contributors are such well-known authorities as Joan Robinson, who examines China's human settlements policies; and Richard Llewelyn-Davies, who considers how architects and planners affect human settlements. As Barbara Ward remarks in her paper, mankind is now at a point where it must realize that there are outer limits to the world's resources, that temporary or local solutions are inadequate, and that what is needed is global responsibility and control of resources. No one concerned about the future of this planet can afford to disregard the observations and warnings made in this book.

These papers were presented at the University of British Columbia between February and May 1976 in preparation for the U.N. Conference on Human Settlements: Habitat '76.

H. Peter Oberlander is professor of regional planning and director of the recently established Centre for Human Settlements at the University of British Columbia.

IMPROVING HUMAN SETTLEMENTS

— UP WITH PEOPLE —

Edited by

H. Peter Oberlander

A series of lectures delivered at the University of British Columbia in preparation for the United Nations Conference on Human Settlements: Habitat '76.

UNIVERSITY OF BRITISH COLUMBIA PRESS
VANCOUVER

IMPROVING HUMAN SETTLEMENTS: Up With People

Canadian Cataloguing in Publication Data

Main entry under title:
Improving human settlements

"Some special lectures and seminars
held at the University of British Columbia
during the first few months of 1976."
ISBN 0-7748-0064-X

1. Anthropo-geography—Addresses,
essays, lectures. I. Oberlander, H.
Peter, 1922-
GF101.I469   301.29   C76-016076-7

International Standard Book Number 0-7748-0064-X

Printed in Canada

Contents

Photo Credits

Cover

Illustrations

following page 42

following page 138

Preface

This book is a record of some special lectures and seminars held at the University of British Columbia during the first few months of 1976. The series was arranged for three specific purposes: to provide an overview of the conditions and circumstances of human settlements, as seen by those concerned with improving living and working in settlements across the world; to illuminate, by choice of topics and choice of speakers, world-wide issues of urbanization and the search for comparable solutions; and to achieve a focus in Vancouver for a discussion of the substantive content of the anticipated United Nations Conference on Human Settlements: Habitat '76.

It was the third of these three objectives that provided the immediate impetus for the timing of the lectures. During the latter part of 1975 it became apparent that the extensive preparations for the United Nations Conference were not achieving some of the desired results, particularly in Vancouver, the site of the Conference. Growing numbers of people were concerned with the increasing politicization of the U.N. Conference under the influence of debate in the U.N. General Assembly and events at other U.N. conferences. It seemed urgent to develop a method and a forum for refocussing public attention on the substantive content of the Conference, and to establish realistic hopes and expectations for a successful meeting. It was particularly important to highlight the technical and professional concerns of those who had originally initiated the Conference, and to begin a public dialogue in Vancouver on the various themes of the Conference and the emphasis it would give to realistic and practical solutions for pressing urban problems. The University of British Columbia, through its President's Committee on Habitat '76, was privileged to accept the responsibility for launching a series of lectures and seminars to take place in the period January to May 1976 on selected topics within the generic concern for human settlements. The President's Committee persuaded a series of academically distinguished speakers with international experience to come to Vancouver, usually for a three-day visit, so as to enable them to present their ideas to a public forum and, in addition, to participate in seminars with a professional or academic audience of teachers and students.

The United Nations Conference on Human Settlements (Habitat '76) must be seen in the continuing sequence of special U.N. conferences that started with the 1972 Stockholm Conference dealing with the natural environment, continued through conferences on food (Rome), population (Bucharest), women's rights (Mexico), and which, next year, will deal with water (in Argentina). The Stockholm Conference focussed the attention of the world on the fragile and precious natural environment and on mankind's obligations to conserve it. It is people in their use of nature and its resources who create the impact that results in pollution or the destruction of resources. In other words, land, water, and air are neither good nor bad; it is our use of these resources that gives rise to concern and reassessment. In addition, it was clear from the Stockholm Conference that man by himself, or in small groups, readily makes his peace with nature and that nature, being exceedingly resilient, can cope with man's demands upon her resources. It is when people live in large groups or at high densities that the questions of limits to human use of the natural environment become crucial. Stockholm demonstrated that it was urban man — man in high density, using space at high intensity — who was the source of a growing disequilibrium in nature and whose activities ought to be the subject of a future U.N. Conference.

The outcome of this recognition at Stockholm was the agreement by the United Nations in 1972 to accept an offer from Canada to host a conference on human settlements and to provide a forum which would examine at least three fundamental areas: mankind's need to husband space and resources in the context of exploding demand upon them; man's ability to devise solutions to an expanding range of worldwide settlement problems; man's awareness of the interdependence and interactive relationship between the needs of people and their environment and the resulting urgent requirement for priorities in the allocation of resources in response to a variety of social, economic, and physical pressures.

The U.N. Conference on Human Settlements: Habitat '76 was a logical sequel to Stockholm, to Rome, to Bucharest, to Mexico City. It would provide a structure within which many of the previously examined special issues could now be integrated for governmental action and intergovernmental or international co-operation. Habitat '76 would emphasize the interdependence of man's use of resources and, therefore, the interactive solutions required. It would put the accent on solutions rather than merely be a renewed recitation of problems or a forecast of gloom and doom; and, finally, while remaining within the context of the United Nations' goals, it would urge national action as well as international co-operation. Clearly, while international co-operation is fundamental to dealing with global issues of urbanization and the interdependence of all settlements across the world, the nation state provides the only effective framework for action.

These basic considerations were in the minds of the Committee as it discussed topics and speakers. It was essential to invite speakers who were representative of different regions of the world and whose life experience and professional knowledge would cover the broad range of issues: the planning and development of human settlements; the social, economic, and political forces at work; and the changing values in the minds and hearts of men and women. Although time was limited, the Committee was fortunate in being able to persuade a unique group of specialists to come to Vancouver and present, within the general context of human settlement, their insights into community building in the developed as well as in the developing world, from Europe to North and South America, from Asia to Africa, in the Arctic and within China.

While each paper illuminates a broad range of concern for human settlements and an almost desperate search for relevant solutions, it is also clear that this worldwide search is beginning to develop analogous answers. Although speakers presented their topics in their own unique ways, the analyses and conclusions often reach answers which are surprisingly similar, regardless of locale or level of current development.

This coincidence of views encourages one to conclude that urbanization has become a global phenomenon and that certain solutions to urban problems, while not necessarily wholly transferable, can form the basis for effective solutions under comparable circumstances elsewhere. Issues of human settlements seem to have acquired a universal character; questions of scale or quality of urban life seem to be the same whether one deals with Africa or Asia or with countries under market economy or centrally planned conditions, notwithstanding the differences of geographic region or socio-economic history. The papers indicate the benefit to be derived from an exchange of experience and the need for many opportunities for such exchange.

While it is too early to assess the success or failure of the United Nations Conference itself, perhaps it is possible to indicate in terms of certain expectations how the Conference has fared and what contribution the papers made. There is growing agreement that in substantive terms the Conference was a success. A broad range of issues was discussed in the context of the sharp political realities of the member nations that attended the Conference, and in the full awareness of global interdependence so characteristic of urbanization. A well-structured agenda, based on extensive preparatory meetings, was thoroughly discussed, both during the official Conference and during the non-governmental meetings at the Habitat Forum.

An unparalleled amount of documentation is now available for detailed analysis by those concerned with informed action by governments or with knowledge and understanding in an academic or educational sense. The Conference passed more than six hundred substantive resolutions, most of them by consensus, dealing with specific points for national action and international co-operation. However, no Conference is better than the delegations that attend it and no international Conference is better than the degree of commitment permitted by each government to its delegation. It is therefore clear that the debate and blunt disagreement that marked certain discussions reflect the prevailing state of affairs in a world divided between the First World, the Second World, the Third World, and perhaps a Fourth World.

The United Nations and its specialized conferences are designed to encourage debate and exchange of experience. The U.N. is not a parliament capable of invoking binding decisions. It can discuss, consider, recommend, but each sovereign member nation must act on its own, within its own political framework. A good deal of popular frustration and cynicism with the U.N. conference process has its roots in the presumption that the U.N. can act like Parliament or Congress. This is not the case. In the company of cynics and sceptics it is hard to be optimistic, but the authors of the papers presented in this book are convincing in their positive and constructive views on the future of human settlements.

In summary, the Conference and its substantive discussion materially raised the world consciousness and sharpened the world conscience in the field of human settlements. There is no doubt that the preparation for the Conference, the Conference itself, and the promise of follow-up have gone a long way to make the issues of human settlements a visible and central concern of most governments and an area of growing commitment to international co-operation. Even the heat of political debate and disagreement merely indicated the importance the world finally has allocated to improving human settlements. Issues and concerns that are of minor importance tend to be discussed with equanimity and politeness; only issues that touch the essence of life and humanity's survival generate heat, outspoken debate, and violent disagreement. Consequently, even disagreements featured in the headlines can be counted as success for the Conference and its agenda by raising issues in the Council of the Nations that ten or fifteen years ago were ignored or judged to be only of academic interest. It may be significant to emphasize that points raised by a Barbara Ward or a Llewelyn-Davies in these pages have been raised throughout the world, by them and their colleagues, for the last twenty or thirty years in professional and technical terms. The nations, and in particular their governments, have now caught up with them. Only now is it possible to relate these issues and their solutions to social and political action and thereby ensure that human settlements will be improved through the action of governments and their agencies, which are able to rally resources and allocate them appropriately.

In this sense, perhaps, these lectures and seminars have played a small role in stimulating public debate in Vancouver. It is to be hoped that this publication will assist in developing a growing understanding of how human settlements work and how our local specific problems, wherever we may be, are comparable to the concerns of those people around the globe who live and work in densely built-up urban communities. It is also the hope of those who put these papers together that they reflect accurately the scope and flavour of current thought on human settlement issues; that they also foreshadow optimistically a commitment to solutions so that the future will be better than the past, and the settlements in which a growing proportion of the world's people exist will be worth living in.

I am deeply indebted to all authors for their contributions to this volume and for their patience with the editor. The detailed editorial work was superbly in the hands of Hilda Symonds, who, in her inimitable way, was able to match the elegance of spoken rhetoric with an expressive written prose.

PRESIDENT'S COMMITTEE ON HABITAT

Dr. H. Peter Oberlander, School of Community and Regional Planning: Chairman
Dr. John Collins, Department of Adult Education, Faculty of Education
Dr. Robert MacLeod, Director, School of Architecture
Dr. Michael Goldberg, Faculty of Commerce and Business Administration
Dr. Walter Hardwick, Director, Centre for Continuing Education (served until his appointment as Deputy Minister of Education, British Columbia, in January 1976)
Mr. Gerald Savory, Centre for Continuing Education

A series of public lectures and its publication was made possible by a grant from the federal government through the Canadian Habitat Secretariat. We acknowledge in particular Mr. J.W. MacNeill (Commissioner General) and Dr. Hugh Keenleyside (Associate Commissioner General, Canadian Habitat Secretariat) for their continuous support and guidance in this project. Central Mortgage and Housing Corporation through its Western Regional Director, Mr. King Ganong, contributed substantially to the publication of the papers.

The editor wishes to record his appreciation of the manifold contributions made by members of the President's Committee for Habitat '76, particularly by its indefatigible Secretary-Convener, Gerald Savory of the University of British Columbia's Centre for Continuing Education.

H. Peter Oberlander

Foreword

First of all, let us define what we mean by "human settlements," for this has been one of my first difficulties. For the layman, this term does not mean much, and each person tends to have his own idea about its interpretation. According to the definition used by the United Nations Human Settlements Conference, this term includes any place where human beings live permanently. It can be two or three isolated houses in a rural situation or it can be a village, a small city, or a huge metropolis like New York, Tokyo, or Calcutta. "Human settlements" is a very broad term. Also contrary to what many people seem to think, this is not going to be a housing conference, important as that aspect may be, because essentially the subject of human settlements relates to all that human beings need to live in one given place.

The origin of the conference was the June 1972 Environment Conference in Stockholm, whose secretary was Maurice Strong, a distinguished Canadian. One of the Environment Conference committees was on the subject of Human Settlements, and, as a result, one of the main recommendations from the Conference to the General Assembly of the United Nations was to convene a further world conference on their subject. In December 1973 the General Assembly approved a resolution convening a world conference on human settlements to be held in Vancouver from 31 May to 11 June 1976.

What were the main reasons why the Human Environment Conference recommended convening this separate conference and why did the countries sitting in the General Assembly accept this recommendation? First of all because human settlements and the human environment are like two faces of the same coin. As soon as you start having any kind of settlements, however small, you start changing the environment, for good or for bad. Wherever you have settlements, you change the air, the water, the soil. For this reason, human settlements are also called "manmade environments." You cannot have any policies in relation to the natural environment if you do not consider the manmade environment, and vice versa. In addition, it is also expected that in the next twenty-five to thirty years, man is going to have to construct as many new settlements — towns, villages, and cities — as are in existence right now. That will mean settlements for nearly four billion people.

Can we stop the population explosion that will require this massive building of human settlements? No, unfortunately. At least not during the next twenty-five to thirty years. Even if tomorrow everyone started having only the number of children necessary for biological replacement, the problem would still exist because we now have the children between one and twenty years of age who are going to start to reproduce. The pyramid is not going to peak until about the year 2000. In addition, life expectancy is increasing in the developing world. This trend is going to offset the gains that can be made by reducing the birth rate. I hope that in a few years we may see some signs that the population of the world will have begun to stabilize, and I also hope that we are going to have a sharp decrease in the birth rate of the world after twenty-five or thirty years. Nevertheless the fact is that even if we do have these changes, these next years will see the greatest increase in population in the world's history.

Bearing in mind that most countries are going to experience some decline in the birth rate during the next quarter century, the important thing is that the consequences of what we do in relation to human settlements will set the style of life for many generations. For example, if we permit a city of thirty million to be established, as will be the case in Mexico City if present trends continue, the consequences will be there for a very long time. The decisions that we make in this regard will not only affect us, and our children, but many future generations and even the future of the planet as a whole.

Another point that was raised in Stockholm and later in the General Assembly is that we are witnessing the most dramatic reversal in the nature of structures and settlement in the history of mankind. Until recently, let us say the beginning of this century, our planet was primarily a rural one. In 1900, less than twenty per cent of the population of the world lived in the cities. By the end of the century, we are going to have an urbanized planet, with sixty-five to seventy-five per cent of the population living in urban centres. This is an irreversible process. In some regions the shift is even more spectacular, as is the case of my region, Latin America. At the beginning of this century, less than five per cent of the population lived in the urban areas. By the end of the century, Latin America will be the most urbanized area in the world, more so than even North America and Europe.

Such massive urbanization will produce physical changes in settlements. It is already causing changes in the social, political, and economic life of the people, and beginning to force the creation of a new society. These are some of the reasons why the one hundred and thirty-eight countries sitting in the General Assembly decided to convene a world conference on human settlements. This is not *my* conference. This is not the conference of the United Nations Secretariat. This is a conference convened by all these countries to discuss the critical problems of human settlements and their possible solutions.

Habitat is not a conference of experts. The experts, at least in their professional capacity, are not invited. Rather, Habitat is a political conference, because by definition any United Nations conference is a political conference. Those invited to the conference are the governments, which I think is the right approach. What is needed to solve the problems of human settlements is not technical expertise or technical solutions. In most cases, the technology already exists. What is needed is political commitment at the international and national levels. This is the message that I have been trying to bring to countries all around the world. The other characteristic of Habitat is that we are not looking for an international treaty on human settlements. This will be the first time that a United Nations conference will focus primarily on recommendations for national action.

This is a delicate matter, because the sensitivities of the different countries must be taken into account even though most of the countries concerned have already made some attempts to deal with the kinds of problems that will be discussed at the conference. Until now, most countries have not had national policies to deal with human settlements. Neither Canada nor the United States has had such a policy. A comparison can be made between this situation and economic planning during World War II. Prior to World War II, economic planning had been very simple. At that time, only the U.S.S.R. had a national economic development plan. But World War II proved that one cannot leave the economic development of a country to the spontaneous market process. Plans are needed to make full use of resources. Now all countries around the world have plans, some of them very sophisticated plans, for economic development. It is hoped that one of the outcomes of Habitat will be to convince politicians and the public about the importance of having national "physical" human settlements plans. Until now, only the socialist countries have undertaken this kind of planning.

When one talks about a physical plan, one must talk about the distribution of the population within a country. A spontaneous process is usually chaotic. One cannot simply wait and see where people are going to settle and then suddenly discover that there is a city of ten million, with problems to be solved that have never been anticipated.

The Habitat conference cannot perform miracles. What it must do is to put in motion a lot of ideas and concepts which if acted upon will sooner or later produce positive results. For example, urban and suburban land speculation is not going to stop on 11 June. Economic groups with vested interests are quite powerful enough to delay socialization of the urban and suburban lands. But Habitat can raise the awareness of political leaders and of the general public in regard to such problems. And these are not just the problems of the mayor or of the city council. They are national problems. Social, economic, and political changes are not self-contained; they affect the entire human settlement.

Conversely, it is not the physical aspect of a city that is important, because the physical aspect is merely the physical representation of the social, political, and economic structure of that community. The problems of human settlements cannot be solved by constructing apartment buildings or super-highways. What has to be dealt with is the basic structure of society.

Enrique Peñalosa,
Secretary-General,
United Nations Conference
on Human Settlements

In 1975 the first meeting of the Preparatory Committee for Habitat was held in New York. This Committee was composed of fifty-six member countries of the United Nations elected by the General Assembly and their task was to pre-pare an agenda and the background documents for discussion in Vancouver. It was at that meeting that I was charged by my colleagues to chair their delib-erations and to guide the discussions that would lead us to an acceptable con-clusive agenda. This agenda was finalized at our August meeting (again in New York) and duly accepted by the General Assembly. It is a twelve-point agenda, but I will concentrate only on three or four points of it because this is where we expect the real action to take place. As Secretary-General Peñalosa has said, Habitat is going to be basically a political conference, not simply a technical conference. This is a point that we feel must be emphasized and we hope that the governments will get the message.

Most of the Vancouver conference will revolve around two committees. The way we envision the conference working is as follows: there will be a con-tinuous plenary session where the heads of delegations, who we hope will be mainly ministers of their governments, will be able to exchange general ideas from their own philosophies and from their own policies on human settle-ments, and try to find out what better situations can be created. Then there will be three committees. Committee One will deal mainly with the Declara-tion of Principles and international co-operation. Committees Two and Three will concentrate on the substantive issues, recommendations for na-tional action. Committee Two will deal with the more policy-oriented issues, and Committee Three will deal with the infrastructural and institutional aspects of the recommendations for national action.

In framing this agenda we have kept in mind that few governments have any integrated policies on human settlements. As the Secretary-General has indicated, since World War II various governments have seen the need for integrated economic development plans. Indeed most of our developing countries have adopted such plans, and in one way or another this action has paid dividends. However, at the same time, it has brought some side-effects which are not always desirable because so often we have tried to copy the economic structures that exist in the more developed parts of the world. In a way, this has been detrimental. It has also been false because the very premises are not the same. Instead of going in more for the kinds of values that would give real satisfaction to the greater community, we have taken the Gross National Product as our standard of development, which in the developing world is an unreal appraisal of progress.

We would like to see a change in policy, so that the economic philosophy is not the sole basis of the benefits that accrue to the citizens, but there is also emphasis on the psychological, social, and cultural aspects and satisfactions of the community. Thus, one of the major issues that we hope that governments will address themselves to is the need to decide on settlement policies and strategies that are not only economically oriented, but also socially integrated. At the very least we hope that some national outlook will develop and some prominence will be given to the question of human settlements in their entirety.

Human settlement planning is one of the other very important aspects that we will expect governments to address themselves to. By this we mean not simply concern about the location of a city, but the making of basic decisions as to whether to encourage growth of bigger metropoli and megalopoli or whether to encourage the growth of smaller urban centres as satellites to cities, or growth centres in rural areas, particularly in the developing countries. This, of course, will involve many other decisions: how to encourage investment, where to place industries, where to have food-growing areas, and what connections to make between one area and another. Human settlement planning is a very involved process which is going to touch on local politics, tribal boundaries, and so on. Such planning will require considerable political courage by governments. Even if we do not expect overnight changes to take place, we do hope at the very least that Habitat will be a launching ground for some very serious thought. We do hope that in the final analysis people will be able to continue this debate in their own countries and in due time get the right decisions made.

The provision of shelter infrastructure and services is another question related both to settlement planning and to the policies to be adopted. These matters will be discussed by Committee Two, where the agenda will be more policy-oriented, more philosophical. They are going to have to cut across the philosophies of governments, but we hope that by emphasizing that this is going to be a political conference, governments will have the courage to make the political decisions necessary to come to grips with the situation.

Committee Three will deal with some very sensitive issues, the first of which is land. The problem of land speculation has already been mentioned by Mr. Peñalosa. Many people have become millionaires through land speculation. You cannot talk about the provision of cheap or inexpensive housing for everyone unless you tackle the problem of land. If you are going to invest a thousand dollars per square foot for land, you cannot build a house that you can then rent for twenty dollars per month. There must be a solution to this problem. The land must be available at reasonable rates so that worthwhile dwellings for the people can be erected. As you can see, this is going to be a very sensitive issue, but one which must be tackled if there is to be any hope for the future.

Public participation is another issue to be tackled. The very people for whom these houses are being built are those who are the least consulted. We hope that in future the public will take a greater part in decisions regarding the types of dwellings they are going to have to live in. We also hope that the public will be able to play a role in the implementation of human settlements planning. In Kenya, for example, there is a system of self-help schemes. We hope that this sort of system can be integrated into the implementation of human settlements in other places.

There are many aspects of these issues, but let us focus here on the problem of slum areas. What are the minimum standards for a house? These are usually defined in city council by-laws and when their details are considered one realizes that some of them are very stupid. For example, Nairobi has adopted English standards, whereby you must have a roof six inches thick in order to support snow. Never have we had snow in Nairobi. But it is in terms of the improvement of slum areas where public participation can come in. Why should anybody be required to have a complete house, or no house at all? According to the building code, you either have a house which meets all the specifications, or else you have something which is not even recognized to be a shelter. The authorities will come and demolish it the following morning. Why can there not be a system where you can gradually improve a house, so that you have a completed one in a period of five years; so that you can have one permanent wall on one side in one year, and maybe after two years you will be able to afford to put another permanent wall on another side? Meanwhile, you can have cardboard around the rest of it. These are some of the things about which we feel there should be greater consideration.

Finally, the question of human institutions, of the management of human settlements, is another issue to which governments should address themselves. I have yet to see a city or a metropolis managed well. I would like to hear of one. If we have to build three times as many human settlements or urban centres in the next twenty-five years, what kind of management do we need? To train the right kind of managers, and to have the right kinds of institutions for human settlements is a matter with which we must deal very seriously in recommendations for national action.

The other very important aspect of the conference is the programme for international co-operation. We believe that the concern for human settlements is first and foremost a question for the given governments, the given municipalities, the given communities. This is where discussion of this matter must start, but, as well, the international machinery must be geared toward assisting local or national governments to implement resulting decisions. The requirements of loans and grants and bilateral agreements between governments should take into account the issues of human settlements. So we will be addressing ourselves to that question. We hope that we can persuade the World Bank to give even greater emphasis to the question of human settlements. Any project that is being funded should have an integrated aspect of human settlement as well.

Father George Muhoho,
Chairman,
United Nations Preparatory
Committee for the
Conference on Human
Settlements

EXCERPTS FROM DISCUSSION

Question: I would like to have some explanation of Habitat Forum.

Mr. Peñalosa: Because of the shortness of time, I did not mention the parallel conference, to which the Secretariat attaches great importance. For a political decision, you need two ingredients. One is the will of the political leadership, but what is even more important is the backing of public opinion. In many cases, a decision cannot be reached, even with the will of the leaders, because of the lack of support and backing by the public. As in Stockholm and Bucharest, we are hoping that the parallel conference will provide unofficial organizations, or an individual who does not agree with the official delegation, an opportunity to speak freely about the problems and solutions of human settlements and so influence the decisions of the official conference. A committee has organized Habitat Forum and this is going to be held at Jericho Beach and will be parallel to the official conference. In addition, there are also one hundred and fifty organizations that are going to be invited to attend the official conference as observers.

Question: I am very skeptical about the position of the Canadian government on this conference. I do not think that they are taking it very seriously.

Mr. Peñalosa: Let me speak frankly. In some ways I think that one of the problems that we need to overcome is the fact that the conference is being held, first of all, in Canada, and second, in Vancouver. Canada is a very affluent country, but it still has problems with human settlements; all your problems are not solved. Canada has two rôles to play in this conference. One is as the host country, because Canada can teach something, but I think also that Canada has a lot of things to learn from other experiences. But it is more difficult to raise interest in countries like Canada, or West Germany, or the United States, because, first of all, people in these countries assume that most of their problems are solved, or if they are not solved, that it is because the politicians do not want to solve them. They also think that they have nothing to learn from other experiences. As for Vancouver, it is one of the most beautiful cities in the world. I think that when the delegates come here, they may forget for a time the problems of the slums of Calcutta or Lima.

In another respect, we have been very lucky, because we have had the strong support of the Canadian government, which has been very co-operative during the preparatory process for the conference. I feel fortunate in this regard, because I think it would be difficult to find another country which would provide the support and co-operation that Canada has shown to the United Nations Secretariat. This is not mere flattery. I think that before the conference takes place interest will rise in Canada. Many Canadians are already aware that a United Nations conference on human settlements is to be held in Vancouver so interest is going to grow. I am optimistic that Habitat will be a great success and that it will be the largest conference ever held under the auspices of the United Nations. I think it will be a success not only for the international community, not only for the other countries attending the conference, but also for Canada and Canadians, and for future political decisions and public attitudes in relation to this subject.

Question: Is it not necessary to have physical demonstrations and exhibitions of things that work? Will there be any at Habitat Forum?

Mr. Peñalosa: At Habitat Forum that will be up to the organization or the individuals attending. I know that some intend to display some exhibits. But your point is a very opportune one because for the first time in the history of United Nations conferences, Habitat is going to use audio-visual presentations to help illustrate the documents and the presentations of the delegates. We have asked all the participating countries to bring to Vancouver films or slide presentations with their experiences, either negative or positive, in connection with human settlement. I think that this is going to be a unique and productive characteristic of this conference. The films are going to show that many solutions exist, that what is most needed is the political decision-making to implement them. Vancouver is going to be the end of the preparatory process and the starting point of the implementation process.

1

The Urban Quest for a Better Life*

Jean Gottmann

Vancouver has acquired a certain symbolical value around the world for people concerned with urban affairs in one way or another. There have been meetings I have attended that have been called "pre-Vancouver meetings," and I have been invited to others that already are called "post-Vancouver," although of course nobody infers Vancouver will have disappeared by then. It has been suggested that what happens at the Habitat conference may not be as important as the excitement generated by the fact that much discussion at the conference is going to take place on urban matters, on Habitat, on human settlements, before and after that conference. There is already arising something that I hope will be called "the spirit of Vancouver" in urban matters, just as some twenty-two years ago a much smaller conference (usually called "the conference on the summit in Geneva") created a certain excitement. I do not presume to foresee or forecast what that spirit may develop to be, but I wish to set before you what my understanding and my hopes are of what the concerns and guiding lines of the conference and that spirit of Vancouver might become.

"The Urban Quest for a Better Life" is, of course, a title inspired by a famous statement of Aristotle at the beginning of his *Politics* when he said (I believe he was quoting Herodotus) that cities were formed when people gathered together first for security, and that people remained in cities for the sake of a better life. So that the raison d'être of the city has apparently been for a number of millennia already, and still remains, the search for a good life. However, there has never been as massive and general a movement of people towards towns and cities, particularly very large cities, as in the last half century.

Because the growth of towns and cities is such a dominant phenomenon of

*Most of the material in this paper was presented at the Nagoya Habitat Conference, in Nagoya, Japan, March 1976, and was published in the report of the Conference entitled *Towards a Better Habitat for the 21st Century: Report, Nagoya Habitat Conference, Pre-Vancouver Meeting for the U.N. Conference on Human Settlements*, Edited by the Japan Society for Ekistics, Institute for Sociological Studies, Toyo University, Tokyo, Japan. This material is re-used here with the approval of the Japanese authorities concerned.

our time, that trend displaces large numbers of people, modifies ways of life, and necessitates a constant renewal of the habitat of mankind as a whole. The problems of urban life have been increasingly in the forefront of the political debate as well as of academic endeavour. The approach to the city has often been theoretical; it has always been rather technical. It has been made to appear that the basic urban problem was one of design, one of pattern involving buildings, roads, horses in the past, or carriages, and now motorcars, parking space, other equipment, and, of course, more particularly, money. It seemed that the physical framework was determining, or would determine, the behaviour of society. Now that the dire crisis is upon us, partly as a result of rapid growth, we have come to realize that it is not only a crisis in transport and housing, but also a crisis in the structure of society. Perhaps it is necessary to remind ourselves that cities are made by and for people and that an assemblage of buildings and roadways without people is, to use an American western term, a "ghost town." Urbanization results from people moving to and multiplying in cities. They do so because they expect to find in the cities that they establish and develop more security and a better life in the future. It is still the same process that Herodotus and Aristotle tried to stress. Today it is a dramatic and massive trend, and it is powered by mankind's hope. To deceive this hope can only lead to tragedy. To help resolve the crisis, we must first recognize the trends that confront the city, and then perhaps proposals may be elaborated for action and for goals to improve our cities and give to their inhabitants the feeling of progress on that road to a better life.

Modern urbanization can of course be best measured by the changes occurring in the size, shape, and function of cities. However, the essential measurement is again that of population. We are confronted with a crisis at present because urban populations increase so fast nowadays, faster than that of the total population of the world. The urban component of the world population rose from thirty per cent in 1960 to about forty per cent in 1975, according to the most recent statistics of the United Nations, and a conservative projection by the same statistical office estimates that it will reach forty-four per cent by 1985, that is, in less than ten years, and at least fifty per cent by the year 2000. This would mean a growth of 600 million for the urban population in the next ten years. The growth will be distributed unequally around the world. In Europe west of the Soviet Union — a small continent, a little smaller than Canada in territory, but now harbouring 480 million people — urban growth will probably add some fifty million inhabitants to the cities by 1985. In the same time, in Brazil alone, a country of about 100 million and also about the spatial size of Canada, the urban population will probably increase by about sixty million. A part of the hundreds of millions to be added to urban settlements will be born in those same settlements. That will be particularly true of the more developed countries. But the majority, especially in the developing countries, as yet less urbanized, will move in from a distance and often from a considerable distance. Even in the better developed countries there are constant and considerable migrations between cities and from certain regions of the territory to others. It has been estimated that about one-quarter of the total population of the United States moved their domicile from one municipality to another within every recent five-year-period, and this high index of mobility is observed in a country where the farming population dropped below ten per cent some time ago, is below six per cent today, and most of the migration from the farms has been completed.

Ten years ahead is a very short span of time. In the case of urban planning, of an operation of urban renewal or urban development of some size, it usually takes at least five years from the moment a plan has been adopted until the real thing begins to rise from the ground. That is the time needed to prepare, to set up the machinery, and to start building. This means that in terms of urban development ten years ahead is the immediate future, about which something must be done right now, especially in this era of rapid change.

In fact, the instability of urban structures does not result simply from the numerical growth of city residents. It results from migration into and out of large cities constantly modifying the economic, social, and ethnic composition of the community. It is increased by the constant movement of transients through the cities; transients who come for diverse purposes to use in some way the services the cities offer. Too often the transients' movement is recorded as sheer tourism, and while it is true that an increasing number of cities and towns attract substantial flows of tourists, the statistics of transient visitors also include large numbers of persons who visit a place to transact business, to obtain information or expert advice that may not be available in every town, and to perform work related to their employment. In the more affluent nations, where a large number of individuals have more than one residence, these often do not officially list as their primary domicile the urban place of abode where, in fact, they spend more time than anywhere else.

Just as the modern organization of urban space favours commuting from home to work over relatively long distances, the modern organization of work favours dispersal of closely interrelated centres into networks of cities. Between these cities there develops a constant movement of persons seeking to do their jobs in the most effective way. There are some statistics, not really satisfactory, about daily commuting to work. There are no systematic counts at all of the movements of transients or of the actual pressures exerted on the facilities and services of a city by the flows of visitors or the "secondary residences" of those who spend most of their time there while being counted officially elsewhere.

Population censuses as now taken need constant interpretation and re-elaboration, and the picture they provide remains doubtful, all the more so as the mobility of people increases for a larger percentage of the urban population. This is true in the more affluent countries of advanced economy where statistical data is usually considered to be the best and most complete. But the society of such countries is particularly mobile and its way of life is spatially more pluralistic. In the developing countries population, demographic, and occupational data are well known to be less reliable, less complete, less comparable from one area to another or one period to another.

If the city is indeed the people, that is, the sum total of the men and women who live in a city or have an important stake in the place because they spend much time there and perform activities of importance to themselves there, then it must be recognized that the modern city is a particularly elusive phenomenon to define, delimit, measure, or even describe with precision. It is very different from the well-ordered, stabilized, homogeneous community that was apparently the town of the past on which urban theory is still based.

In fact, the dynamics of a large, growing city must always have been different from the theoretical image. Large size and rate of growth disrupt order, stability, and homogeneity. In the modern world big size and rapid growth are becoming the rule. It is argued by many experts that the people do not want much more growth, resent the influx of exotic newcomers, and are getting tired of living in cities of multimillion size. The question remains open whether it is sheer size or the mismanagement of large cities that has caused dissatisfaction in these communities and outflow of population from many of them. The loss in number of residents of some larger cities may not be as much a sign of decline as a symptom of mutation — mutation of their function. The modern city is undergoing a social, economic, and political process that can be better understood in the light of a careful study of urban growth and of the resulting mix of people.

Urban growth has now acquired a very complex nature. The real measure of an urban settlement size being population, not area within municipal limits, nor area of floor space available, nor even employment, the measurement of the numbers of people present on the territory and actively participating in the activities of a city is becoming more and more difficult. We have begun to reckon with nighttime population and daytime population. We know that the former, which is supposed to be reported in the census, may decrease while the latter will consume more goods and services and may increase. The nighttime population according to census count is probably an underestimation of the actual number of persons spending the night in the city that has a considerable volume of transactional activities. The census does not count as official residents in the city transients or those who give another place, maybe a country house, as their domicile.

Thus an increase in transactional activities, and it is a phenomenon that develops constantly in large cities today, is likely to decrease the accuracy of the data available on the population trends and the growth or non-growth of a city. The historical heritage or the quality of the performing arts in an urban centre will increase the number of visitors, many of whom may stay overnight or several days. And the workers servicing them may very well prefer, for reasons of cost or congestion, to reside outside city limits in suburban locations.

These are examples of trends of growth which are not easily reflected in the statistical data usually available. Rising affluence of a sector of the urban population determines greater consumption of space in terms of ground, of constructed floor space, and of area appropriated by means of transport. Therefore, in urban centres economic development and even better welfare entail consequences which will cause growth in many urban characteristics, even if the numbers of population should remain static.

One of the essential components of modern development and of economic evolution is increased mechanization and automation of production and services. The mechanization of agriculture and mining chased people from small farms, plantations, mining towns, towards urban centres. That is a well-known, established trend. In these days, the present stage of technological evolution directs the labour force towards the qualified or advanced services that I like to call the "quaternary activities." These are mainly of a transactional nature and cause the personnel engaged in them to move frequently between several urban centres in order to perform their work in a more efficient and well-informed fashion. The cities have been developing their facilities for this sort of visitor, and the equipment required ranges from libraries to museums to hotels, convention centres, world trade centres, computing centres and the like.

This evolution of our ways of working leads to greater specialization and a need for continuing and adult education. It fosters new institutions and new land uses in the city. It also leads to the shortening of official working hours and increases the demand for recreational facilities, indoor and outdoor, individual and collective, in town and at a distance. It also makes the time spent on so-called recreation a period in one's life in which one recreates not only his or her body but also his or her mind, and therefore is closely linked, in fact, to the kind of work that quaternary occupations involve.

Each of these trends would have made a theoretical city grow and evolve with time even if its population were to remain stabilized in number. The latter assumption would of course not be likely to occur in reality. Greater affluence attracts more labour, in both the skilled and unskilled sectors of the work force. The evolution of large numbers of personnel towards the more skilled and quaternary occupations creates, in spite of mechanization and automation, a strong demand for unskilled labour to service the place. And that additional cheaper manpower must usually be brought over from a distance. All these trends increase agglomeration, intensify growth in terms of population numbers and in terms of the requirements of space, buildings, and equipment. Moreover, they increase diversification in the urban agglomeration: diversification of people with consequent inner tensions within the local community, diversification of levels of wealth and power with the inherent oppositions, and conflicts within the same community.

The process of urban growth sows the seeds of discord and strife. This has always been so and the political philosopher longing for order and stability has distrusted and opposed such a turbulent process. That attitude is expressed already in Plato, in the *Laws*. (It is also expressed in Aristotle's *Politics*, in which he discusses a number of passages from Plato's *Laws* and begins to diverge from what the master had taught.) However, this political philosophy, inherited from an ancient tradition, has not been accepted by the citizenry, which has seldom resigned itself to statism, to renouncing growth. Even in stabilized situations, discord and inequity have existed, and people have sometimes preferred growth to continued peace.

Human nature is at least as complex as the nature of urban growth. I arrived this time in Vancouver from the real east, not the east of North America or the regions to the east of it—I came here from Japan. And in Japan, of course, there have been careful studies of the history of Tokyo in the period when Tokyo was called Edo, that is, in the period of the Tokugawa Shoguns, politically a period in which the government tried to apply principles of stability, of no growth, almost as if they were trying to implement the principles of Plato's *Laws*, whether they had ever heard about them or not. By the end of the eighteenth century the population of Edo, despite the policy that stabilized, maintained, and closed Japan to outside influences, reached a figure between one million and, possibly, according to some interpretations, 1.8 million people. If that is true, Edo (i.e. Tokyo) was the largest city in the world at the time. We should not suppose, therefore, that because we try to apply a clear-cut and simple policy that may have been advocated since Plato for some 2500 years, we are going to obtain no growth in cities. It is not so simple. Urban dynamics are much more complicated than that.

The complexity of urbanization around the world today is heightened by the diversity of the processes actually involved in the different areas of the world. In most countries the central parts of cities or conurbations harbour the main transactional activities, and in the vicinity of the business centre are housed the more stable and often the more privileged elements in the population. The poorer elements and newcomers are largely kept on the periphery or in suburban locations. This is not the case, however, in the United States, where residents of central cities are reputed to be mainly the poor, the elderly, the sick, and the underprivileged. With more than one million of its residents living on welfare after having to a large extent migrated from the American south or the West Indies, New York City could be described as one of the largest refugee camps in the world. Calcutta, Hong Kong, and Rio de Janeiro probably have more refugee migrants from different parts of India, China, and Brazil, but these are not taken care of by welfare, supervised and housed, organized in camps, if I may say so, in a comparable fashion.

All large cities have known periods at least in which rapid urbanization caused slums for newcomers to proliferate in their midst. Recently these have more often been kept outside certain areas, although special topographical circumstances may in certain cities inject such groupings close to the urban centre, as for instance the older favelas of Rio and certain hills in Hong Kong. The exodus of the middle class North Americans to the suburbs has not yet gained general acceptance outside this continent.

As cities grow, they need more ground. Recently, they have been voraciously devouring the space around them. Whether by suburban sprawl of one kind or another or by coalescence into one administrative system of heretofore separate nuclei, urban settlements are expanding their area. On the whole, this trend lowers the density of population, although in fact the density of occupation of residential areas at nighttime and of business districts in working hours may increase. This evolution is certainly true of two conurbations as different as Hong Kong and Zurich. On the other hand, to balance the influx of newcomers, and especially of blacks, in their central areas, American cities have been annexing largely white suburban and "rurban" districts to the central municipalities. That is another difficulty in assessing what is actually urban growth in terms of population. By 1970, about a hundred cities in the United States extended over sixty square miles each, and the largest city (I would say in the world) in terms of area was, surprisingly, Jacksonville, Florida, with 766 square miles, inhabited by only 528,000 people. In those cities the average density must be low.

Different solutions can be tried to relieve the pressures resulting from urban growth. The greatest danger arises when growth and urbanization are both condemned and opposed. The population of most parts of the world is not satisfied enough with the status quo to renounce growth in most of its components. With modern demography, technology, and social aspirations, rural dispersal is extremely difficult to maintain, let alone to increase. It would also be extremely costly and wasteful in terms of energy, materials, funds, and time. Solutions must be found to enable urban settlements to improve, expand, and prosper in conditions of high density, of pluralistic coexistence in a versatile city, of peaceful co-operation between its various parts. Present urbanization calls for a new programme with constructive proposals to alleviate the pessimism of recent years.

If large cities are here to stay, society should accept the fact. The idea that we can solve the problems of a large system by breaking it up into a hundred small pieces has never led to workable solutions. It will not work for modern urbanization either. The habitat of mankind is being renewed by migration, growth, technological and social evolution, and by an increasing general will for change. A new order is being sought in the physical, economic, and social structures of the city. At present a strong quantity of chaos permeates habitat. The historians of the future may be able to describe this as orderly creation, but it will depend on us and the next generation whether they will be able so to describe it or whether they will talk of a time of trouble. To its present participants, the process appears rather disorderly because it is so dynamic. The renewal must be helped by the acceptance of specific principles.

For fifty years at least, urban planners have been calling for some well-established principles. They have all agreed that the inhabitants of a city should have access to abundant air, sunshine, and greenery — that is in the famous charter of Athens of about fifty years ago. In older cities this principle has too often been neglected in favour of the provision of better transport and traffic by motorcar and of suburban expansion. Suburbia and the automobile were to supply better access to the countryside and natural amenities. In fact the inhabitants of the favelas of Rio and Recife, of the squatter villages of Hong Kong, or of the Bidonvilles around Dakar, have plenty of air and sun. They need to have less of these gifts of nature and more shelter and healthier homes. To some extent they are offered such a change, but in crowded large apartment blocks where rent and taxes must be paid and rules of behaviour observed. These developments are usually located at a substantial distance from central facilities of employment and transaction. They are also separated from the residential areas of the more established, better serviced population, so that inequalities become flagrant and resentment arises. The situation is better handled in some countries and cities than in others, but some tensions occur in practically all instances.

The large and growing cities form the greatest laboratories for mass acculturation that ever existed. The acculturation works in two directions: the newcomers are learning to live in circumstances of ethnic diversity, high density, higher technology, new and strict regulation. The established, more privileged citizenry is experiencing life with an ethnic variety of exotic, less educated, often underprivileged, frustrated neighbours. Living and working together becomes an unavoidable necessity. Both parties must recognize and apply a way of life and an ethic that will provide a better life for all in the diversified city. Education and mass media must make the situation known to all concerned, its dangers, its opportunities, and how to work for the common good. This could and should be done daily, systematically and generally. It is in my opinion the first prerequisite to the improvement of urban settlements.

In the past the metropolis was often defined as the terminal stage in a long career. Few people were born there, but many died there. As urbanization continues, and as the vast majority of most nations become urbanized, the cities will become self-reproducing communities. They should be conceived and managed for the young as well as for the adults. Each level of the age pyramid must be given a part to fulfil, a role in the city. Only thus can some orderliness and stability be maintained within the dynamic environment of our city and society.

The physical plant is rapidly being renewed. All around the world the rapid sprawl of buildings of all sorts can be observed. The construction industry is, and will long remain, the basic activity of the world, comparable to agriculture or to manufacturing as a whole. It is just beginning to innovate in its rather slowly developing techniques. The last twenty years have seen more new buildings built and more old ones demolished than in any other twenty-year period in history. As an example, the central city of Paris, the Ville de Paris, well known for its stability, its strong conservation policies, its rich area of old monuments, has seen one-quarter of its total built-up area demolished and rebuilt between 1954 and 1974. To demonstrate once more the inadequacy of official statistics, they indicate that the resident population in that central city decreased by 600,000 during the period mentioned, from 2.8 million to 2.2 million, although the number of housing units *increased* by 210,000. Most other large cities have been rebuilt at least at the rate of central Paris. The physical plant of man's habitat is being renewed.

But has this immense endeavour actually been planned and systematically directed? It seems, on the contrary, that it has been the result of diverse and diverging forces, each working for its own purpose. Very little has actually been tailored to the most pressing needs. If the same amount of chaos that has been allowed in the better developed countries spreads through the developing areas where the needs are greater and more urgent, the present climate of urban crisis may evolve towards catastrophe.

The time indeed seems right for an attempt to formulate a new prescription, to regulate the provision of new habitat. Density must be accepted and explained. The present waste of space, materials, and human time and effort must be reduced and replaced with more economic consumption. Despite affluence, a great deal of miniaturization of goods, machines, housing, transport, and space in general used by individuals must take place. This could be achieved if quantitative ceilings were imposed on conspicuous individual consumption. Residences could and should be provided closer to places of work. In areas of high density, public transport must be favoured over individual private transport. The uncontrolled use of the individual motorcar can hardly be allowed in dense, central cities; less obtrusive means of transport such as bicycles can be encouraged.

Policies such as these will not be achieved by decentralization or deconcentration of new towns, which only increase the vast expense of metropolitan or even more, megalopolitan, systems. A major problem will be caused by the propensity of every smaller town, old or new, either to grow and thus establish a new link possibly in a megalopolitan chain, or to decline, vegetate, and complain if no growth comes to it. In the midst of the dynamic urbanization of our time, there are large areas in the Canadian Prairie, in the American

Middle West, in the French Central Massif, in the Brazilian Amazon basin, and even in the northern island of Hokkaido in Japan, where small towns are declining and experiencing difficulty in surviving.

If we seek to encourage growth of settlements wherever possible, we should be prepared to see more and more clusters of urban centres of substantial size occurring. This metropolitanization will progress, and in some cases new megalopolitan formations may arise. Between all these settlements increased complementarity and intensified interchange will develop. The technology of transport and communication will adapt to the new fluidity of our emerging social structure. The fluidity and nomadism of people already requires — in the more affluent nations and will increasingly require everywhere — a more economical multipurpose usage of the diverse components of human habitat. It will be more and more difficult to permit every family to claim exclusive use of more than one place of abode, however fast the percentage increases of people in the developed nations that do have more than one place of abode. New legislation, new customs, and social adaptation emphasizing co-operative or collective usages of space must prevail.

Facts as huge and stubborn as modern urbanization are caused by the convergence of powerful and sustained forces. This evolution came with better technology, mechanization, and automation. It took shape as the people of the more advanced and the more urbanized countries obtained greater freedom from constraining work, more leisure time, more means to consume goods and services, more mobility, and more education. More people flock to large cities, not because they have little choice, but because this is the only choice they know that has opened to many the road to all those benefits. Mankind seeks a new order for its habitat that will allow most to participate in the urban opportunity, and it is because urbanization has brought greater opportunity to mankind as a whole that urbanization is so stubborn and huge a trend.

I do not assume — it probably would be too optimistic and too ambitious — that a huge international conference such as Habitat could consider all those problems or even part of the suggestions I have tried to enumerate. But we may hope, and we not only may, but we *must* hope, that the spirit of Vancouver, which is already here, will blaze a new trail towards a more diversified and complex order in the organization of states and society to allow for more variety and freedom, and for the better life in the urbanized environment.

EXTRACTS FROM DISCUSSION

Chairman: You have made it clear, Dr. Gottmann, that density is with us, and we have to explain it. Perhaps we should tell you that there are people in the audience who would like to take chain saws and go up into the Fraser

Valley and cut down the trees on the Trans-Canada Highway to stop some of the flow of people from other parts of the continent into our region!

One of the recent visitors to this campus was Professor E.C. Schumaker, of *Small is Beautiful* fame. One of the themes he was developing was the concept of intermediate technology and the development of communities of appropriate scale for human interaction. Have you any comments on the contrast between your concept of the ability to live with density, to live with growth, and the views that Schumaker was putting forth?

Dr. Gottmann: I do not think that what I have said in defence of growth and size is in any way contradictory, in terms of urban organization and human community, to the theory of "small is beautiful." Our large cities and conurbations are a mosaic of small communities — how small, how different, how isolated one from another by invisible partitions is up to those communities. But they exist. Vancouver has a number of districts, a Chinatown and other districts, in which communities that represent only a portion of the total population of Vancouver can live in the way they wish. That is part of the freedom of the city, and that should not only be allowed but encouraged, and this does not mean that you have to reinforce partitions. The partitions are up to each community. That is what happens in practice in every city in the world. There are probably more differences between small communities within large cities than within the total community of a small town. I even think that this is one of the reasons why so many young people leave small towns for large cities.

Question: Could we have a little elaboration on how there could be an expansion in central Paris of dwelling units while statistics have shown a falling population in the last two decades?

Dr. Gottmann: I think I have the beginning of an answer. The statistic is that in the central city of Paris in the last twenty years there have been 210,000 more housing units, and that is actual housing units; it does not include hotel rooms (there may have been ten or twenty new hotels built; the total number of rooms would not be more than 10,000, but in any case they are not included in the 210,000 units). Normally 200,000 more housing units, even if families are very small, should have meant half a million more population. Instead of that you have 600,000 less; there is a discrepancy of at least one million people.

When I received a very reliable and precise report with eighty pages of maps prepared not only from computer output but also from checking all data in the field that had been prepared for the city of Paris, I wrote immediately to the man who had directed the survey and asked him how he explained the discrepancy with the census. Basically his reply was: "Well, people live better, they occupy more space, there are more aged ladies that keep large apartments, more widows or widowers at the end of their lives keeping large apartments for themselves alone until they die off, and so on." We may check that with the age pyramid, but basically it seems that a large proportion of the people who occupy those housing units give their domicile in the census as being somewhere else, how many we do not know. The census is not designed to find out the answer to that question. It could be redesigned for that, of course, but that would require convincing all the proper authorities and perhaps even Parliament that it should be done, because one would have to ask some rather special questions about private life.

I have been following up this trend in the last six months because I am interested in the dynamics of French cities and other cities in the advanced countries. It is true not only of Paris. Similar trends can be found in such cities as Lyons and even medium-sized cities of the quarter-million size such as, say, Rennes in Brittany, which show smaller-scale discrepancies but still some. And, if you want to be a little more cynical, and you begin questioning people and looking at certain statistics on the conurbation of Boston, Massachusetts, you may also find that this is not an exclusively French trend. The significance is that there are advantages from the point of view of the weight of one's political vote at election time, and from the point of view of taxation, to declare as main domicile a place in the country-side or in a small town rather than one in the large city. To what extent there are advantages depends on the prevailing legislation. They are numerous in certain European countries, but advantages may exist even in the federal structure of the United States. I do not know about Canada.

There is little doubt that people have better access to their political repre-sentative in a small town or in an area of lower density than in a very big city. It is also certain that there are particular tax advantages. The two together may work in the interest of the municipalities, of the mayors of the small or medium-sized towns who receive more subsidy from a central gov-ernment budget if their census population is higher, so they may welcome this kind of absentee citizenship if it can be justified. Again how large that trend may be is hard to tell, but there is all that population of transients that come to Paris once a week, or once a fortnight, and wants to have at least a *pied à terre*, a place where they can spend a few days during those recurrent but regular visits, or that they can put at the disposal of friends, colleagues, and so on; sometimes their children, if they have grown-up chil-dren — a place for collective use. I have discussed this development with a friend of mine who is an academic, a professor, a banker, and also the rep-resentative on a number of government committees of one of the large cities of France. At one point I asked how it could happen in Paris. "Well," he said, "it's very simple. First of all you know I have an apartment in Paris." And I said, "Well, I am not surprised. You have to go there practically every week for a day or every fortnight for two or three." And he said, "Yes, and I have a daughter who is now twenty and she takes courses in Paris and she can use the place also." He added that his domicile was in a skiing resort in the Alps. He likes to ski all right, but I know he spends much more time either in Paris or in the other city of which he is one of the community leaders, than in the ski resort where he is counted officially. This is not exactly nomadism; it is a pluralism of places of abode because there is pluralism in the places of work, or of recreation, or of family affairs. It is a sort of new urban transhumance. There was the transhumance of sheep and the shepherds were the transhumant people. Now this becomes the way of life of the shepherds of the urban people. I am sorry I am answering at such length but this is a terribly important question if we are to understand what is really happening with our cities. About twelve years ago, I received a telephone call from a friend of mine, a priest who chaired at the Archbishopric of Paris, a committee studying urban matters and housing in the Paris metropolitan area. Basically his problem was that the religious community of the parish was not working any longer as it ought to and as it had in the past because the leaders of the parish were never there on Sunday. They were somewhere else. And that was the problem of the shepherds of the large community. I did not have any solution to offer to help them, but it was the first indication of the trend, and it is interesting that this indication came from the priests, the leaders of the small communities within the large.

Question: You have persuaded us that the case for urban growth is very strong. But if you look at the situation from the point of view of the older residents of cities, then there seem to be some very disturbing things, for example, the fear of crowding of public facilities of all kinds — parks, transportation systems, and so on — changes in their landscape, old neighbourhoods disappearing and being replaced by highrise structures which they consider inhuman and inferior. They see agricultural land disappear which they feel not only had scenic value but provided them with fresh food and produce in season and so on. How can you persuade these people that they are wrong? The result is serious political confrontation at all levels. People say, no, we do not want our cities to grow so fast; we do not want these kinds of changes to happen.

Dr. Gottmann: I believe that there are two aspects to your question. On one hand there are the facts of crowding and of decline of the public services and that of course particularly affects the aged. It also affects small children who are less heard in the community than other people. Of course many young parents have moved out of the central city. In most cities that I know the public services have seriously declined. Partly it is the result of a certain social evolution of our time. All services are declining, and we are now in a society where we have more to do for ourselves. For the aged or the disabled it is not easy; it is sometimes impossible. But the public services have also declined because on the whole we have assumed that the large city is declining, and that fewer public services are needed there; that less has to be supplied; that we should be helping settlements other than the larger city to grow and develop. In many centralized countries, in the case of the largest agglomerations, there is often a definite policy *against* providing services and a policy to discourage crowding. This is true of Paris, London, Amsterdam, and so on — it is a very long list. If we diminish the quality of services in the city, it is again those members of the community that are in the category of the less physically able that feel it the most, and of course they protest. And I cannot see how we can tell them they are wrong. I do not think they are wrong, but they are suffering particularly from two trends. One is a trend toward automation of services — which means do it yourself — and that is a general social trend; it may be reversed some time, but it is not yet going towards reversal and — it is very hard on those who cannot help themselves. Second, there is the trend of curtailing by policy a great many of the public services in the cities, which could be avoided.

Question: You mentioned that cities are badly mismanaged. Have you come up with any ways of attracting higher quality people and of training people that could bring about better management of cities?

Dr. Gottmann: I wish I could answer that positively. In recent years municipal service hardly attracted anybody of higher value than in the past. I do not know whether it is really a matter of the quality of people, or whether it is the general frame of mind, even of those who are responsible for the cities. To some extent it might be the hangover of too old ideas, too old concepts, about what the city is, what it is becoming, where it is going. I do not feel that we have surveyed and actually tried to understand what the trends are. If you look at western Europe, the teaching of planners, geographers, architects, urban sociologists, and the rest is still based on the ideas and work of people who produced their basic work before 1940 — Raymond Unwin, Le Corbusier, and others. Those people were not faced with the evolution and the trends of the last twenty-five years, and possibly some of their ideas were already wrong by 1930. However, I am not concerned with that; I am not an historian; I am trying to look at the present and the future.

Question: In your discussion you gave examples from many countries of the world. Could you comment on policies in the People's Republic of China?

Dr. Gottmann: I wish first that you would tell me a little more about what is being done in mainland China, because like everybody else, I am very much interested in it. I had hoped, with other participants in the conference I have just attended in Japan, that there would be two experts from Peking attending it and enlightening us a little more on what is being done and planned in China. They did not come; what I have heard are two main things. First of all, there has been decentralization and deconcentration of the major cities, particularly Shanghai — probably Shanghai is the largest conurbation in the world today, although the official figures we have are more than fifteen years old. The usual figure quoted is that about one million or at least 800,000 people have been sent away, by order, from Shanghai to other parts of the country. Many of them seem to have been sent to the western and northwestern parts of China. Whether they went to other cities or to establish new settlements that may even be of the rural type, I do not know. That is, of course, a migration policy of trying to increase settlement of an underpopulated part of China and that is a policy that many other countries have followed previously — one of trying to redistribute their population more evenly and to occupy better peripheral or empty parts of their territory.

The second point is more theoretical and in a way more interesting because it may be of more general portent. The information was brought to a meeting held in Toronto last March, by a Japanese sociologist who had been to China and had met with Chinese experts in urban matters. Apparently their view was as follows: that the urban structure should be reshaped in such a way so that ideally all cities would be about equal in size — a fairly big size, I trust. Such a policy would concentrate the whole population of the area including the agricultural population in the cities; the agriculturalists would go out during the day to till the land or tend to whatever work there was in the neighbouring agricultural territory. With modern means of transport that is perfectly feasible. And that seems to be a trend observed, curiously enough, in a number of countries of very different political régimes from China's. These are not very developed countries but are in the developing stage. A recent book by a Turkish geographer on the evolution of Turkish cities has shown that the proportion of the population of Turkish cities employed in agriculture has been rising and, in cities of medium size in Turkey, was often up to twenty-five per cent of the total population. This is almost what the Chinese theory seemed to be aiming at, because, according to that theory as reported by my Japanese friend (and I cannot warrant that it is the only basic theory), every city should have an almost equal number of the main categories of occupation. About one-third would be agriculturalists, one-third occupied in manufacturing, one-third in the services. Also, industries and services would be distributed as equally as possible among all the cities, so that no one city would specialize in textiles, steel, or chemicals; there would be industries of the different categories in each city. As an example, the Japanese expert was given the transfer of certain textile plants from Shanghai to Peking, another very big city, but this was because Peking had had little or no textile industry previously. There is no doubt that this is feasible to some extent, and there is a general desire in the world today (it is part of our egalitarian trend) to establish as much equality as possible between the different regions of a country's territory. However, we have, in fact, seldom succeeded, either in achieving that kind of equality or in improving the status quo. The only thing that we may have succeeded in to some extent in the West is to equalize a little more the average standard of living of the people. But that has been achieved only by leaving very low densities in some areas, such as the Canadian prairies, and agglomerating very high densities in other areas such as the Vancouver, Toronto, and Montreal areas.

Question: This is not so much a question as a point of information and to add to a former questioner's comment about the negative attitudes to some of your ideas.

When you were here in 1963 I became very much interested in the ideas of Megalopolis and have suffered in these thirteen years as a result of being a supporter of your ideas! One of the reasons that I supported your concepts was that you showed us that there was an interrelationship in an entire conurbation, that while there were negative things happening, many positive things were happening. But I found it was very difficult to get this point across to people because of a kind of general pessimism toward our world that one finds in universities, in schools, and in the newspapers, a delight in hating the present trend and showing how badly off we are. I want to give one example. In 1963 I was asked to lead a group of Canadian students on an urban study, and I chose Megalopolis as the study. We took a car and went zigzagging from south of Washington all the way up to Maine to look at Megalopolis, to look with our own eyes as architects at the things you talked about. And two of the students at some of the stops that we made, such as at Levittown for instance, refused to get out of the car, because they were so convinced that it was bad and that I had misled them, having been misled by you. I am just making this comment; I wonder if you have a response to it.

Dr. Gottmann: It is a very good question, because it is a frank question, and I suspect that, alas, my sort of teaching has made sufferers of a number of people. I am convinced in regard to the present trend, in the last fifteen years, in places like New York and Philadelphia and Baltimore and Washington, that there are millions of people who have gone to those places since 1961 and who have lived there better than if they had stayed where they were before — people of several colours. So for whom is it bad and for whom is it good? I did not make them come. They never read my book! They came for completely different reasons. So I am sorry you have had to suffer. I can only add that at times I possibly would have suffered too from what I heard around me if I was not, I suppose, an inveterate optimist. Basically I do not like Levittowns. I had better tell you right away that I think it is a very wrong development from all standpoints, but the person who refused to get out of the car is a man who whatever happens to him is going to suffer much more in his life than you or I.

2

Reflections upon Canadian Habitat

Humphrey Carver

People are going to come to Vancouver from all parts of the world to talk about how they are getting on in building their cities; they're going to talk about their aspirations and their frustrations. There will, of course, be a lot of boasting, because it's part of human nature, part of the territorial imperative, to glorify the place you live in. Even to magnify the enormity of your problems is a form of boasting. But beneath the surface of all the boasting and the trivialities and the complications of the subject there is one question that will interest me most. What are the things of real, ultimate, deep importance to people living in cities? Whether we live in Africa, in America, or in Asia, and however far we have developed in our economies, we are all the same stock of human beings; each man and woman is yearning, suffering, and loving in the same way.

I think it would be useful to discover what these common-to-all, big ultimate things are, for two particular reasons. First of all it might help us to understand, in making our own plans and policies for Canada, what are the really top priority goals for an urban society, sorted out from the trivialities and frivolities. What is it really worth fighting for and spending our money on? As an urban society we have become fat, greedy, wasteful, inflationary, and consequently dangerous to the whole world. We need a clearer view of what we could whittle away and still focus upon the essential things in life.

So I'm going to try, from a Canadian point of view, to say what are, I believe, the big, simple, generally acknowledged aims of life that should shape our urban habitat. To do this, it's useful to start by seeing ourselves as a people who are in the midst of a long historical process of creating human settlements on our continental territory.

THE FIRST SETTLEMENT OF CANADA

If you wanted to go back to the evolutionary origins of our human settlements, you might join in an archaeological dig in Babylon, Palestine, Brittany, or Britain, digging through the layers deposited by generations of habitat-makers. Most of us in Canada came from this long stream of cultural evolution; this is our own past. We are an immigrant stream of city-building folk. To understand what we are doing it doesn't help much to understand the settlement habits of the indigenous native people of Canada, so they are not part of my subject.

Even in the short time we city-building migrants have been in Canada, we have been through successive stages of evolution, at first struggling to survive in the wilderness and more recently struggling to survive in the concrete jungle. Our archaeological deposits, however, are not in layers, but spread out across the surface of the land. Because it is all such recent history, most early Canadian settlements are still in use. It's true that some, like the Gold Rush towns, have already faded into being tourist attractions. But in most rural areas the settlers' houses, the cleared and fenced land, the systems of roads and small towns, are all still part of the scene. Only in a few places of intense city growth have earlier settlements disappeared, buried in the earth. But even in Montreal and Toronto you can't really understand the pattern of streets and property without perceiving that these cities are built upon a pattern of agricultural settlement.

The stories of how the first migrants settled in Canada is our Old Testament, chapter one of Genesis, and the legends have naturally acquired the sanctity of Holy Writ. From our family backgrounds, most of us know some particular little bit of the story — in Quebec, in the prairies, or in B.C. My own thoughts go to a place I know well, on the Atlantic coast of Nova Scotia, a great bay between two headlands.

Champlain dropped anchor here and called it Port Joli. It's had that name ever since, but it is now pronounced Port "Jolly." One summer day, about the time Queen Victoria was born, four small boats came into the bay; they kept close to shore, looking for a good landing place. They found a long solid reef of rock sticking out into deep water so that they could get a boat in, on the lee side, at any state of the tide; then the boats and their contents could be pulled up on the hard shore and up into the spruce woods behind. In these boats were four families — the MacDonalds, the Robertsons, the Leslies, the Stewarts. This became their little settlement, their Garden of Eden. Together they cleared about eighty acres of bush to get pasture and hay for their family cows and horses. They set out a couple of acres down by the sea, to be owned in common, where they could pull up their boats, build their fish sheds, and store their lobster gear. They built four fine houses overlooking the big bay. And, as property has subsequently changed hands, all survey measurements are still made from the original Wharf Rock where they had landed, a place as locally historic as Plymouth Rock was for the Pilgrim Fathers in New England.

Nova Scotia is a community of the sea and, in the dark, out on the lonely grey fishing waters, men seek company. So around each bay there are usually several small settlements which take their name from their position on the water — North East Harbour, West Harbour, South West, and so on. The settlement at the head of the Bay is called The Head; here there is a church, a store, the post office, the community hall. And here is the start of the old road through the woods to the next Head of the bay, where the boys go to find a wife.

One hundred and fifty years after the families landed on the Wharf Rock at Port Joli, the four houses are still there and in good shape. The barns and fish sheds are littered with a deposit of tools, marine gear, and other artifacts dropped where they were last used. The archaeological deposit reveals the steady advance from a stage of survival in the wilderness to the later use of sophisticated engines, radar and ship-to-shore telecommunications, and to a comfortable way of life. It is still a beautiful place, a Garden of Eden, and there are still a few MacDonalds, Robertsons, Leslies, and Stewarts living nearby.

The process of settlement started in many different places in our vast geography. Most of the early settlers arrived in boats, on the sea, up rivers, and along the shores of lakes. So, in the legends and imagery of our Book of Genesis there is always this scene of jumping out on the shore, setting out the warehouses and working area, running surveys for the private lots behind the waterfronts. Within these last few years, most of our big cities, now searching for their historical past so as to get a perspective view of their present and their future, have tried to recapture some of this legend; they have tidied up the old warehouses, restored the beams and chimneys, and found a new pleasure in architectural conservation. So it is in Victoria, Quebec, Montreal, and Halifax.

THE INSTABILITY OF RURAL SETTLEMENTS, THE VIRTUES OF SMALL TOWNS, AND THE INEVITABILITY OF METRO CITIES

Small communities far from cities, by the sea and in farming country, are now in a state of instability. The descendants of the original settler families are under pressure to move from their Garden of Eden, mostly for two reasons. It's important to be on the routes travelled by the big trucks that take fish and lobster and agricultural products to the urban plant and market. One has to be part of the commercial network. Also the children have to go to the big regional school and are not satisfied to travel on the yellow school bus and come home to Mum at 4:00 pm every afternoon. With only two children in the family, life is lonely in the country, and they want to be part of the teen-age culture of the nearby town.

What with the instability of life in the country and the turmoil and tension of life in the big cities, there's a lot to be said for living in a small town. Perhaps the small towns of Canada are the best we have to show in the art of building habitats. We haven't sufficiently appreciated them, learned about them, and eulogized them.

Consider the small town which is a true regional service centre, the focus of life for its surrounding population. Here is the high school, district hospital; the offices of lawyers and doctors; the usual battery of stores, supermarket, hardware, building supplies; several churches, places to eat and to drink. This is the home town of an M.P. or an M.L.A. and a place for political talk and if you stand at the principal crossroads corner of town, sooner or later in the day you are likely to see practically everyone who lives nearby and you could learn to call them by their first names. Many of our small towns in Canada possess all these essential functions of community life. We should cling to them and help them to remain strong and stable.

And what is the destiny of the big metro-regional city, in such a state of turmoil and muddle? In the future, about eighty per cent of our population is going to live in these cities. In my working lifetime in Canada the Canadian population has doubled, from ten million to more than twenty million. The city I settled in, Toronto, is now four times as big. In the lifetime of those now starting on their working lives, the population is expected to double again and almost all this added twenty million people are going to live in metro-regional cities. Though the new generation will have an opportunity to influence what this habitat growth will be like, yet its genesis and its genes already exist, like the body and tadpole limbs of a baby in the womb.

The general configuration, the stereotype of our metropolitan cities, is pretty well bound to be like this, in the era of energy conservation and public transit: at the centre will be the cluster of high-rise towers, a concentration of buildings and people that is the inevitable consequence of rapid transit of the subway type. This feature of Montreal and Toronto will also appear in Vancouver, Ottawa, Calgary, Halifax, and other cities that graduate to this imperial stature. The corollary of the central towers and the transit system will be the series of distribution points where fleets of buses and parked cars assemble to distribute people out into suburbia. And around these distributing nodes will be the suburbia itself, which is the real habitat and the part of a city that is most susceptible to the new ideas and influences of this next generation. Up to now the stereotyped image has been the single family house and lot, which is a tradition carried over from the habitats of small towns and from dreams about those legendary settlements by the sea and in the country, the Garden of Eden.

In trying to visualize what big city suburbia might be like, most people find it very difficult to imagine anything different from the familiar scene of houses and lots. Clusters of high-rise apartments are commonly regarded as a regrettable necessity. Recently the range of acceptable possibilities has included a romantic repainting of an old nineteenth-century house. But most people's tastes in habitat are doggedly conservative. Planners and architects don't have this visualization hang-up and are trained to go back to first principles and then come up with something unexpected. That's what makes them so infuriating to most people who cling to stereotypes and legends.

If you go back to first principles about the nature of big city habitats, you may find yourself looking at two philosophical questions: (1) It's easy to understand that people, in order to survive, need the shelter of a good roof, they need a bed, they need clean water, and they need a loaf of bread. But, beyond this, what are the things in life that make surviving really worthwhile? That is the question upon which depends the design of human habitats. (2) What is the connection between the *human* habitat and the natural landscape, which is the habitat of other living things on earth?

A HABITAT FOR THE FLOWERING OF HUMAN LIFE

Using the terms "habitat" and "human settlements" suggests that we can look at man's behaviour and his environment of life in a detached way, just as if we were looking at flora and fauna and lepidoptera and other forms of life that can be put under the microscope. If you compare man with other creatures, of course the first thing you have to note about him is that he alone has these strange characteristics: an awareness of his own existence in the present moment of time, a consciousness of his past and the perception of a future for which he can plan, self-consciously. He has the strange faculties of imagination, jubilation, tragedy, awe, and love. Man alone has these attributes. And in any review of the ancient habitats of man, what remains to be seen is not so much the shelter that enabled men to survive and dominate the world; most of what remains to be seen, from the past, are the extraordinary works of imagination, the pyramids and temples, the great cathedrals and palaces, the monuments and wonderful old gardens. These are all expressions of ecstasy, worship, and spirit; it is impossible to conceive a man-habitat that does not contain what is so special about this creature.

The works of man that have lasted longer, in the same use, than any other artifact or engineering work are, I suppose, the great mediaeval cathedrals of Europe. It almost seems that, for a time, people in towns and cities thought of church-building as a raison d'être of life. Functionally, of course, these churches served as theatres and picture galleries and concert halls, as well as being places for the quiet contemplation of the tragedies and problems of private life. Though in each era human imagination has found different media and forms of expression — and this is a secular rather than a religious age — yet the same qualities of mind and spirit are still the special thing about men and women; and this has been true of human beings at all stages of development. A South African apartheid township is, I suppose, about the ugliest habitat I have ever seen, a miserable inhuman place, but when you see the Africans gather at the dancing place, stamp their feet in magnificent rhythm and raise the dust, then you know they are great people in their pride and anger and humour.

In 1960 I wrote a book called *Cities in the Suburbs* in which I tried to respond to Gertrude Stein's famous aphorism about Los Angeles, "There is no there there," a comment that has been applied to all stereotyped suburbia. I suggested that each suburban habitat ought to be built around a town centre and that each community should be about the size of a Canadian small town. And what you put at the centre of a suburban habitat, I suggested, should be what is at the centre of human life; at the centre should be the places where people exercise their imaginations and their self-awareness. Where did we all come from? Where are we going to? Think of the tragedy and comedy of this human journey. Schools and libraries and theatres and dancing places and churches and picture galleries and the sound of music are all helpful in extending the imagination.

The point is that it's not much use building a habitat for man, in which he might survive to live like an animal or lepidopterous creature, but in which he had no way of being a man. This is not just an academic fancy but becomes a practical question about spending public money and setting priorities for urban policy. In building a city there are three principal sectors of priority: a city has to work in an economic, productive, Chamber of Commerce sense; money has to be spent on housing so that everyone is raised above the survival level and there is a reasonable equality of life style; money has to be available to set the stage on which people's qualities of imagination, enquiry, and wonder are released.

The same questions of priority in money-spending occur in setting housing policies. We don't struggle to reduce costs and improve the structure of housing merely to provide minimum shelter at a survival standard, as if men were cows in a cow barn, chickens in a chicken factory. The purpose of the struggle is to provide enough space for personal privacy so that, from the beginning, a child can contemplate his innate and private curiosity about his unique place in the universe. I sometimes look at my daughter Jenny's room. She is now twenty-one. But her room still contains the most extraordinary collection of possessions accumulated through her teen-age; the symbols, souvenirs, images, fetishes, "lares et penates," dripping from the ceiling, pasted on cupboard doors, hanging around your head. Of course. That's what life is all about. When we talk about housing costs being too high and about some families having to be subsidized, the aim is not to build shelter for survival but to reach to the infinity of the journey towards self-discovery.

CITIES AND THE NATURAL LANDSCAPE

Let us return to the second big philosophical question about the landscape environment of the habitat and how this may influence our idealizations for designing human settlements. The expression "the concrete jungle" is a good way of explaining what people clearly don't want. What they do obviously want is a green city. It's a curious fact that all the great planner-architect-philosophers who have made a deep impression on their contemporaries have worked primarily on this theme: how to reconcile town and country. One could go back to Thomas More's Utopia of the sixteenth century, to Ebenezer Howard's Garden Cities and greenbelts of the nineteenth century, and Frank Lloyd Wright's Broadacre City; to Le Corbusier's Ville Radieuse and so on to Ian McHarg and the urban environmentalists of today. There's obviously something that runs deep in our Darwinian instincts about this, something hard to explain. In the evolution of Canadian culture, we didn't really get going until the Group of Seven and Emily Carr and the wilderness poets had given us a kind of iconography of our relationship with the natural world. And in this decade a protest movement against the concrete jungle and against the bigness of big cities has sent hippies scuttling into the bush of British Columbia and other parts of Canada and started a romantic migration to a Mother Earth farm, with one cow and the barefoot girls all got up in those draggy long peasant frocks.

In the last few years I have spent a large part of my time trying to save a small lake, just across the road from where I live in Ottawa. A local developer felt that there was nothing wrong in dumping rough fill on the very beautiful marshy, reedy edge of the lake, a famous sanctuary for birds and insects and pond creatures, and converting this into a site for building houses. His right to do so has been taken to court under the Ontario Environmental Protection Act and under the Ontario Planning Act. And, in both processes, the law has upheld the developer's right to snuff out a little treasure of natural habitat, to make a middle class human habitat. We have laws to protect human rights, but we do not have laws to protect the rights of birds and trees and the shores of our lakes and oceans. Perhaps you have come across a little book called *Do Trees Have Rights*. Our perceptions of morality grow and widen. The law is the way in which we sanctify and apply the disciplines of morality; we are only at the beginning of a period in which the law confirms that we share the surface of the earth with other forms of life.

In order that people in cities can have a close relationship with the surrounding natural environment, we will have to set out new patterns of settlement for big urban areas, supported by positive land use laws. There has to be an overall big perimeter pattern for an urban area and there also have to be ways of keeping some of the landscape in the interior urban parts.

The surrounding perimeter pattern is a matter of geometry. The trick is to maximize the perimeter. Let me explain. In designing a house you want to enclose as much space as possible within the *least possible* exterior wall perimeter, because the exterior enclosing wall is the most expensive to build and its exposure to the climate consumes energy. So, geometrically, a circular or roughly square-shaped house is the most efficient. This same principle applied to an ancient fortified city where the aim was to minimize the length of the enclosing city walls that had to be built and then manned by soldiers. So ancient cities were generally circular or square in shape. But if, for a modern city, the objective is to give the greatest number of houses a direct exposure or near access to the exterior landscape, then the best geometrical shape would have an outline of the longest possible perimeter. It would be star-shaped, with long fingers penetrating out into the surrounding open space. This geometrical configuration fits with the stereotype of a modern big city that I mentioned above, a high density core, supported by radiating transit lines with a series of distributing points along the radii. And these points can be identified with centres of communities, each built around a focal centre of life. This is the form of perimeter pattern that seems to emerge most clearly out of actual experience and also out of our idealizations. It then becomes the aim of urban policy to guide city development along these lines. Of course, it has to be understood that rigid patterns are always arbitrary and absurd; the best forms of cities are loose, flexible, and lively, the way plants grow, in adapting to the ecology.

Within the surrounding perimeter pattern of a big city, there is the interior pattern. Here the geometrical problem is in how to use the land space not actually covered by buildings. Canadians and Americans brought to the city from their rural and small town backgrounds, the tradition of the single house on a lot. The prototype was a house with its own yard in which to grow vegetables and fruit for the household, with a yard space large enough to separate the drinking water well from the household effluent in a tile bed. Unless a yard is actually used in this way, it is, of course, an extraordinarily expensive and wasteful use of space. Consuming space has now become a critical element of housing cost, both because of the length of services to be installed and because of the length of trips that consume transport energy. So the original small town and rural prototype everybody loved so much has become obsolete, and new prototypes are required. I think the model for big city housing design should not be subdivision rows of boxy houses and little fenced-in lots, but clusters of houses, each with its own ground level front door, but attached in all kinds of architectural compositions. And the open space should be in the form of meandering ribbons of natural landscape along which you can walk and bike and ski. These might be called "urban trails." They should follow the contours of streams, ravines, and some of the original landscape routes and these trails should link into the larger spaces beyond the city perimeter.

DO WE HAVE FREE WILL TO SHAPE OUR HABITAT?

I want to comment on this question. Are we really creatures of free will, who can make plans and carry them out? Is there any point in becoming involved in this whole subject, feeling that individual persons can really have any influence? There's a lot of cynicism and pessimism about this question.

Looking back over the years, Canadian cities didn't get off to a very good start. When Charles Dickens, a keen observer of cities and city life, visited Kingston, then the capital of Upper Canada, he wrote in his journal, in 1842: "Kingston, the seat of government in Canada, is a very poor town. Indeed it may be said of Kingston that one half of it appears to be burnt down, and the other half not to be built up." The only thing that really impressed him about Kingston was "an admirable jail here," and among the female prisoners behind bars he was quite bowled over by the face of a beautiful girl of twenty, who had been there nearly three years for having taken someone's horse. In Toronto at that time, and well into the twentieth century, the most impressive and far the largest piece of civic architecture, designed by Toronto's most eminent architect, John Howard, was a huge and very grand building of four stories, with classical porticoes and a great dome. This was the lunatic asylum built in 1846. Toronto was long celebrated for being the most boring city in the world and, even at that early date, it simply drove people crazy to live there. And what people felt about nineteenth-century Montreal was neatly put by Samuel Butler: "O God, O Montreal."

Canadian cities started off in a pretty dismal way and until this last postwar period it seemed very improbable that we would ever be in the big league, a country with cities that would really excite people. I think the first perception of this possibility occurred just before the First World War, when the government of Canada set up the Commission of Conservation under Clifford Sifton. And in May 1914 there was quite a large conference on city planning in Toronto and Thomas Adams, then president of the British Town Planning Institute, stayed in Canada for several years to lay the foundations of provincial planning legislation. But little came of this because Canada went through a rough time with the economic boom of the 1920's, the bust of the thirties, and the war in the forties.

But when I look back on what has happened in these last thirty years since 1946, the post-war period, I can only say that the change and the momentum have been extraordinary. Because I was on the scene, I know how the changes came about. I know the steps of progress were initiated by individual people, many of them my own friends. So this makes me an optimist about our capacity to control our own way of life, to shape our own habitat. I have no doubts in my mind that this can occur through the personal efforts of people like you and me, even more than through the actions of famous politicians and other big shots.

Item: In Canada, only thirty years ago there were no planners at all, no city planning staffs, no schools for training planners, no local or national organizations for discussing the habitat subject and very little interest in it. Now this is the most furiously debated public subject and we are just emerging from a decade of confrontation warfare between citizens and planners in all our large cities. That was an experience we had to go through.

Item: Thirty years ago Canada had just set up a housing agency (CMHC) that was given no authority and no money, incredible though this now seems, for improving the habitat of low income people, who need this help most. At that time no provincial or municipal government had any part to play in housing affairs. All that has now changed.

Item: The concepts of regional planning and the two-tier forms of regional government had not yet been thought of. Big city growth had to be looked after with small town forms of management. Since then Canada has been, of all countries, the most experimental in forms of city government.

Item: In 1946 we had no comprehensive programmes of social security and medical insurance and income redistribution, so all kinds of human distress were deposited on the doorsteps of city halls. The poor and the aged were largely dependent upon the charity of voluntary organizations. The building of Canada's social security system began with Leonard Marsh's report of 1943; it has been called "the single most important document in the development of the post-war social security system in Canada."

A social security system is basic to what we are discussing. To build an acceptable habitat for any society begins with improving the conditions of people on the bottom layer of poverty and slum living. The incomes of the poorest families, of old people, and of those who are incompetent for any reason, have to match up with the costs of an acceptable standard of housing. So the presence of a mature social security system is the platform and foundation for a decent habitat. Until this is achieved, you can only do your best with special programmes of subsidized public housing for poor families, old people, and welfare cases. During the post-war period in Canada, over the pig-headed resistance of prime ministers and much of the public, we did succeed in introducing public housing; this was the only way of dealing with the most critical deficiencies in our housing accommodation, while the social security system is still incomplete. But Canadians have generally felt that it would ultimately be better to reach for a social situation in which the incomes of all families, of the aged and the partly incompetent, were supported so that they could share the same habitat as everyone else, and not be segregated in what have been called "ghettos of public housing." This is a healthy and compassionate aim. But I don't think it's fair to deprive poor people of decent housing now, while we gather our morale to act more nobly towards them in the future. (It is useful to go through this sequence of argument in order to explain that one can be a dedicated supporter of public housing now, and at the same time be dedicated to the disappearance of public housing.)

How are we getting on towards being able to create the kind of urban settlement that I described above — big cities with long fingers of urban growth, with open landscape conserved between the fingers, and with areas of clustered housing interwoven with urban landscape trails?

The cluster housing idea started about 1956. It became the particular interest of the Canadian Housing Design Council. Architects and builders all across Canada have now developed a good deal of expertise in this field and the condominium system has really made cluster housing workable. So there is now a wide range of possibilities available between the two stereotypes of single house and high-rise.

We have made much less progress on the conservation of landscape, though the concepts have begun to take shape in British Columbia and in other provinces that have developed environmental protection disciplines and in the Conservation Authorities of Ontario. Perhaps this will be the big breakthrough of the next decade; we need some very large public acquisitions of landscape on the perimeters of urban fingers and for internal landscape ribbons or "trails." We need a financial system by which the senior governments would be the bankers and the acquisition costs would ultimately be paid back as a charge upon the benefiting properties, just as we have always done for other city services and amenities.

In the field of urban management some important breakthroughs may well occur in the next few years when we have thought through the problems raised by the thrust of citizen participation. I feel that there is quite a difference between the forms of management required to *build* a piece of city and the subsequent enjoyment of people living in it and sharing in its management. When a new piece of city is being built, such as one of the new towns on a finger, a certain kind of management expertise is essential; a lot of public capital investment has to be found and managed and there has to be both experience and strong authority in dealing with private developers. This is pretty high-powered stuff, requiring great executive strength and, for this task, a certain type of city government and management is needed. But once a piece of city is established and settled down there should be opportunities for people to run their own affairs at the neighbourhood community scale, in a more intimate way.

I live in a regional city with a population of about 500,000. The neighbourhood community I live in has a population of only 2000 or 0.4 per cent of the whole population. For fifty years my community has retained its individuality as a separate village municipality, and we run our own affairs very competently. We have a reeve and four councillors and only one official who is clerk, manager, tax collector, treasurer. We have our own planning by-laws and a landscape conservation programme. As in a small town, most people know one another and the system is a practical exercise in political democracy. But we are threatened with extinction because we are thought to be too small a unit within a regional system of urban management. To which we reply: "Small is Beautiful." Many other mature neighbourhoods should be allowed to run their own affairs.

CONCLUSION

To return to my starting point: I wonder if people in other countries, at many different stages of economic development and with different possibilities of achievement, would nevertheless recognize the same aspirations for their habitats. Would they find agreement in these three simple propositions:
1. To elevate what is distinctively human in people, it's not just *shelter* we're concerned about. There must be something there of imagination and beauty, a place to dance and sing together with other people, and a privacy at home for discovering how each of us is different and separate from all other people.
2. Somehow the human habitat has to be integrated with the rest of the habitat of life, to see flowers and trees and other creatures responding to the changing seasons.
3. Whatever corporate powers may be needed to build these immense human settlements that are the characteristic of our age, there's got to be a place for every man and woman to share in looking after his and her little bit of estate.

EXTRACTS FROM DISCUSSION

Question: Would you say something about physical composition and social composition, particularly in regard to small towns?
Mr. Carver: I think it is very important that they have a physical composition which people can understand. That is something we try to do. We work to make cities have a recognizable shape and form. With regard to social composition, I certainly have had the experience of working in a particular small town and the enthusiasm that one can get in support for an interesting project just simply bowls one over. In a small town if you are lucky and successful you can get people to work collaboratively on a project in a way

that one cannot do in a big city, really because people know one another and do not have to overcome quite so many suspicions and jealousies of "who's he?" — he runs the garage, and he runs the grocery store, and so on. People already have a place in the small town. However, I do not think we really know enough about our small towns and if we did it would probably help us quite a bit in planning big cities.

Question: You were talking about clusters of buildings that were joined by meandering paths. This sounded very idyllic, but obviously you are not talking about cities with automobiles.

Mr. Carver: I am talking about networks of circulation. There is a rather classic example of this which is Central Park, New York, where a piece of land is so designed that one can move around as a pedestrian, a boat oar-puller, or as a car driver and people do not collide with one another. It's a skill of planning to put into the same area networks of different types of circulation.

Question: What are your observations of the corporate conscience in terms of the financiers of human settlement, the people, the developers who actually make a great many decisions — their motives versus the results of their actions?

Mr. Carver: In a way this is a discussion about the public place; the place of public action in creating the habitat and, in turn, this is connected with the public housing subject. However successful we might be in rigging up a social security system which gave practically everybody access to the same habitat, the free enterprise system naturally is going to operate at the upper levels of that habitat-making because that is where free enterprise has the greatest opportunity for profit, and it has literally no opportunity for profit at the bottom end even when you have set up the whole social security system that everybody has access to. It seems inevitable that one would have to use public action at the bottom end. What I am saying is that there is not any such thing as the conscience of private enterprise and there is no responsibility in the sense that if one starts with the idea of the citizens of a country having rights one cannot claim rights against private enterprise. Private enterprise just does not respond to rights — it responds to profit — that is what it is there for. So that where the private system does not render sufficient habitat in quantity and quality, one can only exercise the rights of the people against the public corporate body. Whether or not you call that the "conscience" of the public corporate body I don't know.

3

The Urbanizing North: Some Comparisons

Trevor Lloyd

My purpose is to draw comparisons between the north polar areas in North America, Europe, and Asia from a rather special point of view. This will sometimes require drawing of comparisons between, say, northern Canada, Greenland, Arctic Scandinavia, and part of the Soviet Union. At the outset I must emphasize that the physical environment is, of course, not the same in all of them, even though they may be in similar latitudes. So if it appears that conditions are more advanced in one area than another, the explanation may very well be a physical one or in part historical, rather than incompetence or basic laziness!

My message about urbanization in the north is simple. Nowadays people there are moving from semi-nomadic, nomadic, or some other scattered existence into a pattern whereby most of them are living in villages, small towns, or even large cities. In other words, they are being "urbanized," as are people of many other parts of the world. This is certainly not the first time in history that urbanization has been advancing so rapidly. Historians will remind us that the Industrial Revolution in Western Europe was a period of intense urbanization when folk moved from the open countryside and from villages to crowd into existing towns and cities or to create new cities and new towns. Crewe, the railway town in England, did not exist before the Industrial Revolution, nor did much of the Ruhr Valley industrial region. In Russia, Kharkov in the Ukraine, for example, was largely a product of that urbanization. Rather later, but still before the Soviet revolution of 1917, Siberian cities such as Novosibirsk grew up in pine forests — with the arrival of the Trans-Siberian Railway. So this kind of transformation is something to which we have been accustomed for a very long time. It is now happening on an enormous scale in many parts of the world — in Asia, Africa, and South America — and there is no reason why it should not occur in northern Canada as it is doing in southern Canada. The urbanization of northern Canada has been paralleled in Greenland, Scandinavia, and the Soviet Union — people in all these northern regions have been agglomerating where they were formerly dispersed.

There are several reasons why the process is going on in the North, and I would like to cite examples to illustrate some of them. There are cases where an area, formerly completely empty and unused, has become a settlement because a mineral occurring there has been developed. There are equally striking examples owing to the construction of a hydro-electric power plant. Usually as far as most of the North is concerned the explanation is the existence of exploitable minerals. In 1938 Yellowknife was created at a point on the north shore of Great Slave Lake, which had never been a significant Indian campsight, although there were Indians in the area. In north central Quebec, in 1954 at what is now the iron ore mining town of Schefferville, there were no native people living. A Greenland example is a small community called Ivigtut, famous for its mining of the unique mineral cryolite. It was never an Eskimo settlement and did not become one; it was simply a single purpose community designed for mining. There are many similar examples in other northern areas.

Another change that has occurred is that existing small communities which already have some raison d'être have increased in size by additions to a nucleus, very small though it may be. Typically this has occurred at trading posts — Fort Smith, N.W.T., was at one time a small trading post; Port Barrow in northernmost Alaska started that way as did also Godthåb, now the capital of Greenland, and Yakutsk on the Lena River in northeastern Siberia. And there are of course other reasons why the northern parts of Alaska, Canada, Siberia, and other arctic lands are now spotted with urban communities, something rare indeed even a generation ago.

In northern Canada we are seeing the creation of an oasis pattern in which isolated, small, or even larger communities are appearing with wilderness or little or nothing between. I believe this will be the pattern of the future; that "emptiness," a sharp discontinuity between the urban areas and the hinterland, is something that we are going to have to become accustomed to and do something about. The reasons for this desert-like pattern are obvious. There is a very small total population in the North, and it is never likely to be a particularly large one. Historically, throughout the North, the population has always been widely scattered, so that when the nuclei were forming, it was natural that the new centres would be far apart from one another. This pattern of settlement is based partly on the hunting economy of the native peoples. Pond Inlet, Baffin Island, Igloolik, in northern Foxe Basin, and Repulse Bay on western Hudson Bay are now three communities of appreciable size. All of them have attracted nomadic peoples who at one time were dispersed over the area between them.

A powerful driving force that has made this oasis pattern inevitable has been a conviction that health, educational, and other social services are essential and that to provide them efficiently, or even at all, communities of a certain minimum size are unavoidable. Policy has favoured urbanization for social and administrative reasons. Another controlling factor in the existence and location of such communities has been transportation, and many of them are found where there is either a change in transportation mode or where routes naturally cross or focus.

So far in Canada we have not evolved an appropriate, or even *any*, system of government that makes it possible to administer a vast territory that is almost empty and which has, or is going to have, scattered urban centres within it. And one can find little in the way of guidance in other arctic areas. The settlement system in Greenland was for two centuries an effective one, but it has now broken down. Originally — I am speaking of the period since the Danes colonized West Greenland in 1721 — there were about a dozen main centres of population, each called a "koloni," having a direct link by sea with Copenhagen. All of them were scattered along the west coast of Greenland at roughly equal intervals at convenient sites from the point of view of a sailing harbour or with good hunting or fishing grounds. Each such centre had subsidiary or satellite settlements tributary to it called "udsteds" or outplaces. Each of these usually had a Danish manager, but they offered much more spartan services than the main koloni. In turn, the udsteds each had smaller satellites called "boplads" (a hamlet made up of a few families). The trade goods reached the koloni direct from Copenhagen and from there were dispersed by schooner to the udsted which had a small trading store. The boplad dwellers would come in their skin boats or by dog team to deliver their catch and make purchases. What of social services? There was a doctor in the koloni, a nurse, or more probably a midwife, at the udsted, and nothing at the little boplads. The same plan applied to schools, churches, and so on. This was a not unreasonable system in an era when a small population depended on hunting from the sea and had to live strung out along a winding coast in order to make a sufficient catch on which to live. There were perhaps two hundred and fifty settlements of one size or another along the coast of West Greenland from Cape Farewell to Melville Bay. But such a system no longer matches the needs of the people. There is now a more centralized system of government in Greenland, with a Legislative Council representing some twelve or fifteen larger communities and a few which are smaller. The old kolonis have grown in size, sometimes quite dramatically. Most of the outlying, third-order hamlets have died, and the rest will probably do so eventually. Some of the second-order communities have flourished, but others are declining. Both the transfer of population and its considerable increase have urbanized the people of West Greenland.

In Canada there was never such a settlement pattern. The tendency had been for the trader, in more recent times usually the Hudson's Bay Company trader, to serve nomads for a distance around him who came in to trade once or twice a year. Naturally, the trading posts were in the best hunting areas. When the missionaries arrived, they usually attached themselves to the same place, and when schools were built, they did so too. Most settlements in the Canadian North were thus located to serve a scattered nomadic, hunting people, and in many cases the modern urban settlement has remained at the old site. In the past twenty or twenty-five years there has been a steady flow of native people toward the larger centres. It was, I believe, inevitable, and it cannot be attributed to deliberate planning by the administration.

It was caused by the force of rather complex circumstances. No one who has read accounts of the deplorable condition of the Eskimos in some parts of the North, when the local food supply ran out and many people starved or when epidemics were widespread, would question the wisdom of reaching the people where they could at least be fed and receive minimal medical services and where children could receive some schooling. It has become fashionable to suggest that the Eskimos should have been left alone. Had this been done, they would almost certainly have died out in many northern areas. Opposition to "modernizing" the Eskimo is not a new idea. It was the official policy of Greenland for 150 years and was applied firmly and effectively.

What might be called a decanting of the new large urban centres back into the hinterland appears to be occurring on a limited scale. There are people who want to continue, at least to some extent, to live the life of their forbears or to follow a way of life patterned on that of their forbears. Needless to say, they still wish to retain ties with the urban society to which they have become accustomed. And, incidentally, they still want to retain the assurance from the various governments that they will not be left to starve to death or to die of disease beyond reach of medical assistance. The result is that there is now gradually being set up a pattern of organized campsights, away from the main centres, where families may go and live for all or part of the year. Expressed in southern terminology, it is rather like having a cottage in the country or an island off the coast or going back to the family farm for a few weeks every year. It is a harking back by the Indians and Eskimos to the old ancestral ways without running the ever present risks that their ancestors could not avoid.

There are already some examples of this "return to the land" that are being given serious study both by independent students and by the governments in Yellowknife and Ottawa. The best-known one is Baffin Island — in the Pond Inlet area and in and near Cumberland Sound. While governments are interested, the moves have been spontaneous, originating among a few leaders who want to retain something of Eskimo culture for later generations but consider this impossible. Had general policy twenty-five years ago been better thought out and calculated to restrain the helter-skelter desertion of the hunting communities, the Eskimos of today would have had access to the best of both worlds. Unhappily, perhaps for financial reasons, government did not take its services to the people where they were but followed a "come and get it" policy, "it" being available in the larger centres.

There is nothing directly comparable to this urge to return to the land in

West Greenland, although it has happened to some extent in the region of the East Greenland settlement Angmagssalik. The Lapp situation in Scandinavia is quite different. (We know next to nothing about the current situation of the 1500 or so Lapps in the Kala Peninsula of the U.S.S.R.) Most Laplanders live in towns or large villages. They are settled people with permanent homes. However, there are also a few thousand nomad Lapps, mainly in Norway, who are nomadic in the sense that they have permanent winter homes but move either up into the mountains or out onto the coastal islands of Norway in the summer. This is a regular seasonal movement along a predetermined route, and it is essential for the maintenance of the reindeer herds. It seems likely to continue indefinitely. The Swedish authorities have taken it into account when arranging schooling for Lapp children. At one time there were even special "nomadic" schools which provided an elementary education without the Lapps having to give up their nomadism. I personally urged something similar on the Canadian authorities in 1947 in order to avoid disturbing the family ties of large numbers of Eskimo children by flying them to boarding schools where they remained for long periods.

As has been suggested earlier, the evaluation of urbanism and settlement in the North is closely linked to transportation and communication. The transportation system, whatever form it may take, helps to determine how goods and people move back and forth; and the communication system determines the movement of ideas and information. This has to be very much borne in mind. It might perhaps be a useful exercise to devise for northern Canada an ideal pattern of population distribution and transportation. Obviously it could only be done in very general terms. That pattern, however devised, could be compared with the facts as they are today, the disparities noted, and the reasons for them traced. An attempt at long-term regional planning of communities could then be attempted. Northern Canada is today the only part of the world's northland that has never been the subject of long-range, overall, macro, large-scale planning, apart from whatever the multinational oil companies do for their own purposes.

Any serious study of settlement distribution would, of course, underline the casualness of the influences that have led to the present pattern. Some of them are historical, resulting in some cases in places lingering on long after the reason for them has vanished because of a kind of geographical inertia. In other places the situation is very dynamic with new, contemporary influences at work. Fort Smith, for example, just north of the sixtieth parallel in the Northwest Territories, exists because there are sixteen miles of impassable rapids on the Slave River. This was the place where people going north got back into the boat after they and their goods had been carried over the portage. The obstruction lay across the main route to the western Arctic. This is no longer so. A road, a railway, and, not least, aircraft follow other routes. Fort Smith should be a dying community with no reason for existence. In the natural course of events, it would eventually vanish. However, governments are sensitive to local influence; so Fort Smith is being perpetuated. It has a large airport, and this is now a kind of "natural resource," giving easy access to the community which is now developed as an educational and administrative centre for what might be called "socio-political" reasons, rather than for the historical reasons which no longer exist.

It is useful here to refer briefly to the Carruthers Commission of ten years ago. Some hard-working administrators in the northern administration in Ottawa concluded that the Northwest Territories should, following the Canadian tradition of hiving off federal territory to create new provinces, be sub-divided. The original North-West Territories lost in this way Manitoba, Saskatchewan, and Alberta. The rest was destined to be "the Mackenzie region," leaving part of the Arctic Islands. A new name was even produced (in Ottawa) for the residual pieces, Nunasiaq, "the beautiful land." Two bills were presented to Parliament to make it effective, but Parliament, on one of those very rare occasions when it really rebels, sent them to committee, where they were roughly handled because the northern residents had not been adequately consulted. Instead of Mackenzie and Nunasiaq came the Carruthers Commission to look into the political future of northern Canada.

The commission produced invaluable factual reports and some recommendations, including one for moving the administration to Yellowknife. It also suggested that it was untimely to settle for all time the political-administrative arrangements needed for northern Canada, because that should grow naturally out of the demographic, social, and economic conditions of an area. Until those were known, it would be unwise to try to devise appropriate boundaries. How different Canada would look today if those who determined the boundaries of new provinces had waited a little longer to match them to economic-political realities. The Carruthers Commission suggested that fifteen years would be a reasonable delay.

When the review comes to be made, some factors not foreseen a dozen years ago will demand attention — including, of course, the Inuit claim to most of the land under discussion. Still unresolved is how to administer a vast area empty but for a dozen or more urban settlements which will be peopled by residents accustomed to a high living standard. And there may be a dozen lesser communities, isolated from each other geographically, linked together electronically (thanks to satellites). What kind of government does one devise for a region where there are a few quasi-municipalities-writ-large in a couple of million miles of potentially rich hinterland whose resources belong to all the people of Canada?

In the space that remains I shall discuss places in northern Canada, West Greenland, northern Scandinavia, and some northern parts of the Soviet Union as illustrations of some of the generalizations I have so freely made.

A physical map of the north polar regions demonstrates that environmental features such as the geological structure are continued across the polar basin, which is in essence simply a hollow in the earth's surface with water in it. The map also reminds us of the contrast between the eastern part of northern Canada and the western part. An important example of this is the diagonally running "tree-line," much farther to the south in Labrador than in the west, where it reaches the Mackenzie Delta. This comment is made by way of a warning not to generalize too freely within northern Canada, let alone between Canada and other northern areas. The Canadian Arctic in a strict physical sense extends roughly from Hudson's Strait north and west to include the northernmost islands. It occupies a very large part of northern Canada, proportionately much larger than in the Soviet Union. This emphasizes how much of the northern development in the Soviet Union has taken place within the subarctic forested areas and not on the treeless arctic tundra.

To assess the kind and speed of change in northern Canada, it is useful to comment on a few places as they looked in about 1940 and again in the late sixties or early seventies. Cambridge Bay, on Victoria Island, in the winter of 1940-41 consisted of the Hudson's Bay Company trading post, the Mounted Police post, and little else. The Eskimos at that time were nomads who only visited occasionally. Today it is a large, well-planned, urbanized community. In 1940 Yellowknife had been in existence for two years. It was a typical mining camp, without a main road along which one could drive. Its main claim to metropolitan status was the only bar in the Northwest Territories. Today it is no mean city, the capital of the Territories, and certain to expand considerably within a decade as a mining, transportation, and educational centre.

Probably the only occasion in the history of Canada, certainly of northern Canada, when the site of a new community was studied far in advance was when the administrative community on the Mackenzie Delta that became the new town Inuvik, today a quite elaborate urban region, was selected.

Greenland presents a completely different set of problems. It is almost entirely an ice sheet with ragged fringes of land here and there on the margins. Settlement has been sporadic and insecure. A thousand years ago Europeans attempted to settle the southwestern corner, and for a time there was a network of settlements similar to those of the time in Iceland and Norway. Possibly as many as eight thousand people lived there. They failed because they were unable to master the environment without constant support from Europe.

People of a quite different origin have continued to live in Greenland for four thousand years or more. They are the Eskimos or Greenlanders. They lived off the resources of the sea, and a typical view of the traditional Greenlander would show a man in a kayak with a seal in tow. That way of making a living has been gradually transformed into commercial fishing — very elaborate commercial fishing — partly because of changes in the sea temperatures. The seal hunter had been able to produce almost everything he needed for clothing, warmth, and food by hunting. But the fisherman cannot do that, and so he has to live where he can trade his fish for all the requirements of a twentieth century urban dweller.

Transportation in Greenland, as elsewhere in the north, has also changed dramatically. Originally it was by umiaq, a skin boat made entirely out of available local resources. Now the important vessel is a trans-Atlantic freighter, for this is what is required to bring in all the resources required when the hunting community has given way to commercial fishing. In Greenland there are airfields which can handle the largest aircraft in the world. They land at Sondrestrømfjord and other airfields. But for internal distribution, the nature of the country makes it necessary for trips between urban areas to be by helicopter. These are to be replaced in time by STOL aircraft using small airports tucked away in the rare level spots.

Now to consider the communities themselves. The small community of a generation ago included a church, a school, the little mortuary back of the church because in winter when the ground is frozen burial must wait; a few Greenlander homes, and no wheels; to be sure an old lady is carrying brush down from the hillside; seal skins are drying; and there are kayaks, on a rack out of reach of the dogs, and shark meat in the foreground drying for dog food.

It used to be said by visitors to Greenland — John Davis among them — that the natives came out of holes in the ground. In fact they lived in semi-subterranean houses, and all the warmer for that. These evolved into wooden homes, some of them with concrete basements, and all built on rock, high above ground. There was never trouble with permafrost in the old days because they always built upon rock. Danish administrators evolved houses which were prefabricated to a standard pattern, designed to provide much better accommodation than the little shack-like houses, which were cold and drafty in winter and contributed to the appallingly high rate of tuberculosis.

As the towns grew in size, it became quite impossible to continue building the same kind of individual houses on the same separate sites as before. Various approaches were tried. At Godthåb there was not enough flat ground available so sites had to be blasted out to provide room for a suburban area attached to the old community. But the steady flow of immigrants from outlying communities was too great to handle. So massive apartment buildings were built by an assembly line-like process. It was found that people from the little villages rather liked to live in these apartment buildings. They have always been in one another's pockets, associated together closely, and seem to have adapted well. One serious problem has been that some of the older settlements are not well located for use as modern Eskimo fishing towns. Even Godthåb is poorly sited. It was an Eskimo community on a small peninsula, where seals could be caught easily. This is no asset for a modern town of ten thousand. There is a shortage of space for adequate housing; no room for an airport; no convenient location for a water supply reservoir, and even the harbour has drawbacks.

Yet some communities have adapted well. A little outpost in South Greenland, Narssaq, which happened to be near a shrimp fishing ground and convenient to cod fishing areas has blossomed as a well-equipped fish packing centre. It seems certain to expand if only because its name Narssaq means "the flat place," a rarity in Greenland.

There are many problems common to all such urban areas. One is water supply. In a very cold winter climate and in a very rocky region it is difficult to provide the fresh water for all the homes. One device is an insulated pipe from which people fetch the water in a barrel or other container; an alternative is melting icebergs, but this is unsatisfactory so far.

Permafrost is not a problem in the southern part of West Greenland, but it is farther north. The solution is mainly a matter of cost. There is a hotel at the Sondrestrømfjord Airport built on eight feet of gravel and supported by piles. It is made of very lightweight, insulated panelling. The hotel accommodates several hundred guests. At Thule airport things are done more luxuriously. A storage warehouse there was built on permafrost. The ground is kept frozen by induction of cold air to overcome any thawing from waste heat. Sewers cannot be placed underground, so they run along the surface in what are called "utilidors." The system is common also in northern Canada, for example, at Inuvik.

In the same latitude in northern Scandinavia the environment is quite different thanks to milder air and warmer seas, although there is the same lack of sunlight in winter, and there are the same long days in summer. Every trace of settlement in northern Norway and Finland was burned to the ground by the Nazis in a scorched earth campaign during the Second World War. I went there in 1949 to learn how, after several hundred years of experience, the Norwegians and Finns would rebuild their communities in the light of modern needs. The planners did their best, but unfortunately, community inertia is very strong, as was the people's desire to return and do things more or less in the same old way in the same old locations.

Scandinavia has the advantage of an excellent and even elaborate transportation system. One can get to the northernmost part of Norway by water, air, road, and a good deal of the way by rail. That is not true anywhere else even in the Soviet Union at Murmansk. In northern Finland one encounters the reindeer and sledge, but for offroad transportation today the skidoo is used. This has transformed the Lapp economy in many ways. Unhappily it has introduced the first article requiring instalment buying, and demands cash for payments each month, as well as to pay for fuel. The reindeer sledge was produced by local resources which cost nothing.

Along the north Norwegian coast shipping serves the purposes that are met by the roads, rail, and air in other parts of Scandinavia, and there is a very good daily service. As all significant towns are on the seacoast and ice does not form in winter, the transportation service is extraordinarily convenient for a region that extends as far north as Alaska.

The largest community in north Norway that was destroyed completely in the war was Hammerfest, a very old seaport city. Planners wished to rebuild it on a new site, because it was wide open to southwesterly gales and had too little space between the mountains and the sea on which to build. Also avalanches damaged the houses. But people insisted on rebuilding at the old site, and that is indeed where the new town stands.

Mining, which has been an urbanizing element in northern Canada, is also of some significance in Scandinavia, notably at Kiruna, in the middle of northern Sweden. Iron ore is the basic reason for the town's existence, but it has developed in other ways as well. It is an important administrative centre, is well known for winter sports and as a summer tourist base, and has developed some manufacturing. The city itself is attractively planned. The town hall has a mine shaft for a campanile, and a real effort has been made to adapt the style of building to the high latitude locale. In northernmost Norway there is also an attractive iron-mining town — Kirkenes — on the seacoast within a few miles of the Soviet border. This town was rebuilt after being destroyed completely in the war.

Northern Finland also suffered seriously from wartime destruction. The town of Rovaniemi on the Arctic Circle is today attractive and reasonably prosperous. A rather picturesque overgrown wooden village before the war, it is now very "Finnish." I watched the town develop at intervals from about 1949 onwards and never could make out the street plan, which seemed chaotic. Then I read somewhere that the architect chose the two rivers that join there as his inspiration and added as a theme the branching antlers of a Lapp reindeer and laid out the street system accordingly. It's a little hard on casual visitors!

Settlement of northern Scandinavia suffers from a serious disability. Despite the Gulf Stream Drift to moderate the climate, local food production is a serious problem, and alternative supplies have to be carried a long way. Costs of importation are very high. Despite the high latitude dairy products, potatoes, and some other vegetables are grown locally. In summer and winter, hothouses supplement other production, but at a price. There is no doubt that winter darkness is also a handicap. Appropriately, Hammerfest was the first city in the world to light its streets electrically.

Let us now give some thought to the Soviet Union. There must be very few people in North America in a position to report at first hand on communities, their planning and population, in the far north of the U.S.S.R. I have seen something of parts of Siberia and have twice visited Murmansk but must take refuge in the claim that Arctic or Central Asian, Soviet settlements are pretty much all the same. Having criss-crossed the country over a period of two decades, I have been struck both by the uniformity of the country and the absence of surprises in its cities.

One still significant contributor to the Soviet urban scene is the Siberian village, a survivor from pre-Communist days. It is a Czarist village, with its long street, the little garden plots, and all wood houses. I have seen Siberian settlements from the train that must have had ten thousand people living in them but which were, essentially, scaled up replicas of villages. The buildings are of timber; there is no town centre of more elaborate structures; the streets are unpaved, water supply is from a shared pipe, and the sewage arrangements are primitive. Better known Siberian cities such as Novosibirsk, Krasnoyarsk, or Irkutsk have replaced most of the old wooden structures but Yakutsk on the Lena, while it has a new main street and city core, is essentially an overblown Siberian village. Access to the heart of Siberia for industrial and construction purposes is not yet easy. In summer, ships in Siberia use the northern sea route, along the northern coast of Siberia. The same ships are seen in Montreal in winter. From the seacoast ships travel in summer along the big rivers, comparable with the Mackenzie but with deeper drafts. There is also a pattern of transportation southward, the Trans-Siberian Railway which crosses the heads of the larger rivers. Transportation northward down the river is also important. There is thus a grid pattern made up of the sea route, the railway, and the rivers linking the two.

A thousand miles from the sea on the River Lena seagoing freighters serve the city of Yakutsk. Eight hundred miles upstream from the city cargo is transferred to and from the Transylvanian Railway. The river harbour at Yakutsk is equipped with a moderate sized seaport and is far more elaborate than any port in northern Canada apart from Churchill. On the contrary, the Siberian highway is far less elaborate, nor is it dependable. It is used heavily for trucking, particularly in the winter when building supplies are brought in for industry and construction. Aircraft are used very extensively in Siberia. As far as one can discern there are very simple arrangements for servicing, most of it being done out-of-doors.

Among Soviet Arctic and Siberian cities many are "single purpose," as, for example, for mining or power industries. Bratsk on the Angara River is one of the latter. The power plant generates almost as much electricity as Churchill Falls in Labrador. It is used for local industries, particularly pulp and paper, all kinds of cellulose, for aluminum smelting, for railway transport and for contributing to the Siberian grid.

Murmansk is a town of 330,000 on the arctic Atlantic coast of the U.S.S.R. It was founded by the Royal Engineers in 1916 as a railhead where goods could be landed and sent inland to support the Russian war effort. It became a permanent town afterwards, but it was largely destroyed during the Second World War. It is now being enlarged and remodelled following a new plan. Its main activity is fishing, but it is also a railroad city, an important defence base, important administratively, and especially in winter a leading Soviet commercial seaport.

A typical frontier community is the electrical power settlement Chernyshevsky in the Lena Valley. Its purpose is to produce the electricity needed, for example, at Mirny, a diamond mining town. Even in such a small community there is a cultural theatre which welcomes visiting dramatic groups and orchestras flown in from Moscow! The town itself can teach a visitor little or nothing about modern techniques of arctic construction. As with most of Siberia it suffers from permafrost troubles. When the whole of an area is underlain by permanently frozen ground, at a depth of a foot or so in summer, planners, architects, and engineers need to follow special principles. Pipes need to be carried above ground. At a road crossing the pipes are carried overhead. Piling is driven into steamed out holes in the ground, frozen in place, and used as a foundation. At Chernyshevsky even a hydro-electric dam has been constructed in this way.

In any remote area, it is very expensive to secure skilled labour (northern Canada and Greenland are no exceptions). So one avoids the use of labour as far as possible, by having much of the construction completed far to the south. Lightweight, prefabricated buildings are made in the south and shipped north, if need be by air. The U.S.S.R. has the same problems but still has much to learn about solving them. Heavy cement sections used at Yakutsk are brought in about a thousand miles from the railway. A good many get broken on the way in. Triple-glazed windows are included in some units, and usually all three panes are broken on arrival. It is not surprising, therefore, that in one of the new oil and gas areas of western Siberia an Alberta company is selling large numbers of their prefabricated buildings for an experimental community being built there. At Yakutsk is the greatest permafrost institute in the world. There is a large scientific staff, which produces an array of publications with a high reputation. The objective of the institute is to ameliorate the conditions of Siberia.

For reasons that are difficult to discover, the quality and design of Soviet buildings everywhere are far below what one would expect. There is certainly a dearth of skilled labour; supervision is inadequate; working people at all levels are irresponsible; and productivity is low. But equally to blame would seem to be the unbridgeable gap between the scientific community which is responsible for research and the construction industry that needs to acquire the results and apply them. From the Lena Valley to the border of Norway I have seen nothing that suggests that the U.S.S.R. has made any major contribution to the planning, construction and utilization of northern communities, with one possible exception. The U.S.S.R. recognizes that some parts of its vast hinterland are for climatic or other reasons less attractive than the heart of European Russia. (One disability is the lack of consumer goods and services of reasonable quality away from the main cities such as Moscow, Lenin-

Plate 1. Teeming cities have evolved under the pressure of population and multiplying urban/industrial activities. Hong Kong.

Plate 2. Changes in world settlement patterns and advances in communication affect the most traditional way of life.

Plate 3. Time-honoured customs yield reluctantly to modern structures and conveniences.

Plate 4. Peoples of all cultures create marketplaces for the exchange of goods and ideas. Kumasi, Ghana.

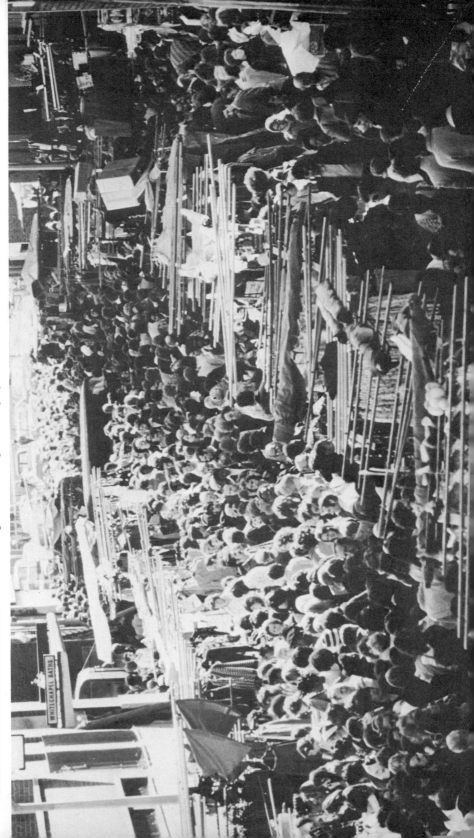

Plate 5. One of the Western world's most famous and enduring markets serving its eternal purposes. Petticoat Lane, London.

Plate 6. In many countries congested trading centres often double as living space. The urban community is an intertwined milieu.

Plate 7. Transportation services groan under the daily ebb and flow of urban life throughout the world. Tokyo.

Plate 8. North American farming communities, dramatically different from the cities, provide local centres of transportation, trading, and communication.

Plate 9. The waters of the world and the life in them are threatened by pollution and industrial abuse.

Plate 10. Waste and swift obsolescence have become characteristic features of industrialization.

grad, and Kiev.) To compensate for the isolation, climate, and other disadvantages and to attract skilled labour to remote places, generous salaries are paid. Taking Murmansk in 1976 as an example: everyone working in Murmansk automatically receives 40 per cent more than for the same work in Moscow. In addition, there is an increment of 10 per cent each six months, so long as the person remains in Murmansk, up to a maximum of five years. There are very generous paid leave arrangements, free transportation once a year to any part of the U.S.S.R., and special vacation arrangements in the south. Prices of consumer goods are about the same as elsewhere. There are also advantages in purchase of cars and other hard to get durables. There is no doubt that the attractiveness of northern communities is greatly enhanced by the generous incentives. Put another way, without incentives there would be far less development in the Soviet Arctic than there is now.

4

Is the Canadian North Properly Populated?

Louis-Edmond Hamelin

In 1972, R.M. Bone collected basic data for a pilot study of northern population in Canada.[1] On the basis of his article and other documents, it is possible to consider some settlement problems in the Canadian North; more specifically, to discuss an optimal situation for settlement in the North. Such a question is less recent in the U.S.S.R. than in Canada. In the Soviet Union, discussions have been going on for some time about such matters as demographic concentration, ways of populating a territory, permanence of habitat, and so on. My purpose here is to explore some aspects of these issues as they relate to Canada.

The North in Canada occupies approximately 70 per cent of the national area. It spreads over two territories, seven provinces, and includes some marine waters, inland and peripheral. But in that huge area, there are only 300,000 permanent inhabitants, plus approximately 200,000 southern Canadians who are temporary residents in the North each year. Permanent residents make up less than 1½ per cent of the population. Such a figure is very low and prevents the North from having a powerful voice in national affairs and from providing a base for services. There are only two members from the North in Parliament out of 265 elected. It is easy to say that it is because the Canadian North is insufficiently populated that it is not better represented.

In that respect, Canada is not in the same situation as northern Scandinavia, which is at least six times more inhabited. Also, as noted by several authors, in many parts of the European North there exists "a strategy of retreat" in the pioneer fringe. In other words, "There are too many people to have jobs within the area."[2]

Another problem about the Canadian North is the size of settlements. We in Canada abuse the term "urban" in reference to the North, there being only three localities with more than 10,000 citizens and none with 30,000. The North is a rather wide archipelago having a number of very small settlements. The accurate number of settlements is still a matter of discussion; there are at least 300 settlements with some municipal (or quasi-municipal) structures; the total number could be around 2,000.[3] If one were to establish means for permanent settlements, one would arrive at 900 people per settlement and a distance of 160 miles between each locality. As shown in Table 1, a majority of present permanent settlements in the Canadian North have less than 300 people.

TABLE 1

Classification of settlements in the Northwest Territories and Quebec*

Number of inhabitants in settlement	Number of settlements		
	NWT	Yukon	Northern Quebec
100	29	26	8
100 - 300	24	10	15
300 - 500	7	4	5
500 - 1000	13	3	7
1000 - 1500	2	0	4
1500 - 3000	4	0	2
3000 - 6000	0	0	2
6000 - 8000	1	0	0
8000 - 11,000	0	1	0
Total	80	44	43

*situation as of 1971, not counting seasonal camps.   Hamelin, 1975

This is the core of the habitat problem in the Canadian North, demographic concentration. The situation is what K. Stone has called an "areally or an uninterrupted discontinuous settlement."[4] Are there too many settlements? If so, should the present number of them be reduced, or, at least, new sites discouraged? In short, should we or should we not encourage the scattering of northern settlement?

Strong arguments can be presented for both sides.[5] On the one hand, one could argue that the number of settlements is already too low, considering the distribution of many wildlife resources; fewer and fewer "urbanized" Amerindians can live in their local environments. One must also remember that the dispersal of settlements ensures a stronger Canadian political presence in the North as a whole; that type of occupation goes hand in hand with sovereignty.

However, other scientists will argue against demographic dispersion. For the modern economy, the dispersed type of settlement seems to present more disadvantages than advantages. Communications are very costly, since distances are great, and the amount of return freight is very small. Settlements which do not enjoy the advantages of regular, frequent air services are fairly numerous; since many of them are not linked by road or rail either, the isolation of the populations involved is extreme. This type of dispersed settlement throughout the North thus necessitates a minimum of services (oil storage, schools, etc.) at a large number of sites; it involves the imposition of an over-industrialized structure on numerous small villages. Furthermore, the turnover of qualified personnel remains at a high level and it is almost impossible to find on the spot the specialist workers and managerial staff essential to local development.

Concentration of population is not the same for every ethnic group. It is at the level of services that the indigenous dwelling can be demonstrated to differ most from those of white inhabitants. The white communities, corresponding to the developed centres, are better serviced than the Amerindian villages. Moreover, the future level of water services will be mainly (but not exclusively) based on the number of inhabitants: four classes have been suggested.[6] Since the largest centres in the North are occupied mainly by whites, and the smallest by indigenous people, these levels of service operate to the disadvantage of the Amerindians. Certain centres, such as Inuvik, have even experienced a certain internal discrimination which is now being rectified.

Another area of discussion is the functional links southern Canada has with the tiny northern settlements. In particular, does the heartland-hinterland theory explain the northern habitat? If borderlands are only to serve the core of a country, if the North is at the disposal of the south, the metropolitan theory is sufficient. In fact, however, in the North that functional concept cannot explain most settlement situations. Only a quarter of northern Canadian settlements can be said to have tight economic links with a big city in the south.[7] Pine Point and Hay River, for example, *should* be in that group, but are not.

Therefore, a majority of sub-arctic and arctic settlements are not in a hinterland position. For these villages, the new concept of "outland," which expresses the looseness or the absence of strong liaisons between southern and northern settlements, is more applicable. Most settlements in the North are outside any profitable economic fluxes; they are also often isolated from social services, so they may be characterized by a high degree of discreteness. Such a situation means that economic planning has not yet succeeded in settling every corner of the North. The huge build-up of local disparities is an expression of this failure.

Another aspect of settlement of the Canadian North related to the preceding one concerns the municipal financing of northern communities. How much can settlements budget for themselves?

Take the example of Pelly Bay, an arctic village of 200 people, for the period 1960-75. Table 2 shows that Pelly Bay is not financially independent. In addition to the data given, the cost of depreciation of capital expenses (in 1970 constant dollars), is 7 million dollars and the deficit is in the order of 4 million dollars. Multiply that amount by the number of permanent settlements in the North and you will have some indication of the total municipal liability there. Essentially, this is the basic explanation for the huge federal non-military budget for the North. Hundreds of millions of dollars have been spent because the great majority of northern settlements cannot survive by their own means. During the Habitat conference in Vancouver we learned that, in Inuvik, only 130 persons among 4000 were significant taxpayers. Elsewhere, the situation is worse. In the North, there is a great gap between the degree of social help coming from outside and economic tools in the hands of Northerners. The "democratic" Canadian North has a paradoxical character, for state intervention is high, a rather more socialist situation. Because of this financial dependence, the problem of the total number of settlements to be sustained is re-emphasized.

TABLE 2
The budget of an Inuit village in the far North

Expenses	initial capital	$1,500,000
	repairs	250,000
	operations	3,750,000
	total	5,500,000
Income	all categories	3,375,000
Deficit		2,125,000

The last factor I should like to consider deals with the mobility of population. Are Northerners too mobile? Mobility is characteristic of the North, even more so than disparity or isolation. This instability of settlements is both an historic and a contemporary phenomenon. Coastal Labrador provides a good example of migrations in the recent past (see Table 3). Although the statistics do not permit a precise study of the changes, nevertheless they reveal the ephemeral life of many settlements. It is the seasonal camps in particular which have been abandoned as a result of local variations in biological resources. During the period considered, the total number of settlements on the Labrador coast fluctuated around 200. Examining the situation at ten-year intervals, one discovers that the positive statistics recorded at the beginning of the century later became negative. The number of settlements exceeded that of those reoccupied, particularly during the Second World War and the post-war period.

TABLE 3
New and abandoned settlements in Labrador 1901-61

Year	Number of new or reoccupied settlements	Number of settlements abandoned temporarily or permanently	Numerical change throughout region
1901	59	14	45
1911	36	29	7
1921	66	31	35
1935	59	60	-1
1945	52	73	-21
1951	14	62	-48
1961	2	33	-31

Source: A.P. Dyke, 1968

The present mobility in the North has particular characteristics. Workers are nomadic to a very high degree. The enormous demand for labour is often only temporary, its duration limited to the period of construction, which lasts only a few years. This is the case with the installation of the components of the infrastructure: railways, harbours, houses, powerhouses, and telecommunication links. After the period of establishment of these installations, only a limited number of workers is required; moreover, these can be recruited easily from among those already on site. Others leave for the south or for new centres in the North. Construction sites often have an irresistible appeal, and the "boom towns" of the Canadian North are characterized by the itinerant nature of the workers. Mobility in the exploitive industries is more serious. Many forestry enterprises, mines, and even tourist camps have disappeared after only a brief existence along the thresholds of the middle north. The agricultural part of Abitibi (in the near North) demonstrates a vast abandonment of the ecumene. Out of 20,000 lots registered during the 1930's by aspiring colonists, the actual number of farms now properly cultivated is only 1500; thus the percentage of viable farms is only about 5 per cent and there has occurred a massive abandonment of settlements. Mobility of population and impermanence of settlements work against any personal involvement in local affairs and contribute to the very low percentage (around 5 per cent) of home-owners in the Northwest Territories.

To conclude, it seems to me that the most important requirement for the future development of the North is for southerners to adjust mentally to northern situations. I have developed that concept in speaking of the northness, or nordicity, approach.[8] Much of the North has to be taken as it is. In the past, settlement policy has not been northern enough, so there have been failures and hardships for many residents. The best way to improve what we are doing in the North is first to change our southern mind, as Stefansson was advocating 50 years ago. After that, we will find the best solution to our northern habitat problems.

Notes

1. Wonders, 1972.

2. W.P. Adams et al., Toronto, 1972 (works by G. Endriss, R. Helle, and P. Poremus); W.C. Wonders, Toronto, 1976 (works by I.Y. Ashwell, J.C. Hansen, E. Bylund, and M. Palomaki).

3. R.J. Fletcher (Edmonton, 1975) suggests that there are more than 1300 settlements for an area smaller than the one considered here.

4. Adams, 1972, pp. 767-68.

5. P. Usher has considered the historical aspect of that dilemma. He has noted that the high number of population centres still dates back to the fur trade era. The real or imagined competition between the fur companies encouraged the maintenance of a large number of posts. Indeed, this commercial era involved a certain concentration and the beginnings of sedentariness of the population. While this evolution towards concentration has continued, the phenomenon of dispersal remains. P.J. Usher, 1971.

6. Northwest Territories, Yellowknife, 1973.

7. AINA, Montreal, 1971.

8. Hamelin, 1975.

Short Bibliography

ACFAS, *La Construction et les communautés nordiques*, ed. by M. Glover. Montreal, 1974, 152 pp

Adams, W.P. and F.M. Helleiner, eds., *International Geography 1972*. Toronto, 1972, 2 vols.

AINA, *Communications Study*. Montreal, 1971, 2 parts (by G.I. Kenney)

Armstrong, T.E., *"Shift Work" in the Arctic*. Leningrad, 1976, p. 115

Bone, R.M., *Northern Settlements and Public Housing in Canada*. Leningrad, 1976, pp. 119-20

Duerden, F., *The Evolution of the Contemporary Settlement Pattern in the Yukon Territory*. Quebec, CAG, 1976, p. 34 (abstract)

Dyke, A.P., "Population Distribution and Movement in Coastal Labrador, 1950-1966," Montreal, 1968 (thesis)

Fletcher, R.J., compiler, *Settlements of Northern Canada: A Gazetteer and Index*. Edmonton, The Boreal Institute, 1975, Occ. Publ. 11

Gordon, A., *Housing and the Social Environment: Northwest Territories and Greenland: A Comparison*. Yellowknife, 1971, 116 pp

Hamelin, L.-E., *Nordicité canadienne*. Montreal, HMH, 1975, 460 pp (English translation by W. Barr)

Larochelle, G., *Report on the Qikirtajuarmiut and Their Relocalization*. Quebec-Ottawa, 1975

Lachance, L. et al., *Systeme resille-coque et préfabrication pour voiles minces en ferrociment*. Montreal, IASS World Congress on Space Enclosures, 1976, pp. 989-97

Northwest Territories, *Proposed Water and Sanitation Policy for the Communities in the NWT.* Yellowknife, 1973, 68 pp

Ostergaard, P.E., "Quality of Life in a Northern City: A Social Geography of Yellowknife, NWT." Vancouver, 1976, 233 pp (thesis)

Slavin, S.V., *The Soviet North.* Moscow, 1972, 193 pp

Rea, K.J., *The Political Economy of Northern Development.* Ottawa, SCC, 1976, 251 pp

Stager, J.K., Report, *Old Crow, Yukon* (presented before the Berger Commission hearings, Yellowknife, 1975)

Treude, E., "Studies in Settlement Development and Evolution of the Economy in the Eastern Central Canadian Arctic," *The Musk Ox,* 16, 1975 pp. 53-66

Usher, P.J., *Fur Trade Posts of the NWT, 1870-1970.* Ottawa, 1971, 180 pp

Wonders, W.C., ed., *The North.* Toronto, 1972, 151 pp (see paper by Bone)

Yates, A.B., "Housing Programmes for Eskimos in Northern Canada," *The Polar Record,* 94, 1970, pp. 45-50

Zrudlo, L.R., "User-Designed Housing for the Inuit of Arctic Quebec," *The Northern Engineer,* 7, 3, 1975, pp. 36-44

5

Issues of Human Settlement:
The Developing Countries

Austin Tetteh

In a recent interview published in the FAO publication *Ceres*, Señor Peña-losa, Secretary-General of Habitat, suggested that the problems of human settlements are not national problems but planetary ones.[1] He emphasized the global nature of the habitat problem by pointing out, for instance, that if Mexico City has thirty million inhabitants by the end of this century and fifteen million of them are without pure water, services, schools, or anything worth having, this is not only a Mexican problem, but a world problem. Similarly, if in the next few decades Canada covers most of its agricultural land with cities that are not producing food for the world, this would not be merely a Canadian problem, it would be a planetary one as well, one which hurts several millions of people around the world other than Canadians.

This view of the problems of human settlements as transcending national and regional boundaries is one we all have to accept if we are to work toward achieving or maintaining a decent standard of life for ourselves and succeeding generations. The decisions we take in our own countries and regions affect human settlements and their relationship to the natural and socio-economic environments. And those decisions have repercussions in parts of the world other than the countries in which the decisions were made.

However, although problems of human settlements are global ones, they do not manifest themselves everywhere in the same form or with the same intensity and the solutions applied to them cannot be universal solutions but must be adapted to and shown to be appropriate to particular problems in specific areas. What appears to be a problem in one area may not be so pressing in another area or may not even be a problem at all in that area. The human settlement problems of the emerging nations of the world are, in general, not the same as those of the more developed countries. Further, where the problems appear to be similar, they do not necessarily exhibit the same degree of urgency and primacy in the emerging countries as in the advanced countries. Consequently the methods, strategies, and priorities for arriving at solutions are apt to be different.

My purpose in this paper is to explore some aspects of the problems of human settlements which are of great importance to the developing nations in general and to the African continent in particular. First, it is important to look at a number of factors and processes which have conditioned the current state of the habitat problem in Africa and in the developing nations. The most outstanding of these are: (1) rapid population growth; (2) rapid urbanization and the growth of urban centres; (3) the essentially rural nature of the African habitat in spite of rapid urbanization; (4) the scarcity of human and financial resources; (5) the subordinate and superordinate political and economic relations established during long periods of colonial rule which still continue to a very large extent in the economic sphere.

The causes of the rapid growth in population are too well known to warrant a discussion here. The most significant thing about this growth is its speed. For hundreds of years Africa and the developing world kept their populations at a relatively low level but, within the past twenty-five years, while the population of the world increased at an annual rate of under 2 per cent, the population of Africa grew at the rate of 2½ per cent per year and that of Latin America at the rate of 2.7 per cent per year. From the relatively modest 1950 figure of 219 million people, Africa by the year 2000 is expected to have a population of 813 million inhabitants. Accompanying this growth in total population is the even more phenomenal and speedy growth in urban population and expansion of urban centres.[2]

Within the last twenty-five years, urban growth in Africa has proceeded at a rate of close to 5 per cent per year, while in Europe population growth has been less than 2 per cent per year. The urban population in Africa has been doubling itself approximately every fifteen years. This increase in urban growth is itself a function of total population growth, in as much as about half the increase in urban population is due to natural increase and the other half is attributable to migration from the rural areas. A significant feature of the urbanization process in the emergent countries is that increases in urban population tend to be concentrated in one or two large cities, and principally in the capital city. In Ghana, for example, the two largest cities, Accra and Kumasi, absorbed over 30 per cent of the total urban population increase between 1948 and 1960. Between 1960 and 1970 the capital city of Accra alone accounted for about one-third of the total increase in urban population.

A more extreme situation exists in a place like Kenya, where between 1962 and 1969 urban population grew more than twice as fast as total population. During that period two cities, Nairobi and Mombasa, accounted for 90 per cent of the total increase in urban population and Nairobi, the capital city, alone accounted for 70 per cent of the urban population increase. This phenomenon of the primate city, in which one city is several times the size of the next one, seems to be associated with certain levels of development, and in time the rate of growth of these cities slows down somewhat while lower level cities grow faster.

The twin processes of rapid population growth and the even faster growth of urban settlements have created many problems, not only for the urban settlements concerned, but for rural settlements as well. In the rural settlements, one observes an increased pressure on land and food resources. Where output per person remains low, and where available agricultural land is limited, the pressure on land becomes a factor of great concern to the people of the rural areas. Furthermore, the rapid increase in population tends to be accompanied by change in the structure of the population itself. With a decline in infant mortality, the proportion of children and young persons in the population increases, thus pushing the dependency ratio to very high levels. In 1985 the dependency ratio, calculated as the number of persons aged nought to 15 together with the number aged over 64, per 1000 of the age group 15 to 64, is expected to be 908 as compared with 575 for the more developed regions of the world. This means that while the total number of persons to be supported in rural settlements has increased, the number of those in the working age groups available to support the rest has suffered a relative decline. And it should be noted that those in the working age groups are those very people who migrate away from the rural areas to the cities to increase the urban population growth. The pressure on the land has led to a fragmentation of land holdings, to unemployment and underemployment, and to low incomes.

Another consequence of the unprecedented rise in population is the effect on those parts of the continent where pastoralism and nomadism constitute the way of life. Overgrazing has resulted in the destruction of the delicate balance between man and natural resources. Overutilization of the resources has created long-lasting effects of artificial drought conditions. The drought in the Sahelian zone of Africa, which attracted international attention in 1975, was not all a result of a natural disaster, namely the failure of rainfall to arrive at the proper time. Part of it was manmade. Before the establishment of nation states, the nomads moved freely across what are now national boundaries. This applied also to those who practised transhumance. With the development of nation states this is no longer the case. It is now much more difficult to cross national boundaries and, within national boundaries, people are actually being encouraged to develop permanent village settlements in arid zones and to ranch in marginal areas where the capacity of the range is low.

Settlements such as those established in marginal areas and lacking an adequate resource base have led to the degradation of the environment by the progressive destruction of the vegetative cover. They have accelerated an imbalance between man and the environment which has contributed to the disasters witnessed in the marginal areas of the Sahara, disasters which could have been averted or minimized had there been appropriate policies of population distribution and physical planning.

With such conditions prevailing in rural areas, it is not surprising that large numbers of young people migrate to the urban areas to seek a better way of life, better incomes, more secure jobs, and perhaps to enjoy some of the dubious pleasures of the city. As has been observed, most of these migrants from the rural areas find their way into the larger cities and, in most cases, to the capital city. The influx of these newcomers into the city, in such large numbers and within comparatively short periods, has created many problems in the urban areas. The size of the influx is usually unexpected and arrangements to provide for housing, jobs, and community facilities are usually for a far smaller number than actually come to live in the city. To give one example, a plan prepared for the city of Accra in 1957 estimated its 1978 population at 337,000 and provision was made in the plan to cater for that number of people by 1978. In fact that figure was actually attained in 1960, eighteen years before the date envisaged by the planners.

Housing, infrastructural facilities, potable water supplies, waste disposal facilities, schools, and medical services are unable to cope with the sudden and unexpected increases in the population of these cities. Overcrowding, squalor, low levels of sanitation, slum formation and shanty-town development, deterioration of public services, unemployment, and sometimes delinquency become outstanding characteristics of the cities. In addition to these problems, one may add the inadequacy of the financial resource base for the cities to cope with these problems.

In spite of the problems faced by the cities, they still remain more attractive in many respects than the rural areas, and thus attract disproportionate amounts of the total investment in the country. In many emergent countries almost all industries are located in the capital city and so the capital city sometimes contains more than 90 per cent of the telephones, uses more than 70 per cent of the electrical energy, contains over 80 per cent of the high-level manpower, and exerts a virtual monopoly over all other manifestations of modern development. The city contains the élite of the country and is characterized by lifestyles similar to those of the advanced countries. Because of the political power exerted by the cities, most of the investment seems to be concentrated in them. To some extent this is a legacy from the colonial past, when the colonial officials invested large proportions of public money in the cities for their own benefit and for the benefit of the businessmen and traders from the metropolitan countries. They usually retained large tracts of the most attractive parts of the city for themselves, and carved out native areas which were generally very congested. Thus, the European residential areas were planned at very low densities and were segregated from the so-called native areas. To a large extent this segregation still exists today, with a new African élite taking the place of the colonial officials and businessmen in the low density areas while the squalor of the higher density areas is hidden from the view of the casual observer by a "cordon sanitaire" of trees, or perhaps is even fenced in by a block wall such as one finds in some cities of the former French colonies.

Many countries have sought to deal with the problems of rapid urbanization by devising policies to slow down the rate of growth of large urban centres. The migration from rural areas to the large towns is seen by some as an evil that must be stopped at all costs. One strategy, which recognizes the positive contribution that urban centres can make to national and regional economies, concentrates on the development of new growth poles, or growth foci, where new investment in infrastructural facilities and amenities can be provided to attract rural migrants. These centres are expected to stimulate development in the surrounding rural areas and to assist in channelling rural-urban migration away from the large cities and thus help to reduce the rate of growth of the latter. They will also serve to reduce the regional imbalances because new employment opportunities can then be located away from the primate city and thus contribute to the raising of incomes in these centres. There is probably little doubt that in the long run this strategy can achieve some redistribution of population. However, its effect in the medium term is another proposition. A World Bank working paper on urbanization points out that, even if a significantly higher rate of growth in smaller towns is achieved, this would have little effect in the medium term on the size of the primate city because the smaller centres start from a very low level of infrastructure.[3]

Other strategies for dealing with the problem of rapid urbanization call for development of the rural areas. They are based on the assumption that the rural person is attracted to the city because of the amenities of the city. It is of course recognized that the city provides employment opportunities that are not present in the rural areas. However, it is argued that as the city already contains a large army of unemployed, the migrant is most likely to swell that army and, therefore, his decision to migrate has probably been based on false expectations. Nevertheless, once he has arrived he stays in the city in order to enjoy its amenities. So, one strategy proposes to provide amenities in the village, amenities normally found only in the city. It assumes that when the rural migrant realizes that these can be provided in his home village, he will return there and not go back to the city.

This view ignores the fact that actually the migrant has a pretty shrewd idea of the conditions in the city. He knows that if he stays long enough in the city he can obtain employment, at least in the informal sector of the economy, and, in due course, can also obtain employment in the formal sector. Even if this does not happen, the chances are that he can still maintain himself comfortably in all sorts of economic activities that are very common in the shanty towns and are referred to as part of the informal economies of these towns.

The view of rural development as consisting of the provisions of a few amenities has been put into practice in many countries, but it does not seem to have produced any significant results. In Ghana, during the 1950's, several attempts at rural development were made by inducing villagers to build community centres, public latrines, schools, village street lights, and other public works through self-help methods. This is very laudable; it does encourage people to provide for themselves through communal labour things which they need, and it has enabled people to be mobilized into a situation where things that the government cannot provide for them are provided by themselves. But the provision of such amenities, though it is a good thing, does not seem to have induced anyone who wanted to migrate to stay in a village, because of the other factors that are responsible for people migrating to the cities. In recent times there has been a greater emphasis on increasing agricultural output in the rural areas and thereby raising the incomes of the people of the areas. However, I do not believe that rural development alone can succeed in checking migration. In the modern world people want to travel, to see new things, to have new experiences. They want to come into contact with other people and to widen their horizons. Such desires cannot be stopped, and thus any policies designed solely to keep people within the confines of a world limited by the boundaries of a small village are going to fail.

What we need to realize is that in most of the emerging nations of the world the rural population constitutes over 60 per cent of the total population. In some countries the proportion is as high as 80 per cent. And so if the overwhelming majority of the people live, and will continue to live for a long time, in rural areas, then the development of the rural areas must be pursued as an end in itself, not as a means to control urban growth, nor as the means to achieve some other end. The raising of the living standards of the rural people, the provision of better houses, of safe potable water, of better health care — preventive and curative — the creation of better income opportunities, and the integration of rural and urban life should form the cornerstone of human settlement policies in the emergent nations. Such a programme should be directed at raising productivity, lowering unemployment, decreasing underemployment, improving the quality of housing, and improving the general health of the people through the control of preventable diseases and the provision of better medical care. The raising of living standards and rural incomes have direct relevance to the problems of human settlement in the rural areas. There can be no lasting improvement in the conditions of human settlement in rural areas unless people can afford to make improvements. If the aim in rural settlements is to improve the quality of the water supply, to pave the roads, to utilize electric power, and to build houses that do not have to be replaced every few years, then an increase in the present levels of income will become necessary.

In seeking to improve the income levels of the rural dwellers, one must not place great reliance on spectacular schemes such as large dams or large irrigation schemes. Experience has shown that such schemes seldom benefit the low income man in the rural area. Generally those who benefit are those outside the area, while a large part of the social, and even some parts of the economic costs are borne by low income people of the area where the project is situated. Sometimes the lands of these people are taken over by these schemes with little compensation, and they may then have to take on employment with strangers from another part of the country or from another income segment. Thus, whereas these large schemes may in fact increase the general level of incomes in the rural area, the redistribution which is essential for improving the lot of the rural person does not always take place. Social objectives may best be realized by helping the low income person to use appropriate technology, the kind of technology popularized by Schumacher ("small is beautiful") which seeks to increase the level and efficiency of the utilization of local human and material resources through the application of relatively inexpensive, simple procedures for problem-solving appropriate to the skill and financial levels and resource potential of the users.

The significant thing about this latter concept is the emphasis it places on the utilization of local resources and the adaptation of technology to the skills and financial resources of local people. It is thus eminently suitable for use in assisting the low income person in increasing his output and with it his income.

The University of Science and Technology in Kumasi, through its Technology Consultancy Centre, has formally adopted this concept. Through the financial assistance of such overseas organizations as OXFAM Québec, it has been providing technical assistance to Ghana's rural people by devising simple agricultural machinery, by setting up rural industries, and also by assisting them to build houses through the use of techniques appropriate to their skill levels.

The adoption of appropriate technology to assist the rural person to increase his output, and with it his income, would ensure more equitable distribution of incomes. The concept of appropriate technology, which has been made famous by Schumacher, ensures the utilization of technology that is most appropriate to the skills, knowledge, and resources of the user.

I have spent some time in discussing rural development because, in my opinion, the habitat problem in rural areas is largely a problem of general development. The problematic variable is the total environment in rural areas, and general development is the key to the amelioration of the rural habitat. Apart from the improvement of general living conditions, the key factor is the greater integration of the rural and urban areas through the provision of better communication, good roads, telephones, public transportation, and other means of facilitating quick contact between settlements. In this way conditions would then be created which would widen the range of settlement choices open to all the inhabitants of the country.

In urban areas the issue of housing, of providing shelter for the many, looms large in any discussion of the habitat question. It is a fact that while no nation has succeeded in housing all its people satisfactorily, the dimensions of the problem in the developing countries are such that many people are apt to throw up their hands in despair and say that the problem is insoluble. During the first half of this century, housing did not constitute a major problem for Africa because the level of urbanization was quite low. It was only when the urbanization process gathered speed in the late 1950's and early 1960's that housing increasingly became perhaps the biggest single problem of urban growth. A comparison of the houses actually built and the housing needs as assessed by several criteria reveals a very wide gap between housing needs and housing provision. In Ghana, for example, between 1960 and 1970 less than one-quarter of the needed housing was being built in urban areas. There is therefore considerable pressure on existing housing, and one response to this pressure is overcrowding. In Ghana in 1960 some 50 per cent of the urban population was living in room densities of three persons or more per room. Those who cannot find a house to sleep in, sleep in public open spaces, car parks, markets, shop verandas, or anywhere they can sleep unmolested. The pressure on housing has also led to the development of shanty towns, which typically consist of shelters made of such materials as packing cases, old corrugated iron sheets, and flattened oil drums. There are usually no infrastructural services of any kind, no water, no electricity, no roads, no drains. The shanty towns are usually the most congested and unsanitary parts of the city, but they should not be condemned outright because they serve a very useful function. These are the areas of the cities which first absorb the immigrants who come out from the rural areas. In these shanty towns they find relatives or friends or people whom they know from their own villages, and they are received into the community and find a sort of home away from home in these shanty towns. At the same time, as already indicated, in these shanty towns there are people who have come from the rural areas and who have been able to get some sort of employment. It may not be employment in the formal sense — all sorts of activities which hitherto have not been well known are found in these shanty towns. For instance, there is a lot of petty trading; there is much craftwork such as the making of baskets and other objects; there is shoemaking; there is even some degree of rudimentary banking service where a lot of people pool their resources and save money, and after a few weeks or months one person gets a large amount of capital to start some little business. Some money may be put out every month into a kitty and within, say, a year or two many people are able to muster enough financial resources to start small businesses. So there are all sorts of activities which go on in the shanty towns.

The high cost of building materials is the greatest factor militating against provision of adequate shelter for the bulk of the population. To reduce the cost of housing and to provide alternatives to conventional housing a number of new approaches have been adopted. These include, first of all, the upgrading of shanty towns or squatter settlements. In this approach such settlements are provided with some of the basic facilities; roads and drains are put in, arrangements are made for the removal of refuse, schools and public places of convenience are made available, and potable drinking water is also provided. In this way the environment quality of the place is improved and people are able to live a slightly more decent life than before.

The second approach is the improvement of environmental quality through physical planning measures. In regard to housing, that is, housing in the wider sense, not merely the provision of houses, perhaps the best known aspect of this approach is what is called the "site and service" scheme. This involves the acquisition of land in the urban areas ahead of the influx of population. The land is then provided with basic infrastructural facilities such as roads, potable water, and refuse collection services. The provision of service plots on which newcomers to the city can build their own houses has become very popular because it enables physical planners to predetermine where new migrants can settle and also because it ensures a functional integration of the new areas with the rest of the city. It has a great advantage over the upgrading of squatter settlements in that in the "site and service" schemes, arrangements are made ahead of the actual influx of the people, and steps can be taken to ensure that people settle in a place near their jobs. Thus it is possible to avoid the conditions found in many countries where shanty towns or squatter settlements are far from the centre of the city, and very far from available employment, therefore forcing people to spend a lot of money on transportation or to walk long distances to their work.

The provision of "site and service" schemes enables the authorities to reduce the cost of providing housing to about 5 or 10 per cent of what it would be if they were to provide conventional housing. That is, the cost of providing these services on the site is very low compared with having to build houses. The acceptance of this scheme also has the advantage that people are mobilized to use self-help methods and communal labour to build their own houses, instead of having somebody build houses for them, which is now quite impracticable because of the high costs involved. Given the opportunity, people will build according to their own resources, financial and otherwise, and, as they obtain more resources, they can add to their houses. They can also build in materials which they can afford. In this way people play a great role in the provision of their own shelter.

Another approach, which however is not regarded as being very successful in significantly increasing the number of houses available, is co-operative housing, which is being tried in Ghana. We have started in the new town of Tema to provide co-operative housing where the resources are pooled and a core house of one room is built and, as time goes on, more parts are added to the house. However, this is not a solution for the majority of the people; it is the kind of solution that is more suitable for middle income people rather than for lowest income people.

The fourth approach to the provision of housing in urban areas is the use of local materials in house construction. A great obstacle in this approach is that instead of using truly local materials we have been trying hard to find materials similar to imported ones because these are usually used in house construction. We have been taught to believe that a good house is one built with cement and roofed with some other material found in developed countries. Therefore, in trying to develop and encourage the use of local materials, we search for local sources of cement or other materials used for building in advanced countries. We thus establish cement factories and industries for the production of aluminum roofing sheets. The fact that these materials are produced locally reduces the cost by only a small margin. We have much to learn from the traditional methods of house construction and the values inherent therein. Where, as in Ghana, mud is the traditional building material, we should consider using it in urban housing. Most of our research efforts therefore should be devoted to making improvements in this material in order to enable it to withstand the rigours of urbanization and of the climate. The main problem with using mud in house-building has been that it absorbs a lot of water and collapses very easily. However, we have been able to protect walls against absorbing a lot of water, and can build mud houses which can stand for more than fifty years. If we look at this as an alternative source of building material I think it will go a long way to solving our housing problems.

A bold policy utilizing these traditional materials will assist us greatly in housing adequately a large proportion of our urban population. But there are some difficulties to be overcome in implementing such a policy. Because of the long period in which we have been led to believe that a good house is one constructed with concrete blocks, we have to change our attitude to these things if we are to succeed. If we are to enable our people to use local materials in house building, then the élite, the planners, the people who have been educated abroad or in the mold of the developed countries, have to learn not to denigrate traditional materials. They must try to see how best these materials can be further used in the urban situation to provide housing for our people. We need a reorientation of attitudes and, if the more favoured classes were to consider using these materials, then they would be able to lead others in this direction.

In speaking about human settlement problems in developing countries, we are speaking about the raising of living standards. In this sense the problems of human settlements in these countries cannot be divorced from the general process of development. If we are to enable people to have better houses, better roads, better working places and more recreational facilities, better health facilities, and better educational facilities, we are talking about the need to increase real incomes as an objective of the developmental process itself. Without increasing earning income opportunities, and thus increasing real incomes, many of our objectives in the improvement of the quality of life in human settlements cannot be realized.

The spatial impact of development is a basic problem. The costs, including social costs and benefits of development activity, ought to be assessed. The question of the "where" of development is as important as the "how" of development. Policies for the redistribution of population, for encouraging the development of growth centres and growth foci, and for the reduction of regional and urban-rural imbalances, pose problems in the allocation of resources. The developing countries are anxious to develop and aspire to enjoy the living conditions of the developed countries. To this end they want to industrialize. They want to have factories and to see smoke rise out of these factories. To industrialize as a means of attaining economic growth is laudable but what are the effects of industrialization on the quality of life in human settlements? The social impact of development is hardly considered in the single-minded desire to achieve economic growth. At relatively low levels of industrialization, these problems are hardly seen by the decision-makers, and where they are pointed out, they are often regarded as irrelevant. But the developing countries must learn from the mistakes of developed countries. Although the latter spend vast amounts of money to correct past mistakes, we unfortunately are not seriously considering avoiding these mistakes ourselves. In the case of developing countries, the financial resources probably would not be available to correct these environmental indiscretions committed in the cause of industrialization.

The economic and social costs and benefits of development should be continually assessed before decisions regarding development are made. Development strategies and objectives should include an evaluation of social costs. All development programmes have implications for human settlement. For example, the building of a dam for the generation of electricity, which seems to be a simple, straightforward engineering problem, has far-reaching consequences for human settlements. It could and often does involve the relocation of several thousands of persons whose settlements will be destroyed in the process of constructing the dam. Thus, the old way of life is destroyed and the unfortunate people are put in new settlements and sometimes have new lifestyles imposed on them. Sometimes there is a reorganization of settlement patterns and structure. In some cases people who are fishermen are no longer able to fish because the dam has been placed at a point where the food for the fish, which used to be obtained at the lower part of the dam, is no longer available and therefore there are not enough fish, so the whole lifestyle of these people has to change. They have to find some occupation other than fishing.

The relocation of people as a result of artificial lakes created by hydro-electric dam projects is, perhaps, the most dramatic instance of the impact of development projects on habitat. All sorts of other decisions affect human settlements in many ways — the building of highways, the building of railways, airports, and, of course, industries — all have significant impacts on human settlements. So do activities such as the declaration of forest reserves, national game parks, and wildlife game reserves. In any country people must try to spell out what kind of settlements and what patterns of settlement they desire, and they must formulate specific policies towards attainment of desired settlement conditions, structure, and distribution. It seems to me, therefore, that in the formulation of policies for development, human settlement problems cannot be treated in isolation. To ensure that the spatial impact of development is considered at the same level as other aspects of development planning and programming, human settlement planning must be integrated with the process of general development planning, the sort of planning done by ministries of economic planning or national planning commissions. In many countries there is a lack of integration and even a lack of basic coordination resulting in all kinds of development activity with undesirable effects, and sometimes even failure to achieve the desired ends of economic growth. It is instructive in this regard to note that national planning commissions seldom include people skilled in human settlement questions. There are few countries in which there are coherent national settlement policies formulated to determine the size, location, distribution, and character of settlements and which work towards the integration of rural settlements into a national system of settlements. What we do have is a number of agencies, each dealing with a dimension of the habitat problem. There are several housing agencies, road development and highway authorities, railway and harbour authorities, and so on. But no single agency is charged with the task of looking at the several interlocking facets of the human habitat and of formulating overall national policies to provide the framework for planning at a local level and for planning the various interrelated factors and dimensions of human settlement. I hope that the Habitat conference has stimulated many nations of the developing world to create such institutions so that the problems of habitat may be considered in a coherent and integrated manner. Specifically, I suggest that a central authority be created in each country, charged with the responsibility of formulating overall national policies on human settlements and with examining human settlement implications of all development proposals. In order to ensure that policies formulated by this agency are implemented and that human settlement implications of development activity are adequately considered, this authority or agency must operate within the ministry responsible for overall national planning, which is usually located at the highest levels of government.

We have approached habitat questions in the Third World mainly as part of the larger problem of development. We have suggested that rural areas must be given priority in such matters because that is where the bulk of the people live and will continue to live for a long time to come. We have also suggested the raising of income levels as a prerequisite for the improvement of the habitat and have suggested that rural settlements must be better integrated with urban centres in order to widen the range of settlement choices open to all people. In all of this, our approach has been that we should seek to improve our habitat from our own resources and learn from traditional methods of doing things. We realize that questions of habitat are very complex and that consequently there are no easy solutions, ready answers. But some solutions do exist, and if we harness our own resources, both material and human, and if we start doing things by making small incremental changes and by thinking small, in Schumacher's sense, we will go a long way to improve the conditions in which we live.

EXCERPTS FROM DISCUSSION

Question: Could you expand a little on your observations about improving communications and transportation in relation to increasing choices and options, particularly in rural areas? I had in mind that depending on when and how this is done, this might be counterproductive and only provide more rapid conduit for people to migrate to the larger urban centres as communications and transportation are improved.

Dr. Tetteh: People who want to migrate into urban centres will do so whether there are fast motor roads or not. They can even walk; in fact, many people do walk from their rural villages into the nearest town, and they walk again from one town to another. So I do not think that the provision of good transport conditions will necessarily increase the rate of rural to urban migration. I put forward the suggestion that we should integrate the rural areas into the urban areas because one of the things about rural areas is the intense isolation. If you live in a village far away from the main road, far away from the world around you, you feel intensely isolated; therefore the urge to get out of that environment where you cannot interact with the rest of the world and where you don't know what is going on, is very great, especially for people who have been to school, who have read some geography. And if it is possible sometimes just to go over to a city, have a look around and enjoy something, even have an ice cream or something and come back, it is better than being totally confined to these villages. In this way the urge to go to town to settle there permanently will not be so great.

At the same time we should mobilize enough resources to increase the choices open to everyone, for the rural person or the urban person to be able to choose to live either in rural areas or in urban areas. I do not believe that we should have a policy simply to keep people in rural areas. People in rural areas should be able to travel. We should encourage mobility. I think mobility, geographical mobility, is also one of the prerequisites, sometimes, for social mobility, and I think that if we are to encourage people to be upwardly mobile, we should also increase their chances of mobility on the ground. And so I do not really think that the provision of good communication systems within the various parts of the country will lead to an increase in rural-urban migration.

Question: Do you feel that the introduction of compulsory primary education back in the early 1960's might have caused a great flow of people from the rural areas into the urban areas, many of whom when they came could not find jobs and consequently moved out into the outer limits of the city, the shanty town areas, and perhaps eventually back to their own villages feeling rather discontented that their dreams were not being realized? Ironically, does the introduction of education, when done suddenly, produce more problems than it solves?

Dr. Tetteh: People have said that. If you are educated your horizons become wider and therefore you demand things which you would not otherwise have demanded if you had not read too many books. At the same time, we ought to consider from the social point of view, and also from the economic point of view, that when you have a country which is developing and you have a large illiterate population, then you are not able to reach the population if you want to make improvements. A young man who is able to read and who is on the farm in a rural area is able to take advantage of improvements in farming practices by reading leaflets or books or pamphlets about growing rice or other crops. So I believe that if people want to raise themselves up from the state of being underdeveloped, education is necessary. It is true that many people who have come out of rural areas are the well educated ones. This is not merely because they are educated, but because they are pushed out of their rural areas by various conditions. There are many villages where the land is not sufficient to provide permanent support in the same position for a large village population. Maybe with the land they have, and given their present agricultural practices, a population of two thousand can be supported. But, if this population rises to three thousand, then serious problems arise. I have been to several villages and talked to the people and often they are grateful that the people who go to school migrate out of the villages. They feel that if these people do not migrate, they will have serious problems in providing food in those villages. So it is not just a question of whether it is people who are educated who usually migrate. This is true, but it is not because they have been to school that they migrate; there are other forces that are much stronger than education which are forcing them out of the rural areas.

Question: Could you say something more about the effects of dam building?

Dr. Tetteh: In Ghana we have tried as much as possible to cushion the social and economic effects of dam construction. We have tried to provide alternative areas for people to settle in, have built houses, have tried to clear agricultural land for them and to provide some inputs and agricultural services for these people. People do not always think about these things at the beginning and do not always realize that they are not just dealing with a straightforward engineering question. I was making a general statement rather than referring to any specific project.

In reply to a question regarding a specific project, Dr. Tetteh continued:

The objective of building the dam has been realized in that we are producing enough electricity for our needs, have been exporting it to two neighbouring countries, and have had offers from a third neighbouring country to buy electricity from us. From that point of view it has been successful. However, at the same time we have had a human problem. This particular scheme involved the relocation of 80,000 people into parts of the country that were not their traditional homes. In this particular case I would say that there has been partial success in that some of the new settlements that have been put near older settlements have flourished. Where the settlements have been put into completely new areas, we have not been able to produce or provide all that we wanted to provide in regard to a certain acreage of land, agricultural services, and to other kinds of services. We have not been able to do all these things and people have not been able to flourish with the result that some of them have migrated away from these new villages into other parts of the country. So that we have succeeded in fulfilling only some of our objectives.

Question: When you were talking about housing options, you mentioned that physical planners were involved in laying out the areas. Do you distinguish between physical planners and social planners?

Dr. Tetteh: Well, I will just call them planners. We do not have a distinction between social planners and physical planners. Most of our planners, at least in the department of which I am head, are trained to look at the problems of human settlements in a comprehensive way, physical, social, economic, administrative. Our planners go out as settlement planners, not as physical planners, social planners, or any other hyphenated planners.

Question: I was very interested in the use of mud in buildings. I come from a part of England where clay and mud were used from early mediaeval times over a kind of basketwork framework and then covered with a kind of application of tar. In a country where there is a high rainfall, houses formed in this way are still lived in five hundred years later. What form of mud house is it that is the traditional one that is being renewed?

Dr. Tetteh: Just ordinary mud worked out with water is used, and they put up about 1½ feet at a time, let it dry, and then build on it again until they come to roof level. Then it is roofed, usually with thatch, and it is probably one of the coolest types of houses possible. The problem is rainwater, which strikes the bottom of the wall and weakens it. However, as I said, we have just found out some ways of protecting the walls to ensure that the water does not seep through, so that these houses can stand for a longer time. I myself have seen houses built of mud which have lasted more than a lifetime where adequate precautions have been taken against the seepage of water into them. As I see it, the problem is one of ideology, that we feel that if we are progressing, one way of showing progress is to build in the materials used by the people from whom we are learning progress. And, therefore, we do not consider too seriously the methods which are used in the villages. Part of the reason is that most of the houses in the villages are quite unsightly so that people look at the houses and do not like what they see. But that is just a question of external finish, and making it look a little more presentable. What is important today is what are the internal values of these houses, what do they represent? They are much cooler than the cement or block houses and their roofs are thatched, which is also much cooler than the corrugated iron sheet. But then there are problems, for instance, of the thatch which has to be replaced very often — once every two years — so probably research should be directed at preserving the thatch so that it can stay much longer and only require changing every ten or fifteen years rather than every two. This is what we at the University of Science and Technology are trying to do, to see to what extent we can prolong the life of these materials. But we still have the ideological problem, the problem of getting people to think seriously of using these materials as alternatives to imported and quasi-imported materials.

Question: Can those second materials, cement blocks and corrugated iron, be produced in Ghana?

Dr. Tetteh: The blocks can be produced but there have been problems with the cement. We have looked for sources of cement and I understand that we have some resources somewhere, but it is very difficult to reach them. The cost of extracting these raw materials is too high, but we do have cement factories which import cement clinkers from abroad and grind them into cement, and we are happy to have local industry. With regard to corrugated iron sheets, these are all imported and it is the same with aluminum sheets. They are brought into the country and cut there, but the main product is actually imported.

Question: It is apparently going to take a large amount of money to stabilize the rural population and to keep them from moving into the urban areas. Where is this money going to come from and how is it going to be repaid?

Dr. Tetteh: I did not propose that we should keep people from coming from the rural areas; in fact I said the opposite. I want the rural population to be able to move freely around the country, and I do not think we can really stop the rural-urban migration.

Question: I am under the impression that you can't meet the needs in the urban areas now. How could you stand an influx of rural population when the majority of your population is rural?

Dr. Tetteh: Some of the strategies are to develop other centres, growth centres, to which some of the population could go. For instance, instead of having one large city, one would have a number of medium-sized cities. Then the people who want to move around would go to these medium-sized cities instead of going to the primary city.

Question: Where is the money coming from for building these other cities, and how is that money to be repaid?

Dr. Tetteh: If some money is available it is suggested that instead of investing it all in a primary city, or in the large cities generally, some of that money should be reallocated to the medium-sized cities. And actually some money is available; some resources are available. It is not that we do not have anything at all. It is a question of where the money should be used.

Question: I believe that Ghana's main export is cocoa. Can you tell me what part that plays in, first, the international trade and, second, the redistribution of population in Ghana?

Dr. Tetteh: As to what part cocoa plays in international trade, I can only tell you that about 60 per cent of our foreign exchange earnings come from cocoa. Thus we depend very largely for foreign exchange on cocoa. The part it plays in the redistribution of population is marginal because there are only certain areas in which cocoa can be grown; these are the forest areas where there is enough rainfall and enough forest cover for the young trees as they are growing. These areas are not very extensive. Cocoa growing has not accounted for much movement of population. A few people could go from one part of the country to the other to engage in cocoa farming, usually as labourers. In the past we have usually had migrants from outside Ghana to work on the cocoa farms as labourers, so that in that case we do not have much movement of population around the country as a result of the cocoa industry. But of course where new areas are developed, as new areas have been developed since the 1930's in the far west of the country, you do get a slight shift of population into those areas.

Question: Would not the world price of cocoa influence a number of people in regard to movement? For example, if the price of cocoa dropped might there be another migration to an urban centre? If the price of cocoa remained high or went even higher might it not influence more people to go to a rural area?

Dr. Tetteh: One of the problems we are having now is that the average age of the cocoa farmer has been rising over the past few years, so that the cocoa industry seems to be in the hands of older people. So, even if the price of cocoa goes higher, I do not think it will really influence people to go to rural areas. In fact, it might encourage migration to the urban areas because if the young people's parents have enough money, then they have something to start with when they go into the town and have a little capital to use while they are waiting for a job. Or they might just take the money to the town and blow it!

Question: Is there any move to relocate the capital to a more central position — the capital *is* still in Accra?

Dr. Tetteh: No, there is no move to locate the capital in another place. It is in Nigeria that there have been moves of that nature. We do not really see any problems with the capital being in Accra and I can envisage a lot of problems if we try to move it somewhere else.

Question: What is the state of Kumasi? Is that a regional capital, a regional centre?

Dr. Tetteh: Yes, Kumasi is the capital of the Ashanti region and is the second largest city in Ghana.

Question: You are suggesting that development strategies have to be a little more selective to be adopted. What success do you see in this regard, working perhaps with an élite which as in most places is perhaps a little more inclined to go the economic route rather than give much attention to the social aspects?

Dr. Tetteh: First there will be a question of education, or re-education, of the people involved.

Question: The problem of birth control seems to be concerning everybody in the world today. What has been done in Ghana as such?

Dr. Tetteh: We have a Planned Parenthood Association of Ghana which is supported by the government. The government has a population policy to slow down population growth and therefore they support family planning measures and make family planning assistance available to anyone who needs it and subsidize family planning devices. People can get the pill or other kinds of family planning products at very cheap rates — a whole year's supply of the pill, for instance, for about $2.00. Ghana is one of the few countries in Africa which has adopted a population policy.

Question: What unique things do you believe Ghana can bring to the Habitat conference?

Dr. Tetteh: Ghana can bring the conference its experience, I think, in human settlement planning; for instance experience in the Volta River project is something which has attracted world attention; experience in building a new town, for instance in Tema; problems in controlling or not controlling the development of shanty towns. I believe that some of these experiences can be shared with other people. The strengths and weaknesses and successes and failures can be discussed and shared with other people.

In response to questions about the use of native woods, Dr. Tetteh commented:

Our faculty has been working on that. We have built a number of experimental houses with wood and we hope that we will be able to establish these as viable alternatives to cement buildings. But there are problems of expense and of the control of rot and termites. Some of these have been solved but not yet quite well enough. However, we now have a Forest Products Research Institute located on the campus of the University of Science and Technology and this Institute is looking into these very problems. We could also explore the possibilities of using wood at least for non-load-bearing walls.

Question: Is there any way that Ghana could benefit from co-operation with Canada and the United States in regard to research and appropriate technology through exchange of people or students?

Dr. Tetteh: I think we can always benefit by obtaining knowledge and therefore I think that Ghana can benefit in the use of appropriate technology through the exchange of students and research workers who are actually working on these problems. Also I think that one should establish a worldwide information service on these things so that experiences of any particular country can be made available to all other countries to use and/or adapt particular devices to their own conditions and their own resources.

Question: What about the possibility of job creation as a cottage industry spin-off of the technological needs along the lines of Schumacher's book?

Dr. Tetteh: We are trying to encourage job creation through the use of these technologies in rural areas, and our technology consultancy centre has established a number of small industries all over the country, first in southern Ashanti and now in the northern part of the country as well. We have soap factories, as well as cloth-weaving establishments using methods which are a little better than the village ones and an improvement on the village techniques so that more is produced for the expenditure of less time and effort. We are doing these things; we have not progressed very far, but we have started. And I think we will be happy to share our experiences with other people and would be happy to hear or to share their experiences.

Notes

1.   *Ceres*, November-December 1975, pp. 25–27.

2.   Figures obtained from *Growth of the World's Urban and Rural Population, 1920–2000* (New York: United Nations, 1969).

3.   The World Bank, *Urbanization: Sector Working Paper* (Washington, D.C., 1972).

6

Institutional Planning Structures

Austin Tetteh

The planning of human settlements in many of our developing countries frequently reflects ideas and practices inherited or adopted from the former metropolitan countries before we achieved independence. These practices and arrangements, which took many years to develop, have by now become largely outmoded and ineffective in dealing with the problems of human settlements, even in their countries of origin. In most cases, those institutional structures we have sought to emulate have failed to ensure that settlements and land are managed for the welfare of all inhabitants.

In many developed countries until very recently, human settlement planning was very élitist in conception and was designed to cater for the needs, interests, and various preoccupations of the wealthy or more favoured classes. Of course some concern was shown for the lowest income classes, and actually a great deal of effort was devoted to alleviating the appallingly unsanitary conditions in which they lived. On the whole, however, planning for the lowest income groups consisted mainly in providing them with access to air and sunlight. But this was perhaps not altogether altruistic, for there was a major concern to prevent occurrence of plagues and epidemics which might spread to areas where the more favoured classes lived.

The habits of thought generated by such practices were transferred to the colonies, where human settlement planning was confined to providing opportunities for the good life for the ruling élite while the indigenous people were segregated in congested native cities. The principal social measure was the institution of public health regulations, chiefly to prevent the outbreak of epidemic diseases. This led to emphasis being laid on the draining of swamps in order to control the breeding of the mosquitoes that caused malaria, the dreaded enemy of the ruling white élite. While such efforts may be considered laudable, they tended to concentrate attention on only one small part of a complicated set of problems. Thus, in the long run, only superficial considerations were dealt with and the real problems of welfare and reasonable standards of living for the inhabitants were neglected.

The institutions which developed were not designed to deal with problems of human settlements in an integrated way. Ghana, where institutions have been created over the past fifty years to deal with the problems of human settlements, may serve as an example to illustrate the type of institutional arrangements which have developed in some of the African countries. In Ghana, the earliest pieces of legislation dealing with human settlements established institutions concerned with public health. As far back as 1920, a central Board of Health was set up with members who were all public health workers, apart from the Director of Public Works. Under this central health board, provincial health boards were established for the provinces and sanitary boards set up for towns. These boards dealt with all matters relating to sanitary works and schemes, including water supply, drainage schemes, housing, markets, sewage, and demolition. Members of the sanitary boards were appointed by the relevant provincial health board, whose members were all civil servants.

Following the creation of the public health boards, the first town planning ordinance was enacted. This ordinance, enacted in 1925, provided for the orderly planning of towns and was designed to control the creation of buildings and the laying out of streets in certain areas in order to ensure that such areas would be properly developed in the interests of public health, neighbourhood amenity, and the general welfare of the community. The ordinance provided for the establishment of a Central Town Planning Board composed mainly of senior public servants from the health and engineering sectors of the civil service. The task of the central board was to prepare schemes in consultation with the Public Health Commission, who were empowered to exercise control over all building operations and to execute schemes within the municipalities. Although the 1925 ordinance had the merit of trying to deal with the problems of towns in a comprehensive way, for a number of reasons its provisions were not implemented. The most important reason was the fact that there were many concurrent ordinances. For instance, there was the town ordinance and the mining health ordinance which gave the directors of Medical Services and of Public Works powers like those of the Planning and Building Commission. These officers preferred to exercise their powers directly instead of discussing problems with the town planning commission, which contained laymen who, they felt, could not be expected to understand the complexities of technical problems. Furthermore, the process of discussion tended to delay action and therefore appeared to these officials to be a waste of time. In practice, layouts for towns and villages were prepared by engineers and officials of the Health and Sanitary departments, submitted through local health boards to the Central Health Board, and then enforced by members of that board (all civil servants) through powers derived from laws or regulations other than those of the 1925 ordinance.

Because the plans were made by engineers and health officials, whose great concern was the improvement of conditions for public health purposes, the emphasis tended to be on plot layout rather than on the comprehensive development of settlements in economic, social, and physical terms. Town planning thus became a spare-time activity instead of the full-time professional activity it should be.

The emphasis on plot layout, and the absence of people professionally trained in the principles and practice of town planning, led to the development of model layouts of the gridiron type simple enough for implementation by health inspectors of limited education. Admittedly, gridiron plans can be admirable where permitted by physical conditions, such as relatively flat land, but in most cases the model layouts prepared could not be fitted into the existing contours, and consequently road alignments went across contours and created erosion problems which are difficult to contain.

During the 1920's and 1930's, many villages adopted the model layouts offered by the health inspectors. The results can now be seen in most of these villages in the extent of erosion, lack of sufficient shade, and inadequate open spaces for social activities, as well as in a certain lack of vitality.

Before 1945 planning consisted largely of piecemeal attempts to deal with the problems of human settlements. Where specific legislation was enacted, the institutional arrangements usually did not permit an integrated and comprehensive approach to the planning of human settlements. Human settlement planning was regarded as a technical matter, to be dealt with by engineers, surveyors, public health specialists, and, sometimes, architects. The Town and Country Ordinance of 1945 sought to remedy some of the effects of previous legislation by creating appropriate institutions with sole powers to deal with the planning problems of towns and villages. The 1945 act is an important landmark in the history of planning in Ghana because for the first time planning was recognized as a major function of government and a town planning law was enacted which was actually put into practice. The provisions of the act still govern planning in the country today.

The ordinance established a Town and Country Board charged with securing the orderly and progressive development of land. This was composed of six to eight members, three of whom were ex officio members and the rest appointed by the Governor of the Gold Coast, as Ghana was then called. Later, after independence, these three members were appointed by the minister responsible for town and country planning. This board was abolished in 1959 and its functions were transferred to the minister himself, who is thus now the sole authority for all town and country planning in Ghana. The actual implementation of the functions outlined in the ordinance is carried out through the application of a series of regulations to legally declared statutory planning areas by town planning committees, appointed for such areas and exercising powers delegated to them by the commissioner or minister responsible for town and country planning. These planning committees are assisted in their work by professional planners provided by the Town and

Country Planning Department who prepare planning schemes and give technical advice to the committees. In effect, this department, a division of the central government, is responsible for the preparation of all local physical plans for both large and small settlements. Thus, through the enactment of the 1945 law, human settlements planning at last has been given the professional attention it deserves. This legislation put planning in the hands of professional planners, and since 1945 plans have been prepared for statutory planning areas and special advisory plans have been prepared for other areas. The legislation created a central authority for planning, with most of its powers delegated to local committees which depend heavily on the technical expertise of professional planners.

However, in the thirty years of operation, certain shortcomings have become apparent in some of the concepts and institutional arrangements created to implement the act. First, there is a failure to integrate planning activity into local government processes. Planning has been viewed as a technical activity performed by technical people. It also seems to be viewed, in practice though not in theory, as a static act — the preparation of a plan — instead of as a continuous process of cyclical decision-making. It is, or should be, a dynamic activity relying on feedback processes from all parts of the real world. The apparent failure to understand the cyclical nature of planning, as an activity subject to continuous review and feedback processes, has led to a situation whereby plans are prepared by the professional officers of the Town Planning Department, sent to the appropriate local planning committee for endorsement, and then sent back for final approval by the appropriate minister. The result is that local plans are prepared by professional planners who are not members of nor in any way connected with the local government. These plans are then sent to the planning committees, whose members are all laymen and who have not been given the opportunity even to understand some of the issues involved in these plans.

Moreover, little opportunity has been given to the people affected by the plans to express their views on proposals. To be sure, the act provides for the views of the public to be sought, but this is *after* the plan has been formulated. Even this concession to the views of the target population is seldom carried out. Where the plan is exhibited for public comment, it is difficult for the ordinary man to understand all those nice maps with their little coloured areas of all shapes and sizes. The social and economic implications of the major provisions are not clearly brought out, and the people are not presented with various alternatives so that they may register their preferences. This lack of adequate knowledge of implications and alternatives is not confined to the public at large. It is also shared by the members of the town planning committees whose responsibility it is to endorse these plans. Furthermore, the requirement of final approval by the minister in Accra before a plan becomes operative presupposes an intimate knowledge of the problems of each local area, a knowledge which no one in the ministry can possibly have. Once approval has been given, any changes, except very minor ones, must receive approval of the minister. Thus the cyclical nature of planning, as a process of action and reaction between planners, the public, and real world conditions, becomes frustrated and the plan is turned into a static fossilized document. What is needed is a process which can continuously monitor change and which responds to changing social and economic realities. The exclusion, in practical terms, of public involvement in the planning process is one of the basic weaknesses of the present administration of planning in most parts of the developing world.

The detachment of planning from the domain of public discussion has led to a situation whereby members of the public are not aware of the various issues and are also unaware of the choices available. It is left to the planner to make these choices on their behalf. Thus, everybody is affected by the choices the planner makes. Most people can only take an intelligent interest in these matters when they understand the reasons behind certain actions: for example, why a city is zoned into various land uses, and why an industrial area, for instance, is located in a part of the town where it will least disrupt the health and convenience of the inhabitants in terms of noise, air pollution, and disposal of noxious solid and liquid wastes. This calls for a system of education in appreciation of the various factors that make a town livable. The usefulness of open spaces, parks, woodlands, is rarely fully understood as necessary for the recreational activities of the people. As a result, such natural recreational resources are often destroyed and replaced by plots for residential housing.

Another aspect of the present institutional inadequacy in planning is the separation of the plan formulation function from the plan implementation and control function. In the cities of Ghana, the town planning department is responsible for plan formulation, while the officials of the city council are responsible for plan implementation and control. Very often these agencies operate from offices which are several hundred metres apart. This hardly leads to an efficient utilization of resources and the creation of the desired environment for living, working, and playing. This is mainly because those who control development are not really aware of the reasons behind certain planning measures and, also because their training does not prepare them to perceive problems from the point of view of those responsible for plan formulation. This arbitrary division of functions leads to a failure to perceive planning as an aspect of local government, and so the planning function is not integrated into the other functions of government. The integration of planning with other governmental processes would facilitate greater co-ordination and a better ordering of priorities within the city government and the provision of budgetary allocations for projects envisaged in the plan. A continuous process of interaction between planning officers and other officials of the city government would lead to more realistic planning and improve considerably the process of plan implementation and control.

A third feature of the institutional arrangements in Ghana for planning for human settlements is the absolute lack of integration of the various decisions affecting human settlements in the country. The minister of works and housing, the minister of local government, the minister of education, the highway authority, the housing corporation, and many other agencies have responsibilities for activities which impinge on human settlements. But each agency does its own planning in its own exclusive office. In theory, the town planner is supposed to co-ordinate these activities, but in practice such co-ordination rarely takes place, mainly because the planner is not provided with the information that he requires for such co-ordination. Even if he had such information he could do no more than compile data for everyone's information. Machinery needs to be created to facilitate such co-ordination and to provide an overall unifying policy to guide the actions of the various agencies.

One example of this lack of co-ordination and integrated approach to the problems of human settlements planning can be found in the field of housing. The various public housing agencies consider it their goal to produce as many houses as possible and they pursue this goal with laudable singlemindedness. This is quite a praiseworthy goal, but in practice they find that because of limited financial resources they cannot do more than scratch the surface of the problem. A less limited view of their task, which would not make them feel that they have to churn out statistics every year of the number of houses built, might have led them to consider alternative solutions for providing shelter. As suggested in my earlier paper, such solutions might concentrate on assisting people to build their own forms of shelter. Also, because their programmes are not integrated with the programmes of other agencies, these housing agencies sometimes build houses before any consideration has been given to roads, water, sewage, electricity, and such services as schools, clinics, police protection, shops, and recreational facilities for adults and children.

A fourth feature of the planning set-up is the fact that while the department of town and country planning prepares plans for individual settlements, there appears to be no overall integrated policy for the development of urban and rural settlements. In the case of rural settlements, there have been many isolated programmes of rural development — build a school there, build a community centre there, or even build a church there. Only seldom have concentrated and co-ordinated efforts been directed at creating opportunities for increasing the income and capacities of rural folk and at evolving a policy of integrating rural villages into a national system of settlements.

The authority of local planning committees does not extend beyond the boundaries of the statutory planning areas. Very often much haphazard development goes on just outside the statutory boundaries. When a person cannot build inside the statutory planning areas because certain conditions are imposed there by planning authorities, all he has to do is to go outside the boundaries of the statutory planning area and then build whatever he likes. This is not a satisfactory state of affairs for human settlements because developments outside the statutory planning areas thus tend to be haphazard and pose serious problems for future settlement development and expansion.

A final deleterious feature of the present institutional arrangements is the lack, on a national and regional level, of overall policies that can provide a general context, framework, or blueprint for planning at a local level. Ghana is regarded as an advanced country in the field of planning, as we have a working central authority for planning created by the Town and Country Planning Act of 1945 and a national planning service manned by trained planners all over the country. However, while we have this well-developed planning service, and while much planning has been done at local levels including the planning of villages, there is actually little overall planning of the country as a whole and the planning that has been done has generally been isolated. Furthermore, statutory planning areas, of which there are quite a few, are the only areas subject to planning control, and outside these anything can happen. So, even in a situation like this where Ghana is quite advanced, in the creation of institutions there are still a number of shortcomings, and one can well imagine that these will be multiplied several times over in those countries that do not have Ghana's experience and where the structure of planning is not recognized as part of the function of government. Some of these shortcomings may be listed as follows: first, the lack of co-ordination in the formulation, programming, and implementation of decisions affecting human settlements; second, the separation of physical planning from the normal activities of local or regional government; third, the overcentralization of planning at the local level. As already pointed out, local planning is done not by local officials, but by central government officials who owe their allegiance and responsibility to the central government and not to the local government, with the result that there is a sort of a divorce, a separation, between those who do the planning and those who actually control and implement these plans. Fourth, there is the lack of co-ordination among the agencies which make decisions affecting human settlements. Fifth, there is an absence of machinery for the formulation of overall national and regional policies for human settlements which, while dealing with problems at national and regional levels, would also provide the overall framework for local planning.

In many countries, there are departments of city planning and agencies responsible for housing, but the real power in terms of ability to effect real changes in the living conditions of the people is held by the ministries of economic planning and finance. Their activities are usually separate from those involved in settlement planning. Many of the economists who work in these ministries have little conception of the spatial impact of the economic policies. They think of settlement planning as an activity practised by a group of people who are in no way related to them except that they may draw maps to show where development projects are taking place. Seldom is it realized that economic planning and spatial planning are two sides of the same coin. The location of economic activity is important in the generation not only of wealth, but also of welfare, and a continual dialogue between those skilled in spatial problems and those skilled in economic and financial matters is therefore necessary for achieving progress and maximizing welfare. The institutions that we now have are unable to create the necessary conditions for improving the quality of life because human settlement problems are dealt with by several agencies unable to co-ordinate their programmes and policies adequately.

In Kenya, for instance, there were thirty main development agencies responsible for planning, financing, implementing, and administering a wide variety of services and infrastructure in settlements. It appears that to counteract this fragmentation of decision-making in matters affecting human settlements, a totally new approach should be adopted in dealing with the problems of human settlements. We need new institutional arrangements which can make possible the creation of central authorities charged with the formulation and implementation of integrated policies for human settlements. Such agencies must be located at high levels of government in order to ensure that economic and fiscal policies are closely integrated with human settlement policies. The creation of such agencies will require the reorganization of local government structures and jurisdictions to ensure that each local authority has the resources, both financial and human, to deal with human settlement problems within its jurisdiction in an integrated way and in accordance with overall national policies, and also to ensure the highest degree of local public participation in the planning process. It is also necessary that institutions should be created at all levels, national, regional, and local, to ensure that physical planning functions are integrated with economic and social planning functions. Institutions are needed that are capable of implementing policies, for it is no use formulating policies when they cannot be implemented — something which often happens when the plan formulation functions are separated from plan implementation and control functions and assigned to different agencies. To ensure maximum success, policy-making and policy implementation should be closely integrated. Those who formulate policies, and those who implement them, must work together in the framing of these policies, and they must ensure that the policies are implemented. At the national level we need a central agency to formulate national settlement policies, one which can back up policies with the necessary budgetary allocations to enable them to be carried out. To leave settlement policy decisions to several ministries and agencies is to continue the present state of affairs where there is a considerable fragmentation of decision-making with regard to human settlements.

Many countries resort in theory to inter-agency co-ordination to provide the coherence of human settlements policies and the integration of them into other policies of development. This has not been successful in many cases because too frequently a number of policies are assembled together into one document with little real integration to form a meaningful and purposeful whole. In some other cases personality and professional difference make it difficult or even impossible to achieve co-ordination. Developing countries have inherited from the metropolitan countries a narrow professionalism which, in my opinion, militates against attacking our problems in the truly interdisciplinary manner necessary to achieve our aims. As already stated, human settlement problems are multidimensional, and if we are to solve them, we must bring to bear on them the resources of several disciplines. Where agencies and ministries tend to be manned mostly by members of one profession, this many-sided, simultaneous attack is difficult to achieve. Each professional tends to defend what he regards as his professional position against all other positions. Economists, architects, engineers, quantity surveyors, and land surveyors — all have their exclusive professional institutions dedicated to looking after themselves and squeezing as much money as possible from the rest of us. Someone said some time ago that each profession is a conspiracy against the laity. This seems to be true today also, and if real progress is to be achieved in human settlements, members of the various professions must go beyond narrow professional interests and regard the development of their countries as their principal objective. They must be prepared to abandon narrow professional interests in order to achieve the true interdisciplinarity essential for realizing the objectives of development and human settlements.

Intermediate between the overall national agency and local settlement agencies, there should be regional and provincial agencies responsible for human settlement matters in their areas of operation. These agencies must form part of the regional or provincial governments. Where development schemes pose problems encompassing more than one region or more than one province, special authorities should be created consisting of representatives from administrations of the regions or provinces involved, but under the general overall direction of the national settlements agency.

Finally, at the local level, planning must be integrated with local government if there is to be a better climate for plan implementation. To ensure the successful implementation of plans and policies, and to ensure that all the suggested institutions are manned by people who can actually "deliver the goods," we need an adequate supply of trained manpower at both professional and sub-professional levels. In Africa today, there is a dearth of professional manpower in the field of human settlement planning. In the whole of Africa there are probably not more than half a dozen planning schools. There will be need in the future to establish more training centres to produce the manpower needed to plan and manage human settlements. We need to train people who can conceive of a human settlement as having multidimensional variables, the problems of which must be dealt with by integrating the knowledge of several disciplines. They should be people who do not have a narrow professional attitude and who do not feel that they have to defend their separate professions against other professions. They should have a commitment to the concept that their profession should be the development of human settlements rather than merely that of being quantity surveyors or any other kinds of restrictive professions.

Apart from the training of professional people in the human settlements field, we also need to train large numbers of sub-professionals for the field. This is because it is very expensive to train professionals and therefore the number of professionals that can be trained by the various African countries is very low. The idea is to give the few professionals several hands — or to extend their hands to be able to do the job properly — by giving them a number of sub-professional people who take a shorter time to train and for whom the expense of training will be much lower than for professionals. We need a large number of people capable of going into the field and helping rural people improve their habitat, people who can help them to build roads, develop rural water supplies and adopt better agricultural methods, people who can do all sorts of things and give advice in various ways to improve the rural habitat. At the same time sub-professionals would be able to assist the professionals working in urban areas as well as those in rural areas. It can be seen that this particular category of workers in the human settlements field is very important for the developing countries because of the large numbers required to help improve the conditions of our human settlements.

The University of British Columbia, through Professor Peter Oberlander, assisted in establishing the first school in Africa for the training of sub-professionals in Kumasi. It is hoped that many more such schools will be established on the continent, so that the practical problems of development at the small community level can be tackled with skilled assistance. A condition for the success of such a programme of sub-professional training is the recognition of the need by society for such personnel, such recognition being expressed in the form of adequate remuneration for their work. If this is not done, one gets a situation where these skilled persons use their training merely as a stepping stone to more lucrative employment. It is important, therefore, that this concept, this principle of sub-professionalism, should be accepted and adopted by the people in general and by the government in order that they will be able to solve their problems. If they do not take this to heart, or if they have only a lukewarm attitude towards it, or they only pay lip service to sub-professionalism, we will not be able to direct the energies of these people into solving the problems which they are capable of solving at their own levels.

In the training of personnel for human settlement positions, the developed countries can be of great assistance to the developing ones. In the first instance they can provide training facilities in their countries for nationals of developing countries. There are many countries that do not have training institutions and the developed countries can give a great deal of assistance by providing places for training people from these countries. However, I think that the ideal solution eventually will be to provide training facilities in the countries themselves, with the developed countries concentrating on specialist or high degree training. In my opinion, it is necessary that people who are going to work on human settlement problems should have their training in their own countries, where they can get instruction by participating in the solution of real problems. The developed countries can also help by establishing new centres for such training in the developing countries, and by strengthening the few existing centres to enable them to extend to more people the training facilities which they already have so that more professionals and subprofessionals are turned out in our own countries to deal with our human settlement problems. The developed countries could help by setting up institutional arrangements and procedures whereby staff could be exchanged with some sent by them to Africa to help the local staff and with Africans received into their own universities on the basis that they would later go back and take positions of responsibility in the universities of the African countries. The University of British Columbia has assisted the University of Science and Technology at Kumasi in the past, and for this assistance we are very grateful. We hope that it will be possible to widen and strengthen these contacts between our two universities in the field of training manpower for human settlements in developing countries.

EXTRACTS FROM DISCUSSION

Question: Because of centralization, in that national plans are with the minister of economic development, how far have they been successful in relation to human settlements in west Africa? Is one of the problems a gap between politicians and academics?

Dr. Tetteh: There is very little co-ordination or integration of human settlement policy with economic planning policy. I do not know of any country which has been very successful in trying to integrate these policies, and what I'm trying to put forward is that there should be a greater integration of economic planning and human settlement planning and human settlement policies. As to a gap between politicians and academics, I do not think there is any significance to this. Politicians are usually advised by civil servants and, in fact, plans are formulated by civil servants, some of whom have recently left the academic field. Also, civil servants can always ask for advice or have studies made for them by people in the universities. While we do not have a great dialogue between universities and civil servants, to my knowledge a great deal of use is made of individual members of the academic community through membership on various committees which the government appoints from time to time.

Question: What are the views of the Ghanaian planners on something like centralization versus decentralization of investment?

Dr. Tetteh: I cannot presume to give the views of Ghanaian planners, but I know that in the past there has been a great deal of centralization of investment, although the mood at present is to try to decentralize. There are other considerations apart from the monetary ones of centralization. In a country or a situation where there is a plurality of groups, and these groups are connected with various parts of the country and located in various parts of the country, there is a situation whereby one wants to appear to be fair to all the people in the country; this is sometimes expressed as correcting regional imbalances. It is necessary to try to appear to satisfy the economic development requirements of most parts of the country. To the best of my knowledge there are attempts being made to decentralize industries. However, it is very difficult to persuade the people who come to start industries to go into the areas away from the main centres because then the costs are very high and they will not be able to sell their products at an economic price. In spite of this conflict, every effort is made by government planners, where possible, to decentralize industrial development in the country.

Question: You mentioned the limitations of the grid planning of the past. How successful has the new town, Tema, been at incorporating new principles of planning?

Dr. Tetteh: Tema happens to be quite a flat territory, so that here this gridiron layout is related to the nature of the land. How successful has the town been? It is very difficult to say. As a town? Physically and socially? The town contains most of the industries we have in the Accra metropolitan area. But there is not enough housing for the people, so that of the 100,000 population in that particular area, about 30,000 are living in shanty towns not very far from the main town, and adequate provision has not been made for the people who are coming into the town. The town is being developed in terms of communities, and a central area has been reserved which, because it does not have large banks and the institutions that go with a city as all these things are still located in Accra, is not yet built on. So when you go to a place like Tema, you have a feeling that there is no centre in the town. Also one finds it difficult to orient oneself because the streets all look similar. The communities have been built with the same house styles, so as one moves from community to community, they all look alike. There are no reference points or any spectacular or distinctive buildings for orientation. It is always difficult to find one's way around in a place like

Tema. Physically I would say that it is not yet successful; of course when everything has been built it may look more successful but it is not very successful at the moment. And socially, too, it has not yet been possible to cater for all the needs of the people in terms even of schools and other services.

Question: Is it a one-industry town?

Dr. Tetteh: No, there are several industries; most of the industry in the area is located in Tema.

Question: The city of Canberra, which has been planned in a series of concentric circles, looks beautiful, but it's like looking at a person without any head — it just doesn't seem to have any feeling; it doesn't have any life. Would you say that the reason is that the people themselves have not been involved in the planning?

Dr. Tetteh: I cannot tell because I do not know Canberra and I have not read anything about Canberra. Maybe you are right and that for a town to have that sort of life there should be some degree of participation by the people in the building of a town in that certain unplanned conditions could exist which would make the place quite lively. It is very difficult, I think, for planners to create that spontaneous feeling of life which characterizes the old towns that have grown in the past. However, some towns have been able to achieve this and I do not think it is a universal truth that the towns that are planned from the beginning are all dry and not very lively. Some of the new towns in the United Kingdom have quite good social qualities. But there is of course a greater probability of having a dead town without proper planning.

7

Strategies for Rapid Growth

Lord Richard Llewelyn-Davies

I propose to talk about the issue of rapidly-growing centres in the developing world. This is obviously one of the most pressing issues facing the world as a whole today, and it happens to be one in which I have some personal experience and in which I am keenly interested. Even this rather limited aspect of the problem of human settlements is an enormous and complex study and all I can do is touch on some aspects of the problems and give you some personal judgments and ideas. I must emphasize that in many instances these are my personal views. The issues involved are highly controversial, and my views are not shared by all experts in this field.

It is common knowledge that most of the big cities in the developing world are growing at a terrifying rate. For example, the city of Bogota, Colombia, with which I have been personally concerned and which I shall use to illustrate most of what I have to say, had a population of 750,000 in 1951. In 1972, the population was 3.2 million, and it is increasing at a rate of 250,000 people per annum. Of course, that portion of the growth which is the natural increase, the excess of births over deaths of the existing population, is exponential so long as the ratio of births to deaths remains constant. The forecast population for Bogota in 1980 is 5.1 million, and in 1990, 8.5 million. Those figures will give you an idea of Bogota's extraordinary growth. There are other cities in the developing world with which many of you will be familiar which are growing at this sort of rate.

Before one can analyze the pattern of growth, it has to be put into historical perspective. The first and most important thing to say about the growth of cities is that it is not a new phenomenon. Throughout the developed world, there has been a rapid growth in urban populations in the past, and many of the features that we see today have occurred — in London, in Paris, in all the great cities of the world. In their own time they too had mass poverty, poor hygiene, illness, social unrest, slums, and squalor. Much of what is written today about the horrifying problems of growth in the developing world was written about most of the historic cities of the world during the eighteenth and nineteenth centuries. Cities were often described and denounced by some thinkers as intrinsically evil and anti-human institutions, which were bad for people and destructive of human life and happiness. They are sometimes so criticized today.

But there were important differences. It is important to recognize that the phenomenon is not new and that there are historical analogues, but it is also important to recognize that the differences are significant. The rate of growth of historic cities in Europe was about 0.5 per cent per annum, compared with 3 per cent per annum for many of the developing cities today. That is six times as fast as growth in the developing cities in the world today. Second, the total numbers involved were, of course, much smaller. They were in thousands per annum, instead of hundreds of thousands. Third, and perhaps most important, on the whole, though not universally, employment in the historic cities expanded at a rate which was closer to the influx of population. But it is important to remember that even in the old historic process of city growth, employment did not always precede or attract growth. In fact, employment was sometimes generated by growth. This is rather an important point. In Britain, for instance, a good deal of urban growth was generated in the eighteenth century by the Enclosure Acts, whereby landowners took over the common lands, the pattern of farming changed from small farms to that of large land-holdings, and the rural population was driven off the land and into the cities, a movement that in effect preceded the industrial revolution. The first phase of the industrial revolution was really one of organized labour in the cities. People came flooding in from the country and by virtue of their concentration were organized to work in weaving mills and similar industries. The development of organized and specialized labour preceded the technological inventions of the industrial revolution which occurred later. Thus, the build up of people in the cities in a sense generated the social changes in the cities that led to increased employment.

Another important aspect of the historic analogy is that, in the developed world, the process of change from an essentially rural population to a concentrated urban population continued progressively until in the developed world today, seventy to eighty per cent of the population is urbanized. Thus, in the advanced, wealthy areas of the world, only some fifteen to twenty per cent of the population is left in rural settlements. If one plots a graph, in which an attempt is made to relate the wealth of the nation to the degree of urbanization, using some measure of wealth such as gross national product per capita as one axis and the proportion living in cities as the other axis, one will find an extremely close correlation between the two; that is to say that the wealthier the country, the more people are urbanized. What would be produced would be an S-shaped curve, at the top of the high part of which are all the wealthy countries: America, the European countries, and so on, those with high gross national products, ranging up to $2000 per capita, and which are eighty per cent urbanized. At the lowest end are the very poor countries of Africa and

Asia, where the gross national product may be a hundred dollars per head or less, and where the proportion of people living in urban areas is five or ten per cent. One important factor is that there is a tremendous spread in wealth in the poorer or developing world. It is important to recognize that there is an enormous spread between the poorest countries at the tail end of this S-shaped curve and those countries half-way up. For example, a country which is thought of as developing and still quite poor, such as Colombia, has a gross national product of about $400 per head, which is already four times the income per capita of the poorest countries, so that the spread within the developing world is very great. However, it should be noted that while most of the countries follow this rather close relation of wealth and urbanization, if one plots the very latest version of this curve which includes OPEC countries, there will be some spots which are not on the graph. For example, one finds that Saudi Arabia, with an income twice that of the United States, nevertheless has a low rate of urbanization. There are some obvious reasons for these anomalies, of course, but the broad, real measure is that urban development is tied to increased per capita wealth. On the evidence of history, one cannot have one without the other. But one may want to ask: why not?

Let us look at the mechanism. What actually is causing the movement that is bringing these vast numbers of people into the cities today? Of course, the mainspring is what is called "the demographic revolution," which is best described by saying that until the end of the last century, the population of the poorer areas of the world was static, or very nearly so. Wars and sickness and a high infant mortality balanced the birth rate with a roughly equal death rate. In the twentieth century, the causes of high death rates have been diminished. With better public health, better nutrition, and so on, life expectancy grows. Wherever in the world there is an opportunity to reduce death rates, obviously it is eagerly taken. But birth rates continue high. Historically there were economic reasons in the cultures of rural societies in favour of having large families. I will not go into all the details, but those of you who are anthropologists and sociologists will know why large families were the rule. So long as these historic cultures continue, the effort to introduce family planning, which throughout the world is being undertaken with great energy, has only a slow and limited effect. As a rule it does not begin to have an impact on the birth rate until the population becomes urbanized and the cultural patterns which led people to want large families are changed. So, in those parts of the developing world where most of the people live, birth rates remain high. The end to the demographic revolution, the attainment of a zero growth rate, is a long way off in the developing countries. Increasing population has to be accepted and coped with for some time to come.

In the cities, the population increase comes from two sources: partly what is called natural growth and partly immigration from rural areas. In most cities, these two causes have roughly split the population growth fifty-fifty. Sometimes it is sixty per cent coming in and forty per cent natural growth and sometimes it is the other way around, but roughly speaking, in the developing world, about half of the increase in population comes from the outside. Natural growth, as I have explained, is simply the excess of births over deaths in the existing population already living in the city, and can only be reduced if and when family planning becomes so effective as to give zero population growth, which is still a long way off in most parts of the world. Immigration from rural areas is a more complex question, and perhaps, in theory, could be prevented. I would like to discuss why, in my view, this movement is really impossible to control.

Immigration occurs because in the rural areas increases in job opportunities do not arise to match the rapidly growing population. There are now in many countries, vigorous programmes of agricultural development, irrigation, improved methods of farming, better supply of seeds and fertilizers, and so forth, but these are slow to bring about the changes and improvements at which they are aimed. When these do come about, they tend, on the whole, to produce more food, which is excellent, but not more jobs. They may even reduce employment by achieving greater efficiency in production per man. Some countries deliberately refrain from moving toward the most highly efficient and modernized forms of agriculture in favour of what is called "intermediate technology," the use of relatively simple and labour-intensive forms of agriculture, but even this method does not get anywhere near to providing for the excess rural population in these countries. A little arithmetic will show why. What one has to do is think of a country in which eighty per cent of the people are living in rural areas. This means that eighty per cent, or possibly more, of the natural increase in population in that country is going to be in rural areas. There are no conceivable advances or changes in agriculture that can absorb these numbers. Perversely, as conditions in rural areas are improved, particularly as regards education, the attraction of the cities becomes more visible and migration, instead of diminishing, tends to increase because people's eyes are opened to the inherent limitations to life in the rural area and they are more likely to move. Eventually, the new generation which is growing up in great numbers has a rather stark choice. They can stay where they are, living at basically a subsistence level, so long as crops are good, and with the very real possibility in many places of intense poverty, starvation, even of starving to death when harvests are bad. Or, alternatively, they can move to the city, where the concentration of industry and trade gives rise to increasing employment possibilities, which, however inadequate, are actually better than those of the rural village.

It is also extremely important to recognize that this movement from the country to the towns is what it is: a purposeful decision by the people who make it. They mostly know what they are doing and why. The more the incoming population to these cities is studied, the more it is found that the people who come are among the most vigorous and intelligent of the rural population of working age. They are the ones who have the energy and the courage to make the journey, which is often very long and hard. It is also becoming increasingly clear that when they do come, they do not move without a pretty good idea of the perils and dangers and difficulties of the city and without some comparison in their own minds between city life and staying in the country. They know from their friends and relatives what life is going to be like when they get to the city. They come as a matter of choice.

We are greatly indebted to two authorities who have studied this movement in considerable detail and have written about it. One is John Turner, who lived with the people in the *barrios* in Peru and got to know them extremely well: another is Otto Königsberger at London University, who has worked in many cities of this kind. It is important not to think of this movement as a kind of mindless rush of lemmings, or to think of the newcomers as subhuman or parasitical, though it is an important political fact to remember that the established inhabitants in these cities see them in this way. In every city where there is a large immigration, there exists a myth that the newcomers are diseased, unintelligent, incompetent, and parasitical. This is very far from true, but it is believed by the established inhabitants and sometimes even by governments.

What can cities and local and central governments do when faced with this explosion in numbers? How are they going to cope with it? There are really three choices. They can keep the people out, or at least try to do so. This I call the "Canute" tactic. They can also ignore the phenomenon; pretend it isn't there; do nothing whatsoever and hope that it will go away. This is what I call the "emporer's clothes" tactic. Finally, they can attempt to manage the resultant urban growth and to use the new population to aid development and increase the national wealth, that is, to use it, as, historically, the process of urbanization has increased the national wealth and created greater well-being for people.

Solution number one, to keep the people out, is very old. According to Königsberger, it was first tried by one of the Pharaohs, who made it a law that Thebes should not expand beyond a certain size. But Tutankhamen, who succeeded him, found that Thebes had already doubled in size, so he repealed the law. In the sixteenth century, Queen Elizabeth I decided that London, which was then about a hundred thousand, was a very pleasant size, and should not be allowed to grow any more. She established a green belt and said there must be no more building beyond the city limits because she did not accept the notion that there was any need for London to grow and did not want an influx of people from the country. That green belt is Hyde Park! In the first five-year plan in the U.S.S.R., Stalin, who ought to have been able to succeed if anybody could, laid down limits for the size of Moscow. I believe it has since trebled in size, despite the incredible weight of authority, and power, to manipulate human life which Russian governments are able to use. When one reflects that the only way to keep people from moving about a country, and coming to live in a city if they want to do so, is to have a system of wire fences, guards, Alsatian dogs, and Pass Laws, as they have in South Africa, and if one is not prepared to do that — very few societies are — solution number one does not really work.

Solution number two, to pretend that immigration is not happening, is, I am sorry to say, the most common one in practice. The results are the cities of the developing world as we know them today. These have an old central area where wealthy people still live and where activity and employment, offices, shops, and the Hilton are all to be found. Around the edge, on vacant lands, along roads, up hillsides, there are shanty towns often without the most elementary services, without roads, water, sewage, education. (They do sometimes enjoy electric light because the people climb up the poles, attach wires to the mains and bring them down into the shanties.) The resulting epidemics of visual squalor sometimes drive governments into the bulldozer tactic, and they send out soldiers, police, and bulldozers and destroy these settlements, or at least the more visible ones, those between the airport and the city and which are thus seen by visiting dignitaries. Of course the only result is that the displaced people move to some other area where they can settle, and hope that they can be undisturbed for a little longer.

Solution number three, to recognize what is happening and try to manage it, is of course what ought to be done and is being attempted with varying degrees of success in a good many countries and cities. Before illustrating some of the difficulties and problems in trying to manage this sort of situation, which are formidable, I should mention one or two other alternatives that have been suggested. One is that it would be better if, as has been done in some countries in the developing world, new towns were created to absorb the rural population, rather than simply allowing them to come and accumulate in existing centres. A famous example of this is Brasilia. The fact is that new towns are a pleasant and delightful way of solving the problem of suburbanization in rich countries. In a rich country, such as England or America, it is much nicer to have a new town, properly organized, with balanced social classes, with employment, theatres, shopping centres related to the homes, than to have great sprawls of suburban growth. But these are really a rich country's luxury. They are very expensive in the provision of infrastructure and, in countries which have little money to spend in handling these problems, they are completely ruled out in terms of cost. Another solution is an attempt to provide in small towns or villages the urban amenities which attract people to the bigger cities. However, here again, the truth of the matter is that if one aims to provide city standards in a widely distributed area of villages, with the same kinds of budget, one is not going to do the same job. Let us take a very simple case: health. If there is a certain budget to be spent on health, and one wants to provide for x million people, and if these people are distributed over hundreds of thousands of square miles, one either has to carry the doctors to the people or the people to the doctors, and the standard of service given per dollar spent on health is going to be far below what could be given if the same numbers were in a compact urban situation. In my opinion, if a nation adopts such a policy, it is condemning its people to acceptance of a lower standard of amenities than is necessary.

In the developing world, if one takes account of the extremely limited amount of capital available to develop a reasonable standard of living for the people, one has to make use of the economies of scale and the existing infrastructural advantages of existing cities. One must expect that people are going to come in and one must try to cope with that problem. As an illustration let us take the case of Bogota.

Colombia has an annual per capita income of $400 per head. To think of what that means as a resource to provide health, housing, education, roads, and so on, for an incoming population shows vividly what the nation and the city are up against.

I have been very critical of the work which most Western planners and consultants have done in the developing world. I think that in most cases where they have been invited in, the plans they have produced, which were basically concerned with the distribution of land use, were a translation into local conditions of ideas that may be appropriate in North America or in England or in Europe, but these plans tend to increase social and economic inequality and impede the very development of the cities that they were meant to help. Indeed, in Bogota, which is built beside a range of mountains which runs from north to south, there was a classical plan developed by Le Corbusier with a concentrated industrial area, a central business area at the foot of the mountains and separate residential zones for the rich living in the north and the poor in the south. That was in fact how Bogota had developed. But in 1972, when I became involved in a study supported by the World Bank there were a number of exceptionally favourable circumstances which made it seem a place where something could happen. There was a history of an unusually progressive urban government under a mayor, Vergillio Barco, who had brought the population of Bogota into participation in a manner which is unusual in South America. He had achieved considerable consensus and acquired public support for expanding social services and for the general improvement of the city.

There was also in Colombia as a whole an unusually far-sighted national economic planning organization, under the direction of a brilliant seventy-five-year-old American economist, Laughlan Currie, who had been driven out of America in the McCarthy investigations. He migrated to Bogota and became the economic advisor to the government and developed with his group of economists in Colombia a series of policies which were unusual in South

America. First of all, they accepted the phenomenon of urbanization and did not adopt an "emperor's clothes" attitude toward it. It was planned that the population coming into the cities would be used, via the development of a housing industry, as an employment generator and as a method of raising the economic status of the country. This involved radical views on housing policy and on land policy. Most unusually, it was decided to limit the growth of motorcar ownership. Currie believed that other South American countries, which had opted for economic growth in terms of setting up assembly plants for cars, were making a mistake, and that the continued investment in highway construction diverted the nation's limited resources from housing, health, and other vital purposes.

The World Bank at that time had adopted, under the influence of some economists there, a rather new approach to its policies of investment in the developing world. Formerly, its policy had been to look at the different infrastructure elements, such as water supply, electricity, or roads, undertake a cost-benefit study and if, by building more roads or more dams, benefits exceeded costs, then the World Bank might provide some of the capital for the the development. This approach did not fully recognize that if in the country or city concerned there was only a limited total amount of national resources available, and that if one put most of it into dams or roads, one would then have so much less to put into health, housing, and education. Therefore, investments justified in the classic terms used by the Bank might actually be inimical to the long-term welfare of the people of the country. But in 1972 the World Bank was prepared to change its policy and look instead at the balance of investment as a whole. Taking all these factors together, there seemed to be possibilities of doing something useful in Bogota.

I have already touched on the nature of the city, the walls of mountains, the old central city, the rich area, parallel to the mountains, going northwards, and spreading out from the city southwards, westwards, the areas of the poor. The whole city is on a savanna nine thousand feet above the sea. When we first looked at the area, sixty per cent of the entire population was living in substandard slums. A few people were in run-down buildings in the old central area, but most were in what were called the *barriadas* to the south and southwest. Those were areas where people coming in from the country had seized land that did not belong to them, or had somehow obtained land and built themselves shacks or buildings and were living mostly without any services or amenities.

There was a sharp distinction between those *barriadas* which were legal and those which were illegal. About half the occupiers had obtained a legal title of some sort to the land on which the buildings were placed. These people owned the land. The other half were in illegal possession, not recognized by the government. They were liable to police action and might be turned out and driven away at any time. In the legalized *barriadas*, despite the absence of government support or services, there was rapid economic growth, a vigorous population which was improving its homes, converting them from shacks into brick buildings and developing fairly rapidly a strong economic life. In the illegal areas, where the people had no sense of permanency, this was not the case. People were depressed, did not invest, and did not try to set up local industries, because they knew their position was unstable. The difference was astonishing.

The process of settlement in the legal areas was interesting, in that there was an established pattern of successive generations. As a rule, when newcomers first arrived in the city they had no place to go but probably had relatives or friends from the village or rural area from which they came who would provide bedspace, subdivide a room, or somehow squeeze them in. So the members of the older generation of squatters were already becoming landlords and making some income out of the newer people. Then the newer people gradually found somewhere to build for themselves, so there was a progressive generational relationship between these inhabitants.

One of the great difficulties for these people was that employment, which was the main attraction of the city, tended to be concentrated in the old centre, or close to it, whereas the settlements were perforce far out. They could not acquire land near the centre, so they had rather long journeys to work. Eighty per cent of the work trips were by bus and there were over thirty bus companies. Bus service in Bogota horrifies transportation experts. The buses are tumble-down, falling to pieces, breaking down continuously, but are highly competitive. If you are standing at a curb, the bus drivers race to get there first to pick you up because they are paid on a per passenger basis rather than on a salary. In spite of all this, the result is an excellent, extremely cheap service, which conveys people back and forth, by and large to where they want to go. There are even two classes of bus: the ordinary bus, already described, and mini-buses, in which one was promised an actual seat. There was rarely a seat to be had in most of the other buses, so that those who were a little better off waited for the mini-bus. Thus, the market had created a two-tier bus system. At the time of our study car ownership was only about thirteen per cent of the population. Apart from the business of travelling to work, there was also a vigorous small workshop industry that had developed in the *barriadas*. People made things. They made or mended cars, cannibalized cars, manufactured things out of scrap iron. There is now a whole literature describing this "informal" sector of these economies. The trade and business that goes on in these areas does not get into any statistics because it is all done by hand-to-hand payment, barter, or cash payment; no accounts are kept, no taxes are paid. So the GNP and other statistics that are supposed to describe the country ignore the informal sector of the economy. Some economists think that it is a significant proportion of the total and it is certainly an important element in raising the general standard of living in the country.

When our team began to study Bogota, the first thing we did was to look at the national budget and consider the total amount of money likely to be available in the nation for the development of Bogota, while this doubling of population was being absorbed. We found investment was split between different uses in the following proportions: transport, 32 per cent; housing, 22 per cent; public utilities, 18 per cent; education, 14 per cent; health, 10 per cent; social services, 2 per cent; and administration, 2 per cent. The 32 per cent spent on transportation, primarily on road construction, was obviously fantastically high, and only achieved at the expense of vital services like public utilities, education, and health. It represented a division of resources which would have been fatal were it to continue. It was clear that by 1980, if this proportion of spending went on, key sectors would have shown sharply worsening standards for everybody; things would have become worse, particularly with respect to health, education, and social services. The population's own priorities, discovered by social survey techniques, were first, employment; second, health; third, education; and only fourth, housing. People did not care very much about being provided with a house. They could look after that for themselves. What they wanted was a job, to know they could get their children to health care, and to know that their children could be educated.

If Bogota had been allowed to develop without any kind of planning, if the whole situation had been left alone, it would have continued its existing pattern, but its problems would have become much more acute. The characteristic city in the developing world, in which no effort has been made to plan for better conditions and improvement, particularly of the lot of the poorer people, is one of concentrated employment at the centre and of a resultant heavy investment in radiating highways so that people can get into the centre. In this kind of city, the rich areas are relatively close in and are isolated from the poorer areas either by zoning or simply by land price. The poor, in their *barriadas* and spotted settlements, live further and further out along the highways, increasingly further from employment and from social services, and with increasing transportation costs. The result is that there is a forced investment in transportation to move people in and out of the centre to the exclusion of other vital needs. There may be some public housing, small in quantity and built on cheap land, far out, and generally above the means of most of the poor — even sometimes of the lower income groups. Often, closer in, land is held, undeveloped, for speculative gain.

The proposals eventually put forward by a joint team made up of Colombians and members of our group were as follows: first, decentralize employment by creating new focuses of employment on the edges of the city. Then develop housing areas closely around these new areas of employment and service and create what are called "new towns-in-towns." We proposed a multipronged housing policy: site and service provisions — that is, by providing land with central services where newcomers could build their own houses; mortgage banking facilities for the slightly higher income groups. Here we had a dispute with our friend and ally, Laughlan Currie, who believed that one should attack the entire housing problem mainly by providing mortgage facilities for the middle class, and that then sufficient disused houses would trickle down to be used by the poor. We examined this theory, and do not believe that it will work. Therefore we insisted on a proportion of site and service provisions.

We were able to demonstrate in Bogota that if one cut the distance between home and employment by creating local foci of employment (cities within cities), one could make sure that the total length of journeys to work only went up by about ten per cent by 1980, and another ten per cent by 1990, whereas if one was to continue the current, unplanned growth of the city, journey length would increase by fifty per cent by 1980. Finally, it was very important to maintain the balance between private cars and public transit, to restrict the proportion of the population owning cars. In 1972, 13,000 people owned cars, and of these vehicles over 9000 were taxis, which in fact were serving as a kind of mini-bus and carrying groups of people to destinations. If that percentage can be held steady by public policy, which is basically by taxing the import of cars, then by 1990 there will be about 275,000 cars. But if the proportion of car ownership went up to what was the common rate in, say, Liverpool in 1965, there would then be over 600,000 cars in Bogota in 1990. This difference would lead to an increase in transportation costs which would be greater than the total sums required by then to provide adequate health service, social services, and administration. Thus, maintaining the policy of restricting car ownership, and therefore the investment in roads, was absolutely essential to providing the new population with reasonable standards of health, education, and other services.

The foregoing is merely an outline of recommendations. There was considerable detail to the study as to how the new towns-in-town should be planned, how sites should be selected, how they should be developed by public corporations which would acquire the land, develop the area, and recycle the increase in land values for the public good, rather than for private gain. Proposals were made on all of these matters and all of our proposals accepted and partially acted upon by the Colombian government and the city of Bogota. However, while the entire set of proposals was formally adopted, I have to end with some degree of uncertainty as to how far they will come through into implementation. The political will to move forward along these lines, which of course is vital if success is to be achieved, does involve some measure of redistribution of wealth and this naturally arouses opposition from some of the "haves," who see some flow of wealth towards the "have-nots." These political obstacles may slow the developments I have been describing. Perhaps I can best sum up the problems and difficulties that cities like Bogota face by saying that since we put in our report there have been four new mayors, five new directors of planning, and the population of the city has grown by two hundred thousand inhabitants.

EXTRACTS FROM DISCUSSION

Question: In regard to the rural migration to the cities, if people are looking for employment, is it not possible to create neighbourhood employment centres in towns where people could be employed in agricultural activities as well as in manufacturing and industry? Could such centres be created in rural areas?

Lord Llewelyn-Davies: First of all, the projected movement into the cities in Colombia, that I have been discussing, is the minimum likely to happen if one assumes that very large programmes for agricultural development, which are in hand and which are internationally supported by the World Bank and the Inter-American Bank, do take place and therefore that the maximum possible number of people remains in rural areas. The assumptions that have been made in giving these numbers for the urban increase are based on the probability that a larger proportion of the rural population is kept on the land by the success of these programmes and policies. That is to say, that the most optimistic assumption about the success of these policies that can be made, has been made, so that if by any chance these policies falter, then the numbers tending to move towards the cities would be greater rather than less. I accept the need and desirability to maximize rural employment and food production in the country to the greatest possible extent. For instance, just to exemplify this, much of Colombia consists of rather high savannas, and these savannas are surrounded by jungles and mountains. The existing population of Bogota can only just be fed by the present savanna capability. It is part of the plan, if the population goes up as expected, to have a greatly expanded food industry in other parts of the country, including the production of dried milk, and so on, because food will have to be processed and transported to Bogota. Calculations have assumed that all of these developments are going to take place and the estimates of the population coming into Bogota do not include all the people who will be involved in them. So I do not think there is anything more that could be reasonably assumed or that could be done to hold people in agricultural employment.

The second part of the question was couldn't you build these new towns-in-town out in the country rather than building them on the edge of existing towns? The answer to that is you certainly could, but it would be very much more costly. This is because the old towns have some available reserves of infrastructure, in terms of educational and health facilities, water supply, and things of this sort, and because the new towns built on the edge of the old towns can share in much of the existing investment in the old towns whereas if they were built on a virgin site, they would have to provide their own infrastructure and this would cost very much more, and cost is a vital factor. I think one of the interesting examples of this is that during the time that the population of Brasilia grew from nothing to 750,000, the population of São Paulo rose by three and one-half million. That's a measure of what you can do with a new town, even when you put very massive and even extravagant investment into a new town in a green field situation.

Question: As your firm has built some of the world's major new towns, I found it particularly interesting that you stated that new towns are rich countries' toys. I was wondering about that comment, but also whether the strategy you applied to Bogota is not applicable to some of the countries with advanced technologies.

Lord Llewelyn-Davies: I think that the countries with advanced technologies have a different problem. The essential transition that is taking place in the advanced countries is the expansion of urban areas from the old concentrated pattern to the larger suburban matrix which Mel Webber calls the non-place urban realm. This is made possible by small vehicle transit, moving in all directions instead of only into a single centre. The resulting suburbanization and diffusion of the city is over a wider area. I think that this can be beneficially managed by new towns in developed countries. If you consider the sort of urban matrix of southeast England, where the population is growing partly from immigration from the north but mainly by natural increase and that there is some movement outward from the old, rather crowded centres, then the question is; is it better to try to concentrate this in new towns and so achieve balance in employment and the mix of social classes, or let it happen directly, following a kind of open market situation? The effect of the latter policy as it has happened around Detroit, and most American cities shows, I think, that there are good arguments for having a new towns policy, if you have the social will in the country and the resources. The new towns policy in Britain basically succeeded in concentrating some, but by no means all, of the suburbanization, and it succeeded in maintaining green space and agriculture and open space threading through the metropolitan area. These are nice things to have. It has not added to the wealth. It may not have made a single English child better educated or better cared for, but it is an amenity, a social amenity and if you can afford it, it is a nice thing to do, I think it is a pity that this opportunity was missed in the United States through lack of will in planning and lack of political structure to carry out planning.

Question: The physical morphology of Bogota, as you described it, was linear; what form did the new plan take?

Lord Llewelyn-Davies: I described it, perhaps, in somewhat too linear terms.

The town itself, taken all in all, is an elongated circle or ellipse. The new form makes it more rounded by concentrating some of the new towns-in-town as close as possible to the old centre, to reduce employment distances. It does not move in a linear direction. It is a sort of semi-circle, if you take the mountains on one side of it.

Question: What would the scale be, north to south?

Lord Llewelyn-Davies: I should think that north to south, from end to end, Bogota must be fifteen miles long, and something less on the other dimension.

Question: Most of our cities today are largely dominated by transportation networks for cars and other means of wheeled transportation. In the future, can the pedestrian network be a more important part of cities?

Lord Llewelyn-Davies: I think that only the older cities such as London and Paris are still walkable. The cities in which you can't walk are basically those that have been designed entirely around the motorcar, such as Los Angeles and Houston, where distances are usually too great between buildings. By the time you have crossed the carpark and found a way to get across the highway and across the next carpark, it is rather exhausting. And you are liable to be arrested for walking about, because, in Los Angeles, it is such a bizarre occupation. I see no reason why you should not have cities which do provide for pedestrian movement, but I think that it would be a mistake to imagine that we will ever go back to such small areas of contact in human life and activity as to exist entirely by walking. I think that being able to move a little further to schools, hospitals, clubs, social activities, and so on, which the motorcar allows, gives real social and human advantages, and will not be given up lightly. I think that you can combine that with a fair degree of access and pedestrian routes by planning, but I do not think that the benefits of being able to "swing out" further will be abandoned.

Question: Was there any public discussion of your plans for Bogota during the process of preparation?

Lord Llewelyn-Davies: Fortunately, the former mayor, Vergillio Barco, had established a lot of communication with the community, a pattern which had never existed before. The matter was tremendously debated and occupied pages and pages in the press and was much talked about on the radio. I wish I could say that I believed it was going to be thoroughly introduced in a reasonable time. I think that it will be done in large part, but I am afraid that it will be done too slowly to have as good an effect as if it were done much faster. One of the problems in many of these countries is a shortage of trained manpower. To build Milton Keynes, which is a city of 250,000, there is, at the moment, a professional staff of 575 people sitting there. I happen to think that this is rather too many, but that is nothing to do with me. When you think that the whole city of Bogota numbers its professional manpower in tens rather than in hundreds, you can see the problems they are faced with in carrying through developments of this kind.

Question: You mentioned that Colombians have not pursued a policy of attracting foreign investment through setting up auto assembly plants. What kinds of policy have they pursued?

Lord Llewelyn-Davies: Laughlan Currie, who is their principal economic adviser, has advised them to use incoming labour force from the rural areas in the building industry as part of the process of urbanization, instead of importing portions of motorcars and assembling them. This will, he argues, in the long run, leave them in a better economic position for a variety of reasons, quite apart from the specific one of saving investment in roads. This is a major economic policy issue for the Colombians, and it is open to question whether they will be able to hold the line on it because the demands for motorcars from the rising middle class could overwhelm economic planning objectives and put Colombia in the same position as many other countries. A whole sequence of problems occur if car ownership rises as rapidly as it is doing in most countries. First of all, there is the diversion of investment to highway construction. Secondly, there is the disappearance or degeneration of the public transit system, because the movement into cars creams off the margin of profit. Thus the poorer sections of the community suffer all the way round. First of all, money that might have gone into services for them goes into highways and, second, their opportunities for getting about the city, getting to work, and getting to the amenities they need, is reduced by the progressive disappearance of public transit. Therefore, according to Currie, the investment in cars tends to increase the disequilibrium in wealth. I am not an economist, but I think it is a rather convincing case.

8

Problems of the Metropolitan City in Developing Countries

I think it is fairly clear, even to those of us who view demographers with some cynicism, that tomorrow's world is going to be definitely urban. The point is that the brunt of this urbanization will be on developing countries. On the average, urban growth in developing countries has been about 4.4 per cent annually compared to about 1.2 to 1.5 per cent in non-urban areas. Even if there is some slight fall in these rates, by the end of the century in the developing countries there will be at least 1.4 billion people in towns of 20,000 and more. This is more than two times the present average and a little more than the present total urban population in the developed world. In essence, so far as the developing countries are concerned, whatever we have of the urban infrastructure — water supply, sanitation, transport, housing, power systems, whatever you like to include in the urban infrastructure — which has been created over decades, will have to be doubled in twenty years. I think this is a problem which has not been fully recognized by most people. It is a problem which we are not, as yet, emotionally prepared to accept. Since the brunt of urbanization will be on those developing countries which are least prepared, resource-wise, this lack of recognition is fairly serious, much more so than for the developed countries.

I have often wondered whether the thinking of the political and social élite in developing countries has not been influenced by some of the things that are visible in cities today anywhere in the developing world. Cities did not invent poverty; they have only made it more visible. Perhaps it is this visibility, this deprivation that seems to be so apparent in the large cities of the developing world, that leads us occasionally to think that what is basically an inevitable process could be reversed. I would like to deal at the outset with some notions which seem to support this opinion. One, of course, is the population policy, decline in birth rates, and so on as a factor working against larger city growth. I think it is fairly clear that whatever the success in any country, including my own country, India, where there is some evidence of determined action in population control, it is most unlikely that, in the short run, this will have any impact on urbanization as such.

In India we have proposed that the 1971 population rate of increase of 2.5 per cent yearly be halved by 1986. Even if we succeed, by the end of the century the population will be close to 940 million, compared with today's population of 600 million. It is also important to remember that we are dealing not only with declining birth rates, but also with high life expectancy, which is apparent to anyone who has watched the developing world for some time.

I think the next notion that still carries much weight in developing countries is that there might be an alternative to rapid urbanization in rural development. Among the political élite, it is still pertinent and fashionable to think that what is rural is simple, and what is simple, *ipso facto*, is beneficial. This is a view that ignores the serious land-to-man ratios in the countryside. Assuming that technological and other efforts to boost production do succeed — and I recognize that they need the highest priority — the question is, will this mean any sizable increases in agrarian jobs? To a large extent, it seems to me that the strategy for farm development in any developing country will have to include as one of its goals the reduction of man-to-land ratios and the development of non-agrarian job opportunities. Surely it cannot be a justifiable policy simply to keep people in the countryside, irrespective of the economic consequences.

It seems to me that the choice before developing countries is not one of stopping migration, but possibly of guiding it, although I do not think this is going to be a major factor affecting the inevitable rate of urbanization. My country is one of the developing countries which has been making a lot of effort at regional dispersal, at correcting imbalances in development between different regions, and so on. Sometimes people talk about limiting entries into cities, and certainly in India we have not been able even to try this out, but I would be interested to know of any success in patently limiting city size by restricting entry. Havana, for example, which was more than one million in 1951, is two million now. China, in spite of all the evidence that one has been able to piece together, still has about eighteen million-plus cities, and the Soviets have ten. In India we have nine and there are seven more waiting in the wings. During the past twenty years, for example, most of the investment that India made in steel, heavy industry, coal-mining, and other basic metals has been in eastern India. Yet the fact is that out of a region of about 140 million people, Calcutta continues to be the home for about 8.3 million people, and the next largest cities are Jamshedpur and Patna with about half a million people each. Jamshedpur has been a modern industrial town in the making for nearly four decades. I am not sure whether the effort towards regional dispersal is going to alter the picture of super-city growth very much in the next twenty-five years.

There is one other view which one hears often, despite clear evidence to the contrary, and that is that doing nothing in the cities, will, in itself, be a disincentive to immigration. Some very distinguished voices have been raised against investment in the city. The most powerful in my country was that of Gandhi himself. He considered every cent that went into Indian cities as tainted money and viewed those cities largely as instruments of exploitation of the rural people. To some extent, Nehru was influenced by this view. African leaders, such as Kenyatta, have also been influenced by it from time to time. While the dislike of the city has been based on some very intense, genuinely humane considerations, the theory that doing nothing for migrants will keep them from coming is one that has been tested again and again and been disproved. You only have to look out from an airplane at any large Asian city, such as Manila, Bangkok, Calcutta, or Bombay, to realize that the squalid settlements and slums there are adequate proof that migration is not halted by lack of water supply, lack of sewerage, lack of shelter, or lack of housing sites. Concern for the quality of the urban environment, or for urban amenities, is a concern that begins at the threshold of prosperity and does not even feature in the reckoning of the migrant or the urban poor.

I am therefore starting from the premise that metropolitan city growth in developing countries is inevitable and that there is no foreseeable trend that would reverse this process in the next twenty-five years. A World Bank survey points out that cities of about 100,000 grow at an annual rate of 12 per cent per annum in Africa, 11 per cent in Latin America, and 10 per cent in Asia. Between 1950 and 1970, Lagos grew from a 0.25 to 1.5 million; Bangkok from 1 to 3 million; Bogota from 0.5 million; Calcutta from 5.4 to 8.3 million. So if today we are talking about Tokyo and Shanghai as megacities, within two decades we are likely to have such megacities around Bombay, Calcutta, possibly Mexico City, and Buenos Aires. I feel that it is time we took note of this phenomenon.

All metropolitan cities in the world have problems. The major problems in Calcutta, for example, are also those found in other cities, including London, New York, Manila — housing, transportation, infrastructure services, and so on. Gross inequities exist in all metropolitan cities. In none of the developing countries does new housing average more than a quarter of what is the annual minimum requirement. As for water supply and removal of human waste, the service provided does not average more than a third of the requirement. In Calcutta, out of 1.5 million households, which represent a population of about 8.3 million, only about 14 per cent of the households have an independent water supply, and only 11 per cent have separate toilets. Assuming that our water system works perfectly around the clock, our capacity is still less than one-third of what is required. If you take transportation, we have in a 24-hour period a 4.5 million transit volume that is handled by a 1.5 million transit capacity. So that is roughly the extent of overcrowding. If you talk about densities, we have more people packed into the centre of Calcutta than live in downtown Manhattan. What I am emphasizing here is that while the problems in all metropolitan areas fall into the same broad categories, it is size that alters the quality of these problems. So far as metropolitan cities in developing countries are concerned, the gross inequities have been compounded by every species of neglect over a period of years. The neglect may vary in degree, but the fact that there has been neglect is undisputed. And, worse, obsolescence is matched only by a lack of investment.

More important, in my view, than this infrastructure deficiency, is the single fact that when we talk of metropolitan cities in developing countries, we are talking about large concentrations of poor people, and about high income disparities. In India, 35 per cent of urban households report a per capita monthly expenditure of less than 30 rupees (that is, less than $4.00 a month). There is no difference in the story of other developing countries — the larger the city, the larger the spread of poverty and the more visible this is, the more sharp is the contrast to the ostensible symbols of urbanization. But the starkness of contrast, instead of leading to a better realization of the problems, and a proper assessment thereof, leads to repugnance. In some of the south Asian countries, we have been taking what we in India call a *pukka* city approach. *Pukka* is a Hindi word that came into prominence in British usage. Anything that is proper and done "the right way" is *pukka*. A city is supposed to be *pukka* when it has a proper downtown, when it has good parking facilities, when the slums are all tucked away, when the roads from the airport are not affected by visible irritants.

Another facet of this problem of repugnance is that municipal institutions have evolved as grudging concessions to local political sentiments rather than effective instruments of urban administration. Besides, what institutional efforts have been made in this respect in metropolitan cities in the developing world have been geared to serving an organized modern superstructure. This institutional fabric totally ignores the vast and pervasive informal sector and the fact that cities in the developing world have done very little to relate their investments to the requirements of the informal sector. Pioneering studies on the informal sector have been carried out by the International Labour Organization. There have also been interesting accounts on marginal settlements in metropolitan cities. These are the two matters on which I would like to dwell at some length.

The I.L.O. study covered six cities: Jakarta, São Paulo, Bogota, Calcutta, Lagos, and Abidjan. In Jakarta, for example, out of one million workers, nearly half are in the informal sector in service activities and petty trades. In São Paulo, which is certainly an example of a modern industrialized city, about 43 per cent of the workers are in the tertiary sector and nearly half of these are in service activities and earning less than the national minimum wage. There has been industry in Calcutta since the 1870's — indeed some of it stems from an earlier date because coal mining and steel manufacturing started in regions northwest of Calcutta in the 1810's. But in spite of the fact that we have a large base of industrial employment, 60 per cent of the manufacturing activities are in petty manufacturing, and 70 per cent of the tertiary activities are in small units. Recently we carried out some fascinating studies of some of Calcutta's informal sector activities. Garment making, for instance, in an organized, large-scale way, really began in a part of Calcutta known as Garden Reach and there is one settlement bordering on a slum which has about five thousand stitching labourers. (I would not call them tailors.) The system works in a fantastic way. There is a set of middlemen who will go to the cloth wholesaler and buy the cloth on a week's credit. This is marked up by about ten per cent, by the wholesaler. The middleman — who takes the cloth let us say on Monday — goes to Garden Reach on Tuesday and engages two or three master cutters who prepare cutting schedules. These people's inspirations are derived from two to three-year-old *Vogue*s or other fashion magazines. In some cases, the master cutters precut the pieces, which in turn are distributed to the stitching labourers, who are paid on the basis of a dozen pieces. Usually a dozen pieces fetch a stitching rate of two and one-half rupees, that is, less than fifty cents. Buttonholes are paid for separately, on the basis of hundreds. The stitching labourers deliver the shirts by dozens on Friday, and these are then taken by the middleman to a market on Saturday and sold. From the income derived he pays the cloth wholesaler at the ten per cent mark-up. Assuming, for example, that one has a family of three or four people working all the time on stitching shirts, the whole family would make something like 150 rupees a month, which would be somewhat less than twenty dollars. I have seen this area, and some of the first sewing machines turned out in the world are in use there, as are some more modern machines. The maintenance cost of the machines is charged to the stitching labourers. One realizes how the economy has been fragmented into so many small segments and how during the past few decades it has been practically impossible for the government sector to intervene in those trading channels. When I talk about garment-makers, it is much the same as it would be for petty manufacturing activities in Bangkok or in Manila.

I feel the aim that we have generally taken in the developing world is one of gearing up organized production. It is only now that there is realization of the fact that there are serious limitations to the job potential that organized industry and organized trade and commerce can offer. This is going to be a major problem, and I think that the survival of the metropolitan cities in the developing countries will depend to a very large extent on how effectively they deal with this informal sector. There are quite a few things that can be done and some of these have been attempted. One possible direction could be at least to reverse the negative policies that we pursue now, consciously or unconsciously. In the developing countries we do have this *pukka* approach, and I think some of these countries are much more harsh than others with their petty traders, their hawkers and vendors. In our responses to small business development, it has been possible for developing countries to give operating capital, but it has not been possible to provide assistance which would integrate and help bring petty trades into the main stream. There have not been many successful cases of city infrastructure investments being consciously geared to accommodate the informal sector. Nor have the training and vocational guidance programmes been particularly helpful. The informal sector and the manner of its functioning are in themselves a sort of kickback to a colonial base. The measures devised so far, bank assistance, purchase of machinery, provision of space, regulation of manufacture, etc. have often tended to undermine rather than assist the informal sector. It is only in the last five or six years that some heart-searching has been going on in the metropolitan cities in the developing world, and to that extent, awareness of the problems is increasing.

With respect to the other main issue, marginal settlements, the Economic and Social Affairs Council of the United Nations has produced a position paper for the Habitat Conference which notes that this is one activity that does not suffer from strikes and goes on round the clock, at a 12 per cent annual growth rate. Whether it is in Turkey, Manila, Lima, or Calcutta, marginal settlements account for nearly one-quarter to one-third of the population. By and large, our attitude to slums and marginal settlements has been negative; we have tended to view them as a pathological phenomenon which should be curbed. Even a strongly humane, liberal person like Nehru was much agitated by the presence of slums and referred to them as "blots on the national conscience which should not be allowed to exist." To some extent, this view also coincided with that of various other interests in India. In most developing countries, until recently, slums have been viewed as an anomaly which should be removed, as something basically detrimental to orderliness, and to growth. Slums have also been viewed as a breeding ground for crime, generators of violence and of radical political forces. The fear of the mob, of course, is an old one, and I am sure that many stories of Calcutta have got mixed up with that fear. There is a long list of newspaper articles and books on this topic; Geoffrey Morehouse's *Calcutta* concludes by hinting that rickshaw-pullers would one day tap their brass bells and signal the revolution that would reduce the city to ashes. One sincerely wishes that rickshaw-pullers would indeed do that, but unfortunately there is little evidence of poor people rising against living conditions in cities. Evidence has been totally to the contrary, as they have demonstrated their ability to endure incredibly low standards of living.

One thing at least seems to have been well established, and that is that slum populations are certainly not the destabilizing influence they have been feared to be. The theory runs something like this: slums are made by urban migrants; migrants, by definition, suffer "urban shock." They lack social cohesion, a community spirit does not develop, and therefore they become ripe material for political leftism and a political participation that eventually leads to radicalism. I would venture to submit that in a slum, if you have to share a bath among, let us say, two hundred people, you have to have minimum social cohesion. It is possible for two families occupying three-bedroom flats and sharing one common staircase to quarrel if that common staircase is not kept clean. It is not possible for three hundred slum dwellers who have to share a bath or toilet to quarrel. Even if they do, survival dictates prompt reconciliation. The instruments of social adjustments are built into slum life. There is very little empirical evidence that slum life goes along with radicalism. An analysis of election results in the slums of Bombay and Calcutta showed that support to the leftist parties was really not any more noticeable there than in other sections of society. In Calcutta the left extremist movement, known as the Naxalite movement, was not something that started in the slums. Its principal force came from middle-class youths. The slums are not in themselves a destabilizing force, nor are they ripe political material. The needs of the urban poor are not political; they are intensely individual. They are work, wages, maybe a roof if possible, maybe a week's credit, and somebody to attend to occasional problems — these are not necessarily political material.

By and large we have seen — and I think this has been one of the most satisfying personal experiences for me in Calcutta — that the marginal settlement is probably the best image of a self-improving community that we have in the developing world. In Calcutta, out of three million people in the central city, we have one million living in slums. Outside Calcutta, in the metropolitan area, we have another one and one-half million. The Calcutta slums are about ninety to one hundred years old. They are not squatter settlements where people came and seized public land. They are settlements which developed in the wake of industrialization, and where there is a distinct three-tier tenancy arrangement of a landlord and a middleman, and a rent-paying dweller.

For several years, we were talking about slum improvement. The planners were denounced as defeatists because we were really not prepared to go ahead with the traditional forms of removal and rehousing. In 1970, after a debate of about seven or eight years, the raincheck arrived, and we were told that slum improvement was "on." Would we kindly go ahead and improve the life of a million slum-dwellers, within one year, and report progress. So we took on that job; we were not able to do it in one year, but in five years we *were* able to provide for about half a million slum dwellers some minimum amenities such as piped water supply, a septic tank base to sanitary latrines, paved pathways, some street lights and some drainage ponds. In addition, play spaces were created by filling up unsanitary ponds. This has all been a very participatory exercise. It is not that all the slum dwellers do a group dance, sing together, carry bricks on their heads and improve their own slums. That kind of thing does not happen because the slum dwellers have to earn their bread; some labour in the port, some are coolies, and some work in other areas. We have engaged contractors who, in turn, have engaged other poor people as labour.

We have found that the most important result of the slum improvement programme has been a political awareness that slum improvement is a good political platform. Members of the legislative assembly are willing to jump on this bandwagon and ask for more! They are willing to stake their campaigns on the basis of additional latrines, water taps, street lights, which I think is an important advance.

Apart from this physical improvement of the slums, we have also found that it is possible to some extent to mobilize voluntary efforts. We have 320 voluntary organizations in Calcutta City. Some of them give slum children a vigorous rub with carbolic soap once a week; some distribute blankets; others teach slum dwellers the virtues of prudence and morality. But the important fact is that there are 320 voluntary organizations with people behind them who find it eminently worth while to work with the slum dwellers. Some of these organizations have formed a loose consortium and have agreed to collaborate with the Metropolitan Development Authority and back up our engineering efforts with social development inputs, for example, a primary school or a health clinic. It has not been possible for the city itself to build a single additional primary school in the past twenty-five years, but individual citizens have built nearly 4000 makeshift primary schools, and the operating deficits have been picked up by the state government. Today if you go into a slum, you may very well come across an industrial worker who after a day's work in the factory spends his evenings conducting some kind of class for slum children. We think that this kind of programme has enriched our experience, and it certainly provides a framework for participation and interaction in the marginal settlements between the Metropolitan Development Authority, the people, and the grassroots political processes. The programme has also helped us understand the true dimensions of the metropolitan landscape and where the thrust should be.

When we think about the physical cityscape of the future metropolis, the conclusion is clear; tomorrow's metropolis in the developing world will not, and need not, be *pukka*; we need not pursue that concept at all. It seems to me that metropolitan cities in the developing world should not be attempting to follow the concept of the land-use master-plan. In Calcutta we rejected this approach in 1961, for two practical reasons: our best maps were at least twenty years old, and, besides, if we had had to start making a list of non-conforming uses, we could have got lost for the rest of the century in land-use registers and in defending ourselves in court actions. We also thought that the infrastructure was more important. In the provision of this infrastructure, some innovation and flexibility was needed. The cityscape definitely should provide for the integration of marginal settlements rather than for their removal.

I would also like to suggest that the present emphasis upon housing as an important function of the city, or as an important goal in urban development, tends to be overemphasized, at least in the context of the developing countries. In my view, cities have numerous reasons to exist. Shelter is not necessarily the most important of them. The reasons for which a city exists need not always be permanent, not always arranged according to a strict order of preference, and they may vary in the way in which they are presented. A city has more enduring functions than housing, such as commerce and trade and manufacture and entertainment. It seems to me that living in a city, first and foremost, is taking part in these activities, not necessarily just building housing. I am not minimizing the importance of housing, but I think that sometimes it does get blown up out of proportion. We do not concentrate enough on the physical environment. When I talk of the physical environment, the crucial task before developing metropolitan cities is one of devising appropriate technologies. After having spent roughly 300 million rupees annually during the past five years, my colleagues and I have reached the disturbing conclusion that it costs almost the same to lay one foot of sewer in Calcutta as it does in New York. There must be some other way of reaching water; some other way of disposing of human waste; some other way of disposing of garbage. Here again I feel that the developing countries will have to help themselves. Though I have not been to a planning school myself, I have a very strong liking for coloured pencils. My engineering friends have very strong likings for World Health Organization standards. Among us, we are quite capable of running up some very frightening estimates and bills for our state and national authorities. It is clear that we cannot afford to do this. In terms of housing, we have five hundred experiments going on at any given time to discover cheap housing. We do have a lot of scientific talent, but it still does not seem to be possible for developing countries to devise cheap, realistic alternative solutions to their problems. This is something where international assistance cannot be of much help; as a matter of fact, it is extremely difficult for intermediate technologies to be pursued if propagated from abroad. The search has to be essentially within countries.

I also feel that innovation and flexibility are urgently required in our governments and funding arrangements as well. Municipal institutions have been regarded as cradles of political action, but that political action meant participation in our country's freedom struggle. The Calcutta Corporation is one of the most hallowed municipal institutions in the world, but the mayors of the Calcutta Corporation have often been the presidents of the Indian National Congress. It is difficult to fight for a country's independence and run a city government at the same time. To some extent, this is true of other developing countries as well. Again, if you take into account the fact that the metropolitan areas have come into existence over several decades and are all a mixture of small and big municipalities, you will also find the colonial hangover. In the past, it was in the interests of a provincial government to keep municipalities weakly financed as creatures of a provincial government, merely as keepers of birth and death registers, as street-sweepers, and so on.

When one deals with a Calcutta of five hundred square miles and a hundred municipal entities, Manila, with a dozen entities, Jakarta, with a very large region, Bombay, with half a dozen settlements, Karachi, which also has several municipalities and non-urban units at its fringe, the question arises, do we really need city halls? It does not mean do we really need participation. This is not a mutually exclusive question. It is time we made up our minds: we cannot pay homage to Pericles and Baron Haussmann at the same time. Given the fact that metropolitan cities have multi-level, multi-sectoral problems, their administration should also have a multi-level, multi-sectoral view.

In the case of Calcutta, the Calcutta Metropolitan Development Authority came into existence because of municipal bankruptcy. There was no reason for us to come into existence but for the fact that the municipalities had failed to do what they were assigned to do. But the situation varies from one city to another. In the case of Bombay, for example, the Greater Bombay Municipal Corporation has been doing a fairly good job in its own jurisdiction.

Recently a Bombay Metropolitan Regional Development Authority has been set up which is not a substitute for or superimposition over the Bombay Municipal Corporation. Along with the B.M.C. and other municipal bodies in the region, the B.M.R.D.A. has been fashioned as a federative body entrusted with certain metropolitan level functions. In Madras another metropolitan type body has been established by the provincial government mainly for metropolitan level planning and development co-ordination. There could be a number of other alternatives in organizing the governance of metropolitan cities. It is not necessary that these bodies be shaped in the classical style of a legislative or deliberative council and an executive wing with the province or some other power acting as an umpire. Such councils are not the only means to secure participation, political or otherwise. I mentioned the participation we get at the grass roots level in the slums of Calcutta. I am told that in Lima there are over a hundred mayors, one for each of the barriadas. The non-official mayors are also elected and hold power more effectively than the official mayor. So it is quite possible to think of participation in ways other than through a council or an elective hierarchy. At the metropolitan level there is, of course, the need for funding, executing, planning type of bodies, but these could very well derive their political mandate from the province itself. If legislation is involved at the metro level there could well be a segment of the provincial legislature. Elective hierarchies are not the only means of participation and these need not be replicated at the metropolitan level, just for form's sake. For instance if there were to be a Greater Vancouver Metropolitan Council, its members in their background and approach could not be vastly different from members of the British Columbia legislature from the same geographical area.

The same innovative approach should apply for finances as well. All over the world, certainly in the developing countries, the metropolitan cities are recognized as great engines of production, as major contributors to the national economy. But, with the exception of the city-states of Hong Kong and Singapore, which quite wrongly are often cited as examples to be emulated, the funds generated within metropolitan cities are not available for appropriation within their respective jurisdictions. It is important to realize that so long as the metropolis is viewed as a generator of wealth there is an implicit case for that wealth to be shared for the sustenance and upkeep of that metropolis. A recent study of municipal finances in Asian cities indicates that per capita municipal revenues for Asian metropolitan cities accounted for only eight per cent of the national income, compared to about thirty-five per cent in the developed countries. Yet, I read the other day that, when the mayors of United States cities met in December 1975 to discuss in depth the changing economic needs of their cities, the number one proposed solution was more revenue-sharing by the federal government. Obviously the American President's admonition about prudence in City Hall had not weighed much with the mayors. With taxing powers reserved almost totally by the federal and provincial levels of government, the case of metropolitan cities in developing countries for revenue-sharing is even more compelling. What needs to be recognized clearly and fully is that given their role in the economy, and the pressures encountered from migration, dominance of low income households, increasing costs of servicing a city, inelastic and inadequate taxing systems, and so on, the metro city in the developing world cannot be left to fend for itself.

In this, as in other respects, we do have as I have repeated before, the problem of size. But since size is something we cannot do much about for the immediate future, we should at least recognize the true dimensions of the problem. It is not something of which we should despair. It is necessary for us to think and devise solutions, carefully and deliberately geared to the requirements of developing countries. The opportunity to do so is available now rather than later. But the basic goal, the purpose of the search for the solutions, has to be quite clear. In my view, a very personal view I should add, the task ahead need not be the City Monumental nor the City Beautiful. It need not call for aesthetically pleasing, visually neat solutions. I feel sure that it is within the competence of developing countries to devise and produce solutions which would bring about at least a certain livability if not a vast attractiveness.

EXTRACTS FROM DISCUSSION

Question: In 1940, Chinese cities like Shanghai and Peking had the same problems as other Asian cities. Can you compare those cities with the present-day cities in other developing countries? Has there been any improvement, and can you apply the same solutions to cities such as Calcutta or Bombay?

Mr. Sivaramakrishnan: The relevance of the Chinese experience is something that has been posed to us quite a few times. It has not been possible to get accurate information. What one has been able to piece together is that some limitations on entry have been made; that it has been possible to relate housing and other facilities to employment; that these facilities indeed move with employment; that there is some strong evidence that participatory processes at local levels make day-to-day existence reasonably controlled. While I should certainly be very happy to receive much more detailed information, it is not clear to me whether large city growth as such has indeed been contained, as claims have been made to this effect, and also, what success there has been in developing diverse job opportunities outside the city. Further, assuming that participatory processes are, of course, taking place and are well regulated, who does the regulation? Do all participatory institutions at the local level contain arrangements for conflict resolution? Is there a series of brains, or some super brain that monitors and ensures the success of this process? It was my hope in coming here that I might learn something of the Chinese experience, as I understand that Habitat Forum will have some special programmes. Generally, the information available is very scanty and I do not regard myself competent to draw comparisons on that basis.

Question: What aspect of attractiveness in the cities will have to be sacrificed in order to assure the proposed policy of livability?

Mr. Sivaramakrishnan: I do not know if I should attempt a poetic and simplistic answer. The smile of a slum child, for example, might be a compensation for several of the art galleries, and things like that. When I talk about livability, I am not calling for a sacrifice of attractiveness. I am calling for a departure from the monumental; I am calling for a very conscious effort which would help us avoid investing in some very prestigious projects that developing cities still consider it necessary to do.

Question: How much Haussmann would you trade for how much Pericles?

Mr. Sivaramakrishnan: Pericles is out of date. I am tempted by some of Haussmann's methods, but I don't think that in the long run it is a choice between Haussmann and Pericles.

Question: How much Lutyens versus how much Geddes? How much Geddes would you want? How much Lutyens would you sacrifice?

Mr. Sivaramakrishnan: Should we take an architectural view of cities? Is it not possible to take some other view? Neither Lutyens nor Geddes really dealt with the kind of problems we are facing today. Lutyens would say that "liberty will not descend to a people; the people must rise to it." It is not just a question of exhortation to people but understanding their real needs and abilities. Models are not readily available. They will have to be searched for, worked for very consciously in each city. Take for example the barriadas of Lima. Quite a few barriadas might have been considered visually unattractive, but as income levels have improved and as people have been able to effect home improvements themselves, the barriadas have become distinctly colourful. In Calcutta, for example, if you come during October and November when the annual Durga Puja is held, a kind of resurrection depicting Mother Goddess vanquishing evil, you will find that Calcutta is a most attractive city. Tinsel and paper and bamboo frames bring about that visual attractiveness and there is gaiety in the streets. Yet the streets and byways are there with all the evidence of deprivation and decay and the grind of daily existence comes again when fiesta is over. There are no ready indices of attractiveness or indices of imageability. It is something that will have to be worked out consciously. What would be the imageability and the visual attractiveness of ten thousand community latrines, for example? The solution need not be architectural or physical. There might be other solutions. Livability itself might be the most attractive. When you are dealing with the problems of solid waste removal, or pavement dwellers, or crowded buses, isn't improvement there an attraction in itself? I am not sure at all whether we are confronted here with a choice of attractiveness versus something else. Such value judgments and systems as we have been able to piece together from a variety of past experiences do not seem to hold good. The Indian New Town is an interesting example. We have built a hundred of them. Few people know this. We built them all in the image of Howard and Geddes, and of quite a few British new town planners; we all wanted to have garden cities, but most of our New Towns are neither gardens nor cities. We have a terrible problem of maintaining the "one-acre cauliflower patch and one-house" concept. I don't know whether that is attractive; whether it would not be more attractive to have entirely different kinds of structures and some other form of commuting to the factory for work. There is an opportunity available for metropolitan cities to devise some very specific solutions, and that is why I feel that it is a process of anguish and search that we have to undergo ourselves.

Question: Would you like to comment on Moscow, and the inflow and outflow of people and the regulation of them? Can these methods be applied to developing countries?

Mr. Sivaramakrishnan: I don't see any virtue in keeping people confined to certain locations. I think we in developing countries have been willing to make a lot of sacrifices, compromises, tricky emotional, political, and physical adjustments. I don't know whether keeping people in particular locations and preventing their movement is in itself a solution. There is once again the question of size. Assuming that in the developing countries we do succeed on the rural front, what is really going to happen to the population? Will they all get jobs on the farms? Will there be enough land for all? Surely there cannot be sharecroppers on non-existent land. There will have to be some other settlements. Call them "metroville," "agroville," call them any name you want. And these are not going to be very far from the large cities and they will have to be serviced. So I am not very sure whether entry limits into specific cities by itself will provide a solution. Take Calcutta, for example; our rate of migration has slowed down since 1961. Compared to Bombay, we have a lower rate of migration now. Does that mean that this by itself has been a solution? And when you are talking about large populations, isn't there a natural base for internal increase as well? When you have eight million people, assuming you have zero migration, this eight million itself is quite capable of giving you some additional people. An entry limit is all right if you have a kind of frozen situation or near-frozen situation. You could perhaps do it in a two hundred and fifty mile island like Singapore and say "No Entry." But if you have a very large country, and also have the basic problems of economic development and income improvement, you have to have mobility. To regulate or control that mobility you need to commit the inadequate governmental machinery and you also need a highly trained political process to support this kind of a system. At any rate, by itself, it is no solution at all.

Question: What are you doing to improve transportation in the cities?

Mr. Sivaramakrishnan: Transportation is an extremely important consideration in the city, and perhaps one of the tools that is available for guiding and shaping the future metropolis. A choice has to be made between location of employment activities on the one hand and high commuting costs on the other. Here again I feel that it is very easy to fall into high expense solutions. The city of Calcutta is building its first tube railway, to be completed in 1981. It is three years behind schedule and is going to cost us twice what was estimated. We are of course somewhat consoled by the fact that nowhere in the world has any tube railway been built according to schedule or according to the originally estimated cost. The simple fact is that even after the tube railway is completed, we are going to be pretty much in the same position as we are now because the surface transit volume will have picked up. So today we are wondering whether we shouldn't be investigating other alternatives. Should we not be trying to think in terms of shifting office locations? Have we exhausted the possibilities of alternate locations within the metropolitan area? I am not talking about a mini-Abercrombie plan for Calcutta, but of relocating within the metropolitan area. It is a fact that many cities in the developing countries do have space. Are we giving the needed priority to public transport? Is it necessary to go through the same processes as European and North American cities before we officially condemn the private automobile? Is it not possible for us to anticipate some of these steps? In Calcutta I find that official thinking in this regard is rapidly changing. About two years ago, if I had suggested that all ministers should not be allowed to drive their cars right to their offices, but should walk about a furlong, I would have lost my job. Today, the thinking is somewhat different. In Calcutta during the past three or four years we experimented with a system of minibuses. We found that minibuses were perpetuating the same individual route economics of private, long-distance buses. We are now saying that minibuses should perform a supplementary role. We should have shared taxis. We should have different kinds of transportation. Public transportation policy might be a very important tool available for planners in the developing countries. It seems to me that perhaps in this area, rather than in other areas there might be some opportunities for some satisfying interactions because here at least technology seems sufficiently advanced, and the potentiality for the transfer of expertise also seems to be high.

Question: How much are your views supported by the central government in India? There were recent reports in the paper about efforts to move slum dwellers outside the city and there was some rioting. Obviously, this is a direct contradiction of what you think should be done. How much support is given to your views?

Mr. Sivaramakrishnan: In 1962, when we came up with a proposal for slum improvement, we were thrown out of the finance minister's room. In 1965, when we asked for funds for a pilot slum improvement scheme, we were given the funds, but before the experiment was completed, the funds were withdrawn. In 1969, slum improvement was respectable. In 1971, as I mentioned, slum improvement was on. In 1973, the slum improvement concept was picked up, and extended to most of the metropolitan cities in India as part of a national programme of minimum needs. So today I would say that compared to the position that prevailed about ten years ago, the improvement of slums and their integration is definitely a part of public policy. But at the same time, in certain cities, some decisions have been taken to remove slum dwellers and relocate them. You are specifically referring to the incident in Delhi. While this particular incident has of course been noticed, it should also be remembered that over the past fifteen years, Delhi has provided something like nearly 85,000 open, developed plots for slum dwellers and future migrants. Delhi has had the good fortune of having publicly owned land to which future migrants could be brought and where construction labour could be settled. It is in the relocation process that we have had this problem. About four months ago, Bombay completed a massive survey of all its slum population. Bombay slums are different. They are sort of squatters' slums and are operated by middlemen. Most of the slums are located on lands belonging to the Bombay municipality and Bombay government. What Bombay has done, having taken a total census of the slums, is to relocate certain slums, which, according to them, are on prime city lands. But with regard to the rest of the slums, they went through a system of photography and passbook issue and direct rent collection. We were quite amazed to find that the total rent that is realized from the slums of Bombay per year amounts to 500 million rupees. This has been brought almost en masse into the housing stock. In Calcutta we do still undertake a bit of slum removal, but that is in connection with some of our other development schemes. In one area where we tried to undertake slum removal and finance rehousing through cross-subsidies and work out everything very economically, we landed flat on our faces. Madras is the only city that has attempted limited amounts of slum removal and rehousing, but there again, they have not been able to alleviate the problem of slum growth. So I would venture to submit that individual incidents need not be regarded as departures from policy. On the other hand, there is clear evidence, in contrast to what happened before, that it is not feasible to have slum removal as a public policy. I would say that this is perhaps one of the welcome shifts in public policy in India. I would not say as yet that the scene is ripe and everyone is a convert to slum improvement. All politicians are the same, and prefer to lay foundation stones for new housing estates rather than latrines for existing slums. It is difficult to persuade all of them at the same time.

Question: Would you care to comment on the effectiveness of your government's plan in the field of family planning as it relates to the population pressures in the metropolitan areas?

Mr. Sivaramakrishnan: The national population policy aims at reducing the birth rate from 2.5 per cent in 1971, to half that in 1986. Recently, some very important decisions were made in consultation with state governments. One of them, of course, is stepping up the outlay on family planning. The second important thing is in regard to central assistance; decisions have been made that division of tax income between the centre and the states would be pegged at current levels, not on future population, thus avoiding the possibility of disincentive. The third is that while the national government itself is not going in for compulsory sterilization, it has left it open to the state governments to undertake such a programme. The history of family planning programmes, as everyone knows, has been very uneven in India. I would only say that during the past few months, there has been considerable evidence of a determination that did not exist before. One can only hope that this determination will last. There has been a slight decline since 1971; the 1974 figure is around 2.3 per cent, compared to 2.5 per cent in 1971. This is still slender evidence to advertise, but it is quite clear that both at the national and the state government level, the population measures are receiving much more attention and importance than they ever did in the past.

Question: In your talk, you predicted the population of India would be about

940 million by the end of the century. What kind of prediction are you making for the big cities of India?

Mr. Sivaramakrishnan: Million-plus cities, according to an assessment made by the central town planning organization, will number about twenty. There are nine now; seven more will cross the mark by about 1986. There will be four or five more thereafter. As for cities above one hundred thousand — from the present number of about 160 — these will probably number about 400. Urban population itself will be about 28 per cent. These are the projections, but I am not very fond of using these figures. I think it is fairly clear that even if the existing metropolitan cities are going to be doubled, then my grandson's job is well laid out.

Question: You mentioned moving the rural population back into the rural areas. Is this really possible?

Mr. Sivaramakrishnan: If you are talking about taking out existing populations from metropolitan cities, no, I do not consider that possible. But if you are talking about establishing new urban focal points which would at least deflect future migratory streams, yes, this has to be a very important part of the urban policy. I feel that there will be opportunities for doing this.

9

Views on China's Habitat Policies

Joan Robinson

It is appropriate that in this series there should be a talk about China because both the problems and achievements of China in the sphere of habitat are remarkable. I am not an expert on China, but I did start visiting the People's Republic about twenty years before Mr. Nixon did, so that I have seen it through a number of phases. Every time, one learns more respect for the tremendous achievements as well as for the tremendous problems that they face in that country. To sum up, the situation with respect to habitat in China is that there are no shanty towns, there are no slums, there are no families living in the streets as in Calcutta or Bombay; the great cities are being limited in their rate of growth and the major part of the population is living and flourishing in the villages where their ancestors lived.

Of course, the question of settlement is bound up with the whole problem of economic development, and particularly with the relation between agriculture and industry — the relation between country and town. The economic policy of China has been concerned from the start with the problem of the need for balance between agriculture and industry.

At the beginning, partly under Soviet influence and with Soviet aid, the Chinese made great strides in laying the foundations for heavy industry. Although they did not perpetuate the Soviet direction, this was a necessary foundation. The Great Leap Forward in 1958 is generally represented in the West as a stupid idea and a failure. I think it was not a stupid idea; it was an important experiment to see whether by rousing the energies of people it was possible to break out of underdevelopment at one step. In that respect the Great Leap was disappointing, but it did show how much work remained to be done. It had great achievements to its credit, but at the same time, as the Chinese freely admit, they made many mistakes in that period and they were caught off balance by the bad years of climatic disasters which followed and so, in 1961, they were in real difficulties. Nevertheless, one of the greatest achievements of China's economic policy is that the country went through this period of scarcity without inflation. They preserved economic discipline throughout the difficult years; afterwards, from 1962 onwards, they achieved steadily improving harvests and gradually got out of the woods. However, during this period, they had necessarily to reconsider their economic policy, and it was at this time that the slogan "agriculture is the foundation and industry is the leading factor" was adopted. The Chinese abandoned the Soviet notion of heavy industry at all costs and of plowing back the products of industry into industry and allowing agriculture to fall behind. Their policy has been the reverse.

The basis for heavy industry was scanty. In the northeast, in Manchuria, the Japanese had developed an industrial base but a great many of their installations were stripped away during the last stages of the civil war and had to be reconstructed. Then the Chinese started new centres, for example, big steel complexes, and machine-making complexes, so that they would have a foundation for developing industry. Industry was then to be devoted to fostering agriculture. This is an important clue to Chinese achievements in the sphere of human settlements, that is to say, in allowing people to live in the country and preventing the drift into cities which has been such a disastrous consequence of so-called development in most of the third world.

Land reform has already been completed. To a large extent, it took place spontaneously. During the civil war, in northern China, the peasants rose up and got rid of the landlords and organized the distribution of the land. In the rest of the country land reform was carried out systematically after liberation. A system was introduced whereby the land in each village was to be redistributed among the families of the village. The land was taken away from the landlords and distributed among the landless workers and, where there was more to go around, to the poor peasants. The landlords, of course, had now become landless, and were given a share as well in the distribution of the land. The Chinese measure land by the *mou*, which is about one-sixth of an acre, and this distribution of land was of the order of two or three *mou* per head. The holdings created were tiny, and it was clear to everybody that this did not provide the basis for flourishing individualist agriculture, therefore, the move towards collectivization went much more smoothly in China than it has done anywhere else. By gradual stages, the peasantry was brought into the system that is now the rule in most of the country, that is, the system of agricultural communes. Communes were formed as a result of the enthusiasm generated by the Great Leap, and consisted of an amalgamation of neighbouring cooperatives. The co-operatives, which were units of perhaps a thousand families, were then joined up into units of perhaps ten or fifteen thousand people. The point that I want to emphasize is that these people had their own land, their ancestral lands, which had been given to them in the land reform and which were now pooled and reorganized.

The organization of the commune is a brilliant invention. It arose out of problems that had been created by the distribution of land and the development of the co-operatives. A commune is organized in three tiers: the basic unit is a team, which might be the fellow workers from thirty or forty families living in the village. Each team has its own piece of land and its task is to cultivate this. The teams are thus in charge of the regular agricultural production. They are then grouped in brigades which in turn have certain tasks. For instance, a brigade will run the building team, to which I will refer later; it will run a brick and tile factory; it will be in charge of the grinding of grain, thus relieving thousands of women of the task of stamping out the grain every morning. Brigades are then grouped within the commune, which is the organization that is the point of contact between co-operative agriculture and the national organization. The commune is in charge of any large-scale activities. By this means, the Chinese have succeeded in fitting the tasks required to the appropriate scale of operation.

The formation of the communes was drastically put through the wringer in the bitter years. Many modifications were found to be necessary as the Communists learned from their early mistakes. However, the importance of the communes in this period was that they nursed people through a situation which in the old days would have been one of famine in which millions of people would have died, millions of families been dispersed, and devastation created, as has happened time and time again in the history of China. This time they were nursed through the crisis and the structure of the agricultural community was kept intact.

Meanwhile, as the agricultural development went on, a great growth in industry was taking place; and this development was on the principle of "walking on both legs." That is to say that those types of production, such as an iron-steel complex, which must be built on a large scale and with great investment per man employed, were instituted in a thoroughly modern manner. At the same time, while automated installations of the latest types were made, a great number of operations continued to use old-fashioned labour-intensive methods. Those industries were created with very simple techniques and very little investment. The people themselves could gradually mechanize to some extent out of their own savings, and gradually raise their level of production. In this way the horrid dilemma which exists in third world countries between installing modern industry and finding employment for the people was overcome. In fact, in principle the problem of unemployment had been solved; that is to say, everybody in China has a place in society, a right to an income, a right to social security. This is not full employment in the sense that everybody has a high level of production. There is a great deal of employment at a very low level, and what a Western businessman would call tremendously overmanned concerns. But from the social point of view, we can say that the Chinese achieve full employment by this means. The development of industry will go on and gradually more and more of the labour force will be equipped with sophisticated machinery so that the modern industry "leg" will be gradually strengthened and the low-level production in small-scale, labour-intensive industries will eventually be absorbed.

In a similar way, the relation between town and country in China went through different phases. During the Great Leap, there was a strong emphasis on industry; many people came into the industrial cities. During the bad years, they had to be forced to return to the country where they could get their food. The slowing down of investment resulting from the difficult years meant that the cities also had to be reduced in size. A definite policy that the great cities should not grow was adopted. Shanghai, for instance, is to be limited to ten million people. The central core of Shanghai is a little over five million, and greater Shanghai, including the satellite towns which have grown up around it, is to be limited to ten million. The way this is done is related to the method of recruiting labour when installations are established. For example, when a new factory is to go into operation, housing will be built at the same time and workers will then be recruited from the country. The enterprise will be given the right to recruit so many people from a particular district and the people are brought in with their families and neighbours. Thus, there is not the terrible disruption which has often occurred both in capitalist countries and in western communist countries in the process of uprooting people from the country and drawing them into society. In China, this is done in such a way that the structure of the society is maintained even when it is being transformed into an industrial society.

Through this approach, the housing needed in the cities is partly provided in connection with the industrial enterprises as new enterprises build housing estates to accommodate their workers. But housing requirements are also being met by cleaning up the old housing. I remember very vividly a visit to Shanghai in 1957 when someone who had known Shanghai in the old days commented about a particular quarter where it had once been a common sight to see corpses thrown out in the morning and said that no westerners would ever have dared to go down those streets, which were wretched filthy places. By 1957, such streets had been rehabilitated; neighbourhood committees had been formed and people had helped one another. They had mended the roofs, cleaned up buildings, cleaned the street, cleaned the alleyways, and the city had provided waterpipes at the corner of each street. Such community enterprise has continued. In 1976 one would not see such a primitive way of clearing the slums. By now there has been a great deal of rebuilding and rehousing and settling people, but always with this care to settle people in neighbourhoods where they can work together and help each other instead of flinging them from many different places into one heap.

The problem of Shanghai is a very formidable one. To some extent the Chinese have succeeded in reducing the pressure on the central urban core by the creation of what we would call satellite towns, with a belt of agricultural land between the city and the outside towns. They have built housing, factories, schools — all that is needed for a community — so that the population can be scattered in this way and the tremendous pressure on the central city relieved. All this has taken place against a background of a rate of growth of population which is as high as any seen in the third world now.

After restoring the structure of society, and after providing an excellent medical service and social security for everybody, the Chinese had a big drive to keep the birth rate down. But, of course, getting the birth rate down does not mean immediately stopping the growth of population because the number of families growing up from the earlier period of rapid growth are coming along and pushing the solution to the problem into the future. Meanwhile, the problem of settling the people, keeping them in the country, and limiting the size of cities had to be undertaken not only with an exceedingly dense population to begin with but also with still rapidly growing numbers. The Chinese have to work on the problem of limiting cities from both ends. It is not only a matter of preventing people from coming in until there are jobs and housing ready for them, but also one of pushing people out because the natural increase in the cities is still going on. The process is achieved partly by sending teams out to reproduce in the back areas the kinds of sophisticated installations that have been developed in Shanghai. Skilled workers from Shanghai are sent out and they train the local people; by this means industry is being spread all over the country.

Another policy followed is that of sending so-called "educated youth" into the country. Educated youth means young people who have completed secondary school. A general rule is that everybody should work in the country for two years between school and higher education, or between school and being recruited into urban jobs. The hope is that a good proportion of them will stay in the country, and some of these young people volunteer to go to remote and difficult parts of the country, to settle there and work and to help raise the educational level of the backward place. This is, of course, a lot to ask of ordinary families. There has been a considerable amount of trouble about this policy. Those people who are strongly imbued with the spirit of socialism and the ideals of Mao have gone willingly, but, in the ordinary run, families still try to cling to their children as they do anywhere else. The regulation has now been altered so that when the children are sent to the country, unless they volunteer to go to some remote place, they can go somewhere near home and so keep in touch with their families. This policy is a way of preventing the development of a problem which is also perhaps beginning to be apparent in Canada, but which is very marked indeed in countries such as India, namely the problem of unemployed intellectuals, of people being educated to think that they deserve jobs at a level where there are not enough jobs available. This is a chronic problem which arises from the spread of education. We are all in favour of education, of course, but it does create great problems of fitting the needs of the community to the supply coming out of the educational institutions.

This problem of intellectual unemployment is precluded by the Chinese system. People go for their period in the country, many of them stay, and then when their turn comes to be recruited for industry or to be recruited for some other kind of job, they are brought in to a job where they are needed. So the problem works from both ends, but it is also a contribution to the long-run ideal of Chinese socialism, which is the breaking down of the three great differences: the difference between rural and urban life, the difference between agriculture and industry, and the difference between work by hand and work by brain. This is a programme for a hundred years, perhaps a thousand years. But here the Chinese are making a start by getting the population mixed up in this way and getting the educated people to feel that there is a duty and a pleasure in helping their countrymen who have developed quite a different style of life from their ages of traditional work as peasants in the country. Furthermore, peasants also are being educated, so the sharp difference in educational level is gradually being eroded, but it is not something that can be cancelled out in twenty-five years.

The development of industry is under the national plan. The Planning Commission sketches out the twenty-year plan broadly, and implements it in five-year and one-year stages. Planning authorities deal with the whole country as if it were a chessboard and work out where installations should be put and how development should go on. The general aim is to allow the industry that is already developed in the great coastal cities, in Peking and so forth, to continue as well as the natural growth on the spot from reinvestment, but in addition, to ensure that the new big installations are put in different places throughout the country. The purpose of this is gradually to bring to the country an even development, or a much less uneven development than that which was left from the semi-colonial period, when industries were developed by foreign powers on the coast and the interior of the country was left alone.

The chessboard, the development of industry in remote parts of the country, goes hand in hand with a financial system which is continuously draining off funds from the rich provinces, provinces where there is a high value of output per man. This policy allows large subsidies to be paid to the backward parts of the country, particularly to Tibet and Sinkiang but also, in many places where there are national minorities, areas that have been neglected or areas that have particularly difficult terrain. These are now receiving subsidies and receiving investment from the money that is made in the already developed parts of the country, particularly in Shanghai, and which is not at the disposal of those particular cities or districts. They are not allowed to keep the fat to themselves; their funds are directed towards development in other parts of the country. The spirit of the slogan "we must combat egoism and eschew privilege" is not only valuable for the individual in guiding his conduct, but also for the guidance of financial and economic planning.

In the communes, there has been much creation of arable land. China, having had a long history of relative peace and good order interrupted by periods of turmoil, developed an enormously high density of population in that part of the land suitable for cultivation. Even animals were lacking; the land was cultivated entirely by manpower. To restore a better ratio, it was necessary to create more land for agriculture. This was done by irrigation, by terracing hills, by curing waterlogged or saline land by leeching, and by bringing transport into remote places so that new land could be cultivated. In all these ways, the Chinese have been increasing the supply of arable land. We hear of "turning labour into capital"; this was turning labour into land. In the remarkable system which was developed, the large schemes, such as the large river control scheme, were carried out under the national plan and by organized teams of workers. In addition, a great deal of small-scale land improvement has been carried out by the communes. In the slack season of the year, when agricultural work is not pressing, they organize teams of volunteer labourers. Funds are provided from their own accumulation to pay for any expenses, such as buying drainpipes, and so on. Then, with advice from engineers or government advisers as required, the commune will work out an appropriate scheme for a project which they will carry out by working during the winter. Expenses are allocated to the different teams according to the land that will be benefited. The team in effect has the equity on a particular piece of land. The benefit which they get from this work is that the next year their land will be easier to work, will have a better yield, or will be available for better crops. The cost is merely a matter of working in the slack season instead of being idle. Assuming that one has enough to eat, that is enough calories to enable one to work all year round, this is not really a cost. One might as well be working as sitting under a tree! At one time, people did not have enough calories, and they had to sit under a tree during the starvation months because they were just not able to work. As soon as there is sufficient food to live and to work on all the year round, then such schemes are something for nothing because the work is going to result in an improvement of the land. These are necessarily short-term schemes: it would not be possible in this way to undertake long-term schemes, of five or ten years, but the short-term schemes are really giving the people something for nothing.

There is no extra payment; thus there is no inflationary pressure caused by doing this work because the income of the team comes from the crops produced. The individual is rewarded by work points; if he volunteers to participate in one of these schemes, he gets more work points. Work points give him a claim on the income of the team. So the work of improving the land and creating a greater supply of land is carried through without generating the kind of inflationary pressure that has been the big impediment to schemes of this sort in many third world countries.

Development of the backward areas in China is not only an economic and technical problem, but also a human problem because there are certain national minorities, people who in the past have regarded the Han people, the main Chinese people, as aliens and enemies. These now have to be made to feel that they are all part of one nation. This has been an important element in the problem of handling the development of national minorities. I was fortunate to get some insight into the problem the last time I was in China. I visited Yunan, an area where there is an autonomous prefecture of some Thai people, Siamese people, who had been washed up by history into this area and had lived there for centuries under archaic feudal conditions until the liberation army came in. When it did, it did not start to tear down the Thai institutions; instead it showed the people that there was another way to live. It did not arrest the feudal lords or treat them as criminals, but rather simply let the system crumble under the influence of a different style of life. By this means the army managed to get the people to accept and to delight in the same system of socialist agriculture, to share in the educational system, the health service, and advantages that the town people were enjoying.

I mentioned that the Chinese are presently having a big drive to try to get the birth rate down. I do not know how Mrs. Ghandi is going to get on with her compulsory sterilization programme, but in China the most effective element has been the removal of the need to have children as a means of providing social security. In the country, everybody is guaranteed a livelihood. Most of the old people live with their families. The usual pattern is for the grandparents to live in the house with the young couple, and the old granny is very useful in minding the babies and helping in the house so that the young woman can go out and earn work points with the team. If there is someone who does not have a family, he nevertheless has the five guarantees: food, housing, clothing, medical attention, and a decent funeral. These provisions are made through the welfare fund of the team. The immediate effect of the liberation was a big increase in medical services; this was even further extended after the cultural revolution. Thus the terrible anxiety to have children to support one in old age is removed.

The cultural revolution has great achievements and good legacies to its credit, but unfortunately it got out of hand in the end. It ended in dissention. The movement was wound up, and there was a return to good order afterwards. One particularly good legacy is the health service in the rural areas. One of the slogans that Mao evolved was to the effect that hospital medical attention was concentrated too much in the cities and that too much was provided for those who already were the privileged people. Medicine had to be taken to the country. So doctors went out and helped to train medical workers, the "barefoot doctors," and some also settled in the country. Every village now has medical workers and every commune has a little hospital. The big hospitals are available for difficult cases. Mass diseases have been practically stamped out. The place in Yunan which I mentioned had a severe problem with pernicious malaria and was almost being depopulated, but the disease has been overcome. Ordinary malaria still occurs because Yunan borders on Burma and Laos and some malaria comes over the frontier so that it cannot be eliminated altogether. Generally speaking, however, malaria, cholera, and leprosy have been stamped out and the death rate has been reduced to Swedish levels. So the framework now exists within which it is possible to mount a big campaign for family planning, late marriage, and small families. This movement is apparently having considerable success. As noted earlier, one cannot stop the growth of population just by getting the birth rate down because the peak in the birth rate which occurred after liberation means that vast numbers are still coming to the age when they must be allowed to have their two children. Thus, the growth of numbers is still an important problem and the drive for developing agriculture must continue. In September 1975 there was a conference on this problem. The aim was to raise most districts to the high level achieved already by the best districts and at last to overcome the problem of feeding the people. These are the enormous problems which China has faced. It was not a simple matter, but progress has been sufficient to instil confidence in the future.

At the present time, the main drive is the mechanization of agriculture. Sometimes people who have learned some economics say, "Why do they want to mechanize agriculture? They've got surplus labour." This, of course, is the kind of remark that people make if they have been brought up in the capitalist world with private property. The point is that if the land belongs to the people who are going to work it, and the machines belong to the people who are going to operate them, then it is not a problem of displacing labour, it is a problem of assisting labour. So mechanization is going ahead and has a number of aspects and a number of advantages. First of all, it does increase productivity. It is not true that mechanization merely displaces labour. Very often, by getting the crops in quicker, it is possible to have two or three crops where there was only one before. Mechanization can also increase yields by improving ploughing. Secondly, it is a very powerful incentive to the collectivization of work. It seems that in the Soviet Union the peasants are interested only in working on their private plots. In China, the private plot is gradually disappearing because it is more convenient to put a private plot into a field with the others where it will be ploughed by tractors. Then it ceases to be a private plot; it is simply a bit extra on one's rations. In places where these ideas are newer, for instance in Yunan, an area of national minorities, private plots are still allowed and there is a good deal of trade at local fairs. The policy of the government is to bring people into the modern life gradually instead of trying to push them into it ahead of what they are able to understand. Mechanization certainly helps; even in the areas of national minorities, I saw bulldozers levelling the fields. Once the fields have been levelled, a different kind of cultivation becomes possible and yields go up.

In the mountains, there are numbers of wild people, some of whom were quite unknown before and who lived there entirely isolated, with their own language and their own customs. They are being helped by mechanization to use modern methods for cultivation. Formerly, they would burn the forest, stick in a seed with a digging stick, and wait for the crop to come up. The result was a very small yield and a very low income, but it required very little work. These people have now been shown how to make terraced fields, how to make dams in the little valleys where they live, and how to use water for irrigation, or even for electric installations. They are provided with walking tractors (small tractors invented in Japan but now widely used in China) so that they can find their way from the stone age to modern mechanized agriculture in one jump.

A third point about mechanization in China is that it is an important contribution to the long-term aim of removing the three great differences among the people. It means a big change in the life and in the attitude of the young people in agriculture. Formerly they thought peasants were one kind of being and industrial workers were a higher type altogether. Now they are realizing that they can be involved in industry, and they have a lot of little factories on the communes. They learn to handle machines and acquire the book-learning necessary for engineering work. This development is contributing in an important way to breaking down the three great differences and is also one of the important elements in keeping the people in the country, thus preventing the desperate problem of people being driven from the land and living on crumbs in ghastly slums around the cities, a frequent scene in all the underdeveloped world.

There is not space to enlarge on another aspect of the revolution, but I must at least mention it, namely that the revolution in China was much greater for women than for men because previously the life of women in China had been very oppressed. Now women are formally liberated; they have equal rights with men and opportunities to take advantage of them. But it takes a long time. The girls are still more shy than the boys. The women's revolution is not yet complete, but the opportunities for women are open, and anybody who wants to do something is able to try it. The revolution in China is an enormous one, Half of Heaven, as the Chinese say, and it is a big contribution to economic development, social development, and to education.

Another issue, which I cannot deal with in detail here, is the question of pollution. There is still a good deal of pollution in China particularly because of old-fashioned installations belching out smoke. New installations are set up with great care. The Chinese do not talk in terms of pollution, but rather in terms of avoiding the three wastes of air, water, and materials. The water is cleansed. The chemicals are taken out of it and used for fertilizer, and the water is then made available for irrigation, resulting in a large saving. Similarly, poisonous chemicals are taken out of the smoke and made use of, and all kinds of scraps of garbage are used. Bio-gas plants are being installed. By avoiding waste the Chinese also keep the country clean.

I was interested in the effect of the cultural revolution on the organization of planning, particularly in the change from lines to areas. The line organization is an organization of an industry, for example, iron and steel, machine tools, textile manufacturing. Following the Russian pattern, the Chinese had a system by which there was a ministry in Peking which was in charge of the industry. There were always lower level industries where people were free to establish small works of their own, but the main industries were organized under a ministry. After the Cultural Revolution, the organization was changed, although it was still planned. The main disposition of raw materials to the various industries is in the national plan, as is the destination of goods. As stated, the individual province or city does not keep its fat to itself. Goods are distributed over the country, the counterpart to the distribution of finances. As far as production is concerned, it is now the concern of a local or area organization. This is obviously helpful in many ways. The different branches help one another out and co-operate in various ways. Also it is important from the standpoint of avoiding waste, or as we would say, of avoiding pollution, because there is a natural tendency in China, as in more developed countries, for engineers to want to get on with the job of production. They find it rather a bore to have to take a lot of trouble to avoid pollution or avoid destroying amenities. Once production is the charge of an area organization, its interest is on the side of preserving the amenities of the district, and it will curb the engineers' independence and make them use the technology which will prevent pollution.

The interest in Habitat is a sign that we are beginning to realize what problems our so-called advanced Western economies have created for themselves. We have a great deal to learn from China, if only we are not too conceited to study what she has to teach.

EXTRACTS FROM DISCUSSION

Question: Why do you suppose that China hasn't made a commitment to attend the Habitat Conference?
Professor Robinson: This is part of their general foreign relations. What the

particular issue is here, I don't know. They do go in for some things, yet not for others. I don't suppose that they really feel that they have a great deal to learn.

Question: You mentioned the point system for the workers. How are the points allocated?

Professor Robinson: In industry, there is a regular system, inherited from the Soviets, of eight grades of wages, according to seniority and skills. The spirit of the cultural revolution was to reduce the differences. This the Chinese regard as a long-term thing; you can't suddenly deprive the higher paid workers of the benefit of the scale, so they work at that very gradually. But the work point system is used in the co-operatives. Points are recorded in a book in which everybody enters what job he has done and what points have been earned. Then there is a periodic settlement which is supposed to be once a year. The total team work points are summed up as is the income of the team which will consist partly of grain and partly of money because cash crops are sold to the state (e.g., cotton and tobacco). The surplus of grain above that needed for their own consumption is sold to the state at fixed prices. The grain is given out to the families in advance on a ration scale and they pay for it with work points at the annual settlement. Monetary income is distributed according to each individual's points. There is a good deal of individual incentive in this system. People have a motive for working hard, but there is also a collective pressure because the income of the team as a whole depends to some extent upon the amount of work individuals contributed. Anyone who says, "To hell with this! I don't mind if I get any money or not," is a bad neighbour. There is pressure for everybody to work for collective reasons as well as for individual ones. This is the system under which income is distributed in the communes. There are differences among the communes because some are richer, some for instance have easier land to work and therefore have a higher output per head, so that when they have taken off the amount they need to eat, there is a larger amount left over to sell. They then have the advantage of being able to import more goods and get more houses built, and so on. Thus there is a tendency for uneven development in different parts of the country. This is a problem which also has to be looked at.

Question: Are there economists in China? Is there a place for economic research?

Professor Robinson: The Chinese have a sort of philosophical study of the Marxist classics, but for the rest, they study the way the economy is working. Students are sent out to a commune at a time when the work points are being distributed, or they are sent to a department store to examine the structure of prices of consumer goods, and so on. Examining the reports the students write is a way of keeping a sort of general survey on how the economy is working and what problems are coming up.

Question: Your description sounds incredibly Utopian. Is anything going wrong?

Professor Robinson: The Chinese have immense problems. First and foremost they have the problem of ensuring that they really are going to be able to feed the population as it grows. They have, of course, political problems. Every economic decision made is the subject of the "struggle between two lines," because every decision made involves the balance between good order, discipline, structured control, on the one hand, and spontaneity and democracy on the other. Regular problems are constantly being discussed, sometimes resulting in strong clashes.

Question: In a 1972 article, you wrote that it appears that China is following a trend opposite to that of the U.S.S.R. in reference to bonus points and profit drives. How do you feel that subsequent events have affected this trend?

Professor Robinson: I think the Chinese are always pushing. Last time I was in China, after writing the pamphlet referred to, the theme was the dictatorship of the proletariat. This was being studied in terms of concrete problems such as the problem of the eight-grade wage system. An eight-grade wage system isn't really true socialism; it has some bourgeois elements. The Chinese hope to overcome this bourgeois character by gradually getting the people at the top not to accept a higher wage when they get a step up and by distributing the benefits of increased productivity to the lowest income groups.

I was interested in this very primitive community — the Thai community I mentioned earlier — primitive in the sense that they have only very recently come into this game. They said one of the problems concerned the tractor drivers. A tractor driver feels himself to be a very superior man. When he has hauled a load, he sits there and expects someone else to unload the heavy stuff that he has brought. This is an element of "bourgeois rights" which must be curbed. This pressure to fulfill the ideals of socialism is continually going on and is continually up against a counter-trend because it is not possible to run a huge, modern country without having a hierarchy of command, and if there is a hierarchy of command, it is terribly easy for it to slip into being a hierarchy of privilege. This is a counter-tendency against which the dictatorship of the proletariat has to fight continually.

Question: How much decision-making power does the local body have regarding choice of commodities to be produced?

Professor Robinson: The little collective industries in the communes can do what they like. They usually work for their own needs, such as minor equipment needed for agriculture. In the cities, neighbourhood groups can set up little industries. One of the outlets for the newly liberated energies of the women, including housewives who cannot go away to a factory, is to set up a little business and start producing. They might get in touch with a regular factory and make components to order for that factory. There is a tremendous amount of spontaneity at the bottom of Chinese society, but, at the same time, the main lines of the economy are controlled by the official overall plan. This system is from the bottom up and the top down. That is to say, the plan is always discussed at the bottom level. It is discussed first on the basis of proposals made at the bottom. When the plan is finalized, it comes down, and the enterprises enter into contracts. These contracts have to be fulfilled. The contracts are discussed with the workers or the peasants who will be carrying them out, so that they understand what they have undertaken to do. By this means, individual responsibility is combined with the national plan.

Question: The implication of the comments you make about China is that to deal with the question of settlement and decent human settlement patterns we have to deal with production and distribution and how they are organized. Do you think it is possible to solve the problem of human settlements if you only deal with it purely on the technical level?

Professor Robinson: No, I think every technical question is an economic question, and every economic question is a political question, and every political question is a moral question.

Question: How are the original plans co-ordinated? Is this done on a regional basis or a specialized basis?

Professor Robinson: The national plan covers a list of important commodities, that is to say, all investment goods and main consumption goods such as bicycles, textiles, radios, and also more sophisticated goods. There is a fair distribution throughout the country of the various products. At the lower level, there are provincial plans where the people are free to organize production at that level. At the county level — the county level is very important, because it is the link between the communes and the provincial and national organization — there is a good deal of independence in what they do with their group of communes and how they help them.

Question: China is essentially a closed society in which there is intense ideological conditioning. How much dissent is there against such conditioning and how much re-education is going on? Does anybody know? What form does this take?

Professor Robinson: I think every society is one of intense conditioning. Consider how much we are conditioned. The Chinese all the time are carrying out political education. For instance, the children in the playschools are taught to clean the place up after themselves and not to expect to have a servant clean up after them. This is political conditioning.

Question: What do you know about work camps or reinstitution centres? Is there any information about these or what happens to political dissenters?

Professor Robinson: During the cultural revolution there was a tremendous outburst and a number of people, including some of my own English friends, were arrested. They have all been released now. As you know, many of the Chinese leaders who were criticized, such as Teng Shao Ping, have been released and restored to their positions (note: He has since been demoted again). But there was a great deal of dissent at that time.

Question: Is painting flourishing as an art in China?

Professor Robinson: The old painters were working up until 1964. During the cultural revolution, they did not exhibit their private paintings. There was a deplorable period when they were influenced by socialist realism; posters were put up in the Soviet style. Now they have much more in the Chinese tradition, the sense of design, good form, even in posters. The most interesting thing is the new peasant artists. They have developed peasant schools of painting and woodcarving which are really delightful. They retain that Chinese sense of form, but they are very vigorous and optimistic. They make pictures of fields yellow with corn or pink with blossom, and the little people working, climbing up the hill, and so on. It's quite a new form, but at the same time it has a very Chinese quality in the design and colour and sense of placing.

Question: Please explain some of the reasons for expanding the boundaries of cities to incorporate large areas of the surrounding countryside. Is this being applied to more and more cities?

Professor Robinson: Shanghai has the rank of a province, and it includes the surrounding agricultural area, as is true also of Peking and Tientsin. These are three cities which rank as provinces and which have their communes within that unit. There are many towns scattered all over the country. Communes are linked to the national economy through the counties.

Question: You referred to national minorities. Could you elaborate on them?

Professor Robinson: The important ones are Sinkiang, Tibet, Mongolia, and the Uighur Republic in the northwest. These are very large units. The ones I saw were very small units. There was an autonomous prefecture of the Thai people, and there were little pockets of people living in the mountains, some of whom had come from extremely primitive conditions. The general policy has been to show them a way to live, to release them from serfdom, poverty, and primitive conditions of life by showing them that there is another way to live and so bringing them in. From the way these Thai people were talking, I thought the policy seemed convincing. But, of course, if you have a feudal estate, you might not quite like it when your land is distributed to the peasants. There must have been people who resented it. But, on the whole, it seems to have elicited a sufficient spirit of co-operation so that even the feudal lords are accepting it.

10

Thought and Action in Architecture and Planning

Lord Richard Llewelyn-Davies

I want to talk in a somewhat philosophic sense about what has been happening to architecture and planning during the years in which I have been engaged in them. I think my starting point is a paradox, namely, that the great founders of the modern movement, Gropius, Corbusier, and others, did much more to destroy an outworn order than to establish a new one. This remark sounds rather ungrateful, but I think it is generally true that people who demolish the intellectual basis of a long-established system of doing things usually do not act out in their own lives and actions the actual results of the intellectual hatchet job they have done. Voltaire and Rousseau were revolutionaries in thought, but not in action, and they would certainly have found the French Revolution most uncongenial. Bertrand Russell and his generation did not need to apply in their personal lives the freedoms which they bequeathed to us. I think this is true about the founders of the modern movement in architecture and planning. I think that when you look at the way they worked, they all designed, to a surprising extent, in the renaissance tradition, using rules of balance and geometric proportion, though they had demolished forever the credibility of this old system. Thus, my generation and that of those of you who are younger have from them a gift of freedom and the job of making something new.

When I think of the former group, the one who was most conscious of this vacuum was Mies van der Rohe. Throughout his life he sought some comprehensive basis for design. His central philosophy can be expressed in his saying, "architecture belongs not to the age, but to the epoch," by which he meant that architecture should reflect the spirit of a major historical period, a sort of *zeitgeist*. He was very much opposed to attempts to base design on short-term influences and rejected altogether the idea that new materials and methods of building were themselves enough to generate a new architecture. He also said that he believed that our epoch was the epoch of science and technology. He sought an architecture which was appropriate to that epoch, but in an intellectual or even spiritual sense. His model was the gothic period, when, he believed, cathedral buildings responded to and were generated by the reflected spirit of their age.

I want to take up this idea and to look at the interaction of ideas about the nature of the world with the work of architects and planners. I think it is true that the bulk of our ideas about the nature of the world with which we have had to deal have been generated by science and technology. In trying to do this, I am somewhat encouraged by the work of the Edinburgh geneticist, C.H. Waddington, who wrote a fascinating book showing how painters from the post-impressionists up to the present day were profoundly influenced by scientific ideas. He traces the history of modern painting in parallel with the development of science through relativity, atomic physics, and the biological, statistical concept. But there is an important difference which I have to take into account, in trying, as it were, to use his method and apply it to architecture and planning. The development of new techniques and methods in science hits architects and planners at two levels, both practical and conceptual. Whereas the invention of new paints did not really mean much to painters — the developments of science affected them through their skins, changing their view of the world — technology and science did have a considerable impact on the practical aspects of the work of architects and planners.

Most of the theories of contemporary architecture are taken at the practical level of the impact of the new ideas in the world. Functionalism is a theory at this level. Banham, when he tried to relate the genesis of modern design to environmental and mechanical engineering, was working on the same basis. I am not belittling the importance of these direct impacts. They are real, and very important, but they have been well discussed and well documented, and I do not think they fully explain what has been happening in the hearts and minds of architects and planners. I want to deal, therefore, with that part of modern design which cannot be explained by the development of new technology, but which reflects a more general perception of the world by architects and planners.

Nearly all schools of architecture in the west were originally based on Beaux Arts theory of design, which I think reflects a technological rather than a scientific view of the world. Moreover, when the Beaux Arts was founded, it was the great age of engineers, who, in the nineteenth century, using well-established physical and mathematical methods, appeared suddenly as men who could change the world. Their dramatic achievements — railways, bridges, and dams — are extremely exciting. They proceeded from a very narrow and rigorous basis in theory to the boldest action. Earlier, each step forward in building had been a matter of trial and error. You tried a new idea in construction, and if it did not stand up, you tried again. But the Forth Bridge was built from theory. It was conceived and built without resort to trial and error, which was a glorious, heroic, and inspiring act. I think the Beaux Arts was intellectually dominated by the dramatic achievements of the engineers. One can see this link in the way the Beaux Arts organized education. First, students went through a very rigorous training in the elements

Plate 11. The desperate search for more resources demands sudden cultural changes and endangers indigenous people, often uncomprehending and remote from settled parts of the world.

Plate 12. Complex expressways spell efficiency and speed, but disruption of established settlements is the price extracted from the unsuspecting and often uninvolved.

Plate 13. North Americans still favour fully detached houses for individual families; the Americanization of the world carries this preference to its four corners, but at considerable cost in land and services.

Plate 14. A decade ago the Habitat complex at Montreal's Expo '67 demonstrated a rational alternative for housing families while maintaining privacy, variety, and individuality.

Plate 15. Compact cluster housing is another contemporary answer to large concentrations of people in major centres.

Plate 16. Cities have always attracted people; the rate of growth has escalated exponentially. Resettlemen designed to quicken urban growth, is often a mixed blessing. Kowloon.

Plate 17. Rapid urbanization frequently leads to improvised squatter dwellings, exacerbating the problems of poverty, particularly for the young, the old, and the weak. Bogota.

Plate 18. Port and transportation facilities are essential requirements to entering world trade. Ghana.

Plate 19. Communication systems like this radio and meteorological installation in India are a vital link between developing and developed nations.

Plate 20. Self-help is an immediate way to improve life and harness local resources; it also involves the consur in determining his environment.

of architecture, which are identified as columns, arches, domes, and so on. This stage took several years and corresponded in their minds with the engineer's basic training in mathematics. Towards the end of his course, the architect was allowed to design buildings, but within strict limits. (After training as an engineer, I went to Beaux Arts for a year, so I am speaking partly from experience.) Design was seen as the art of arranging a limited repertoire of elements to suit a "programme." Possible arrangements were classified and subject to a set of principles which were the rules of composition. I think this system was an unconscious imitation of the laws of physics, which govern the designs of an engineer.

There are a lot of other elements to the Beaux Arts system which because of its immense vitality is a matter of continuing interest to architects and planners. It survived so long because of its elegant simplicity. It was entirely self-consistent; it could be rigorously taught, which gave it immense strength. But of course it did not fit the real world, and Gropius and others demonstrated that that was so, just as Kepler and Copernicus had done for the previous cosmogony.

The Bauhaus accepted the task of freeing us from the rigid system imposed by the Beaux Arts. And in this task it was fantastically successful. Its influence extended world-wide over the whole field of design work. Succeeding generations have had to find some framework in which to work and to teach. I think that for inspiration they have looked towards concepts which evolved in the world outside, most of which, in our time, had their origins in science.

The twenties and thirties were the great age of atomic physics. The first image of atomic physics was the atomic model, the nucleus surrounded by electrons. Behind this familiar array of coloured marbles connected by wires, lay the important idea that any substance, however complex, a bit of wood, a piece of bread and butter, could be analyzed down to a number of limited, self-contained basic particles connected together by lines of force. This extremely powerful idea influenced both architects and planners. For architects, I think it encouraged the analysis of the building's function, and even today, when faced with a problem, architects start scribbling; their scribble consists of a number of blobs connected by lines. Each blob is a functional entity and the line is a functional connection. These look remarkably like the old atomic diagrams. This practice, I think, helped architects to develop a much more rigorous, functional analysis of their buildings. But, when taken too far, it also on occasion could have an undesirable result, because it tended to make architects believe that it would be right to design each section of a building around a rather narrowly-defined function.

Some modern buildings appear to consist of a number of separate blocks linked together by tubular corridors or staircase towers. These are oversimplified physical expressions of intellectual analysis, or of the atomic model. Buildings which take this idea too far generally have a short useful life, because they cannot easily accommodate changing functions. It is important to note that this model did not really challenge traditional architectural ideas because the atomic model is essentially hierarchical, with a dominant element, the nucleus, and subordinate parts. This is, of course, an acceptable Beaux Arts idea. It also had hard edges; everything was sharply defined and not subject to growth or change. Everything was in balance and remained so over time.

I think a very good example of this is the 1929 story of the architectural competition for the first League of Nations building. This was a famous, world-wide competition, which was won by Le Corbusier with a design that was very analytical; it split up the building. Instead of building a massive block in the classical tradition, the design split it up into its four functional parts: secretariat, meeting rooms, and so on, designed in the Le Corbusier idiom. The League of Nations rejected the Le Corbusier design because it looked too modern, and amidst international outcry, they handed the design over to four traditionalist French architects from the Beaux Arts who had failed in the competition but who were then given the job. They immediately used the Le Corbusier plan and concept dressed up in historical form, which resulted in the building that we have today. The important point is that they could do so because there was no fundamental incompatability between the Le Corbusier concept and their traditional ideas.

If we turn to planning, the atomic model, of course, was a profound influence. Planners have always been baffled by the inchoate amorphous organization of the city, and the atomic idea suggesting that you could make a simple analysis was very attractive to them. Earlier books and articles on planning are studded with diagrams which look exactly like the atomic model. There is the capital city, which is a circle of fixed size. The surrounding new towns are even called "satellite towns," and there is generally a single line connecting the satellite town back to the centre. There is a lot of empty space all around, as there is in the middle of an atom, which is of course the green belt.

Even in the design for new towns, which started to come out about this time, the model was reproduced on a reduced scale. Each neighbourhood was enclosed; there was a great debate as to how many people made the neighbourhood. Was it eighteen thousand or nine thousand? In any case, you had to have a neighbourhood, it has to be enclosed, there had to be a minor green belt surrounding it, and once again it was linked to the city centre in a "one only" manner. There were very few cross-links. A lot of towns were built on this model. It was even imitated in the United States as late as the fifties and sixties, where it was suddenly discovered and thought to be a wonderful British idea. Of course, as we now know, the richness and complexity of urban life were poorly served by these simplified layouts.

While architects and planners were using these concepts, in physics they were being found inadequate to describe the observed phenomena. Heisenberg's principle of interdeterminacy acknowledged that the behaviour of fundamental particles could only be described in terms of probability. One could not tell simultaneously where an electron was and how fast it was going; the more one knew about one aspect, the less one knew about another. From then on, very few laymen could follow the development of ideas in mathematical physics, but a very new and different picture of the world began to emerge which influenced the thinking of everybody in every sphere. The new world which emerged was very complex and not susceptible to precise or definite description. One had to understand it through statistical mathematics. You really had to decide on the basis of probability rather than on certainty. This was very uncomfortable for a number of people. You could say something was as likely as two-to-one, or as unlikely as a million-to-one, but still it was not certain.

This new view of the world was found very indigestible, especially by architects. Despite the fact that in their daily lives architects make decisions on probable consequences, it was hard to swallow uncertainty as the basis for design. It is easy to understand this reaction because there has been a very long tradition of determinate thinking, beginning with Plato and continuing right through to Newton, which is deeply imbedded in Western culture and seemed as steady as the Rock of Gibraltar. When one looks, for instance, at the writings of Doxiadis, one of the first who tried seriously to understand and relate to the new world, one can see how hard he found it to break out of this Newtonian, cause-and-effect, linear thinking and how this hampered his powerful intellect.

At a practical level, the concept of statistics had a rapid advance in design method, and some of the working groups in England began to work on problems of fluctuating demand, a perennial problem for architects, and showed how these could rationally be solved by probability analysis. We began to learn that the idea of buildings tailored to an exact specification for use was a mistake, and that often the shifting and changing patterns of human life could be better met by a loose-fit design. A friend of mine, a French doctor who worked in France, decided that the best possible hospital would consist entirely of rooms the same size and he christened it *"l'hôpital banal."* There was a lot of sense in it. At the conceptual level, when one is thinking in terms of composition, the idea of indeterminacy really challenges every canon in traditional architecture. It is impossible to use traditional design theories of balance and symmetry or proportion in buildings which had to be planned to accommodate uncertainty.

Of the great early architects of our period, I think, Mies van der Rohe, although he never spoke or wrote of this theme, was unconsciously affected by it, and he tried to invent an architectural vocabulary which would respond to it. He always divides his façades into halves and quarters and never by uneven numbers (never by thirds or fifths or by the golden section), so he gets a regular and neutral pattern, which proceeds to infinity and has no centre. The analogies between his work and Mondriaan's have been commented on. Mondriaan's paintings are not designs from the frame inwards, as are practically all classical compositions. They run off the edge of the canvas. Mondriaan even paints round the edges of his pictures to show that he does not intend them to end anywhere but rather to spread out in space, like a bit of painting cut out of space. They do not have a beginning or end.

Le Corbusier and Gropius showed little interest in the design problems which this view of the world raised at a theoretical level, but they were both involved, to some extent, in trying to cope with these problems at a practical level because they were involved with prefabrication. If one has to manufacture panels of a certain size and buildings have to be made by adding them together, one cannot design a building of any fixed proportional system because one does not know how many of the bits he is going to use. Le Corbusier's famous proposal to use Fibonacci series (1:1:2:3:5:8:13:21: . . .) symbolizes his attempt to bridge the gap, because the numbers of the series are additive: each number is formed by adding the two previous numbers. So one could make components in these sizes and always add them up and get one of the other numbers in the series. At the same time, by chance, as one gets into the slightly larger numbers, one finds that each pair of numbers is related to the golden section. Le Corbusier felt that by basing prefabrication on this series he could have his cake and eat it, too.

There are very real and serious problems concerned with design for uncertainty and change and a new discipline which is different in character from the one on which traditional architecture has been based is needed for this purpose but has to have similar potential. In looking for this discipline, architects began to look for models in the biological sciences. The planners, on the other hand, found the idea of uncertainty and change much more easy to swallow than did architects. Many of them were originally trained as geographers, economists, and sociologists, and they were more sceptical and speculative than architects, who have to be strongly action oriented. Planners were already familiar with statistical methods and theory and became accustomed fairly early to the idea that they have to try to understand and plan for the future, but cannot control it. So they found themselves more at home in the post-Heisenberg world.

Mel Webber, who works at Berkeley, soon realized that the modern city was unlike the old centralized image of the city, and refers to it as the "nonplace urban realm." His argument is that patterns of life and work are now spread across large urban and suburban areas and the strongly-focused city is a thing of the past. Jean Gottmann made a similar point when he was studying the megalopolis on the eastern seaboard of the United States.

At a much more detailed level, Stuart Chapin and his colleagues at the University of North Carolina, in studying the actions of individual people, by micro-behavioural studies, showed, for instance, that the concept of a single neighbourhood did not make sense any longer, because each person in the family lived in a different neighbourhood with different "swing out" of activities from his home. In place of the old atomic model of separate, identifiable towns and neighbourhoods, we began to see a picture of the city region as a continuum in which, here and there, were concentrations of activity. Communications were seen as a kind of mesh which covered the entire urban area, strands of the mesh getting closer together in areas of high density and spreading out in areas of thin density. This is a fundamentally different concept of the city from the earlier atomic one. A very witty and brilliant exposition of all this is given by Christopher Alexander in his essay "A City is Not a Tree."

The first attempt to express some of this thinking in actual planning occurred in the work of a team in which I was involved in the planning of Milton Keynes, a new town about fifty miles northwest of London. This plan has often been described, and I will not describe it here, but I would like to list some of the assumptions on which the plan is based because, at the time, they were controversial. The first assumption is that the future is uncertain; it is not possible, indeed, it is presumptuous, for planners to try to predict what sort of life people will want to live twenty years ahead. (This proposition, though perhaps it seems obvious today, five years ago was strongly opposed by most European planners.) Of course, having said that, you still have to build the city. You have to put down roads, and sewers, buildings, power lines, and so on, and the important thing is that every time you make an investment, every time you take an action, every time you build something, you are closing off alternatives to the future, shutting off a number of options. It is all very fine to say that the future should be left wide open, but one cannot take a step without closing it in. So the problem now is how to find criteria by which the various choices or possible futures can be ranked, and a choice made, not between precise futures, not laying down one only, but by saying, "This, and this, and this are those choices most worth protecting." This is not impossible. There is even some theoretical work about it, and one can, to some extent, describe the future in terms of probability and try to plan for a certain number of defined options. The practical result is that, for example, instead of having a tree-like hierarchy of roads, sewers, and other services, in which there are a centre and branches and all development relates to this tree — one can only put small things at the ends of the branches and big things by the trunk or the roots — there is, instead, a more universal mesh which spreads over the entire area of development and which gives roughly equal access to all parts. For example, Milton Keynes' plan permits the removal of industry or housing, or a change in densities, or a shift in the plan as it is developed, in order to react to changes in society or economics. But such flexibility is within limits set by certain rules. Once one has designed the chessboard, as it were, there are certain rules of the game within which one has to work. For instance, the spacing of the streets as a network implies certain limits to density, and so on.

It is true that the plan for Milton Keynes was possible because we had technical tools of a more advanced type than planners had had before, particularly in the form of systems analysis. But in looking back, I think it is fair to say that the whole idea would not have come into our minds had it not been for the general picture of the world which had been emerging quite outside the technical developments within the architectural and planning professions.

Architects, especially when they are designing large buildings — universities, hospitals, and public institutions — are faced, on a smaller scale, with very similar problems to those of town planners. But they have a much harder job, because unlike the town planner, they cannot design a chessboard and then walk away to leave the town council or subsequent generations to play the game. Architects have to do the whole thing themselves. They have to find a discipline which will enable them to control and manage change. This is hard, because our traditional architectural training has been in designing objects once and for all. Biology, which was the most rapidly developing branch of science in recent years, has familiarized us with the idea that growth can be something that follows an established pattern, can be described mathematically, and can result in great beauty. D'Arcy Thompson's book on growth and form, published in the forties, had a powerful impact on many architects. He showed how growth generated the actual physical form of many living things, shells, antlers, trees, animals, even animal skeletons. Architects were extremely excited by this discovery and tried to employ the mathematical disciplines of growth which D'Arcy Thompson analyzed in relation to design. But it was soon found that the analogies were not exact. Peter Cowan, at London University, studied the actual growth and historic change over a period of time of buildings such as cathedrals or long-established hospitals and universities, and he logged how they had changed. He was able to show that the growth patterns were not really comparable with those of biological forms; buildings grow in fits and starts. He was able to develop some mathematical treatment for their growth, but this work is only beginning. In recent years, many architects have been working on design theories which accept and express change and are trying to find appropriate building forms. My own partner, John Weeks, has worked on these theories. His published papers about them call attention to the analogies that lie between the problems faced by architects, contemporary painters, and even by musicians such as John Cage.

So far I have discussed ideas which have been emerging from the physical and biological sciences which dominated our epoch until lately, as Mies van der Rohe had predicted. Since the explosion of the atomic bomb, science has come to be seen in a much more baleful light. The use of science and technology for deliberate, destructive purposes in war, and its rôle in disturbing and damaging the natural environment have caused a revulsion in feeling. Architects and planners are themselves now under attack, certainly in the developed world, as agents of undesirable change. We are accused of carrying through developments which are destructive of traditional culture, natural amenity, and even of human well-being.

But I think it is also recognized that science, architecture and planning are all really directed, either for good or for evil, by society and its institutions. Thus, the sciences that deal with society have become a new and major focus of interest to architects and planners. For architects, the relevance of sociology, psychology, and anthropology are obvious; they yield insight into the human activities for which we have to provide the shells. They also provide a means by which the social requirements for building can be measured. Much of our work today is for social groups rather than for individual clients, and the specifications for building to meet social needs calls for the skills of social science. Again, I think the social sciences have brought valuable criticism to bear on some established architectural ideas. The criticism, for instance, of tall, high-rise blocks for low-income families with young children has resulted, I think, in the elimination of this form of development from the housing policies of many countries.

The social sciences have become a major source of practical support to both architects and planners. Planners in particular have been using the tools of social science as part of their *armoire* for a long time. More generally, the social sciences have underlined the diversity of human society and its tendency to change. I think this is important because the architect's first response has sometimes been to look for a stereotyped model of human behaviour, to assume that all human groups, once described, are the same everywhere. The influence of anthropologists, who have shown how varied social patterns can be and how different societies can flourish in an enormous variety of different physical environments, has been a healthy factor in increasing the scepticism of architects and planners about their ability to change society by changing its physical envelope. I think we have become more modest as a result, and I think that that has been good.

We might think for a moment about the following lines from Milton's *Paradise Lost*:

> The moon whose orb through optic glass,
> The Tuscan artist views;
> At evening from the top of Fiesole,
> Or in Veldano to descry new lands,
> Rivers or mountains in her spotty globe. . .

The "Tuscan artist" is not an artist as we would use the term, he was Galileo. Milton, when he was travelling around Italy, visited Galileo and referred to him in *Paradise Lost* as quoted above. For Milton, and all his contemporaries, the words artist and scientist had the same meaning. There was no distinction. There was a complete integration, of science and art and of thought and action. Many architects were scientists for part of their lives, and vice versa. Christopher Wren was a disappointed scientist who only took up architecture at the age of thirty-five when his rival, Harvey, discovered the circulation of the blood and Wren decided that he probably would not make his name in physiology. In the middle of Milton Keynes, there is a small village in which there is a very beautiful church; the architect was Thomas Hook, a contemporary of Wren and another founder member of the Royal Society. Nobody has ever thought of Hook as an architect; he was a famous scientist. He invented Hook's Law, which connects stress and strain and which was the basis for most of engineering. But he took time off and designed a church, and a very nice one, too.

Similarly, throughout the Renaissance, the architectural view prevailed. Rudolf Wittkower has shown that the scholars, artists, scientists, architects, and astronomers in the Renaissance had an identical picture of the world as a system governed by the mathematics of harmonic numbers. That was the music of the spheres. They believed that because a certain sequence of numbers led to harmony of the chords in music, this was the key that would unlock proportion and science. They believed in an integrated theoretical basis for all the arts.

In those days, architects did not really need to make a conscious effort to understand the spirit of their time, as Mies van der Rohe said we should, because it was inside themselves. Today, the intense specialization of knowledge and the rapidity of its development make it very difficult for a professional architect or a planner to have this easy, natural relation to his epoch. I believe, as Mies van der Rohe did, that we need to seek this understanding as a basis for our work. I do not think we are as yet succeeding in this. Much of the architecture that one sees today, like the paintings of Andy Warhol, is an instant response to the stimulus of some limited and short-term aspect of our culture. I think that however talented such a designer may be, his work is bound to be ephemeral. Of course it could be argued that that really is the spirit of our age, the throw-away container, the discarded beer can. But I do not accept this view; I think that there is a longer, deeper swell in our age that we can try to understand and discuss. C.H. Waddington gives a list of insights into the nature of our time which I think are important. First of all, he says, "We now know that the observer does not wholly make what he observes, but that his intrinsic character colours it; that there is no strict subjective dichotomy, and that the painter is in his painting, and the scientist in his science. We know that chance plays a rôle amongst the fundamental mechanisms, and that everything has a feeling for everything else."

Finally, on a more down-to-earth level, and I think this is very important, and perhaps links with Habitat, we do live in surroundings that we make our-selves and conditions that we make ourselves; we don't live in a state of nature that we have to accept in its entirety. I do not agree with Ian McHarg that man is a planetary disease.

In various guises, I think, these ideas are present in nearly all contemporary thought. In seeking to understand them in this sense, many different people in different disciplines with different perceptions have come together to interact. Architects and planners cannot escape the need to move from thought to action. We have actually to design and construct buildings in the cities, and these structures impose constraints on the people who live in them. It is not enough to recognize diversity and uncertainty and change; we must find a way to express these problems of our age in the manner which best responds to them.

For me, at least, the supreme excitement in architecture and planning arises from the interaction of thought and action. For me, the true heroes are those men who are able to move from one to the other. People like Brunel, the engineer, or Nansen, who had a theory about polar drift across the polar ice cap and who designed a ship and locked himself into the ice cap to see if his theory was true. And Bagnold, a soldier, who explored the Sahara in a Model T Ford, resigned his commission, and invented a method for studying the physics of blown sand in the laboratory, and later led long-range armoured columns through the Sahara to attack Rommel in the rear.

I would like to conclude with a statement from Mies van der Rohe. He said, "Reason is the basis for all human work. I throw out things that are dear to my heart, if I find that they are not reasonable."

EXTRACTS FROM DISCUSSION

Question: Was the new town of Milton Keynes built on the fabric of an old town?

Lord Llewelyn-Davies: Practically all the English new towns were, and did in fact have fairly substantial populations in towns or villages there already. Milton Keynes had in it the town of Bletchley, with a population of forty thousand, which compares with the two hundred and fifty thousand in the final population. It was a larger indigenous group than in the case of most other new towns, but none of them were in green field situations. In all cases, there was the problem of the integration of an existing town with the new incoming population. There are various myths about incoming populations to new towns which are rather general. One is that the people are those with the lowest IQ in the country. Another is that they are addicted to crime and drugs. In fact, none of these things are true. The problem with new towns is that they attract an élitist group of energetic, bright young people who want to better themselves, and therefore, you don't get a balanced social mix, not enough dropouts and people with low IQ's will come.

Question: You mentioned uncertainty, probability, and indeterminacy which I believe to be anxiety-provoking. How about the obverse in the work of some psychologists where there is increasing emphasis on the human need for diversity and for uncertainty in the sense of surprise?

Lord Llewelyn-Davies: I accept the idea of latent anxiety. I think that is true. I think that there is a need in most people, an emotional need, for some feeling of order, or management or control. Most people would find complete uncertainty very hard to live with. Therefore, while part of the problem is to devise the rules of the game to permit the maximum degree of pleasurable variety and change, this should not leave people feeling as though they are floating into space, which is disturbing and unreal. In practice in our work, the amount of variety that can be provided for becomes less and less, as you proceed with the essential decision-making involved in action.

11

The Great World Transformation
and the Next Twenty Years

John Platt

I want to talk to you about the great world transformation through which we are passing and the directions in which it may take us in the next twenty years or so. I think the best way to start is by emphasizing the enormous speed and scale of the technical changes of about thirty years ago. In communications, for example, we now can talk by sight and sound around the world with the speed of light. If you compare this speed with that of about a hundred years ago, with the speed of horses, the speed of ships, or even the speed of the first locomotive, the difference is a factor of approximately 10^7. In energy we have some current crises, but if you look at our available solar or uranium energy, if we mined the low-concentration uranium rock, our total energy supplies are much greater than the coal energy that was available in 1940 — perhaps 10^3 times more than we thought we had then.

In weapons, from the twenty-ton blockbusters of 1944 to the hydrogen bomb of 1954 was a jump by a million times, about 10^6 times in a single decade. In travel, many of us have travelled at very nearly the speed of sound on jet planes that simply did not exist before about 1940. It is a jump from the speed of horses by about a factor of 100, and if you go on to the speed of the Concorde, or on up to speeds in orbit of 17,000 miles per hour, the speed is a hundred to a thousand times greater.

In data processing, when I was a student at Northwestern back in 1935, there was something called a depression in the United States, and they hired us students, at 50¢ an hour, to do calculations for the physics department or the library. I was hired to multiply things on a desk computer. When I wanted to multiply by 47, I would crank 1-2-3-4, and then I would flip the column lever and crank 1-2-3-4-5-6-7. In that year, 1935, we got an *electric* desk computer. It was a Friden, from Sweden, and it wasn't any faster than I was, but I wasn't as tired at the end of the day. Since that time there have been many "generations" of computers: electronic, micro-miniaturized, solid state, and so on. The difference in speed from 1935 is at least a factor of a million (10^6) and maybe much more than that.

One can go on and on in this way in many other areas — take exploration: since 1953, when Hilary and Tenzing climbed Mt. Everest, people have gone to the top of the highest mountains and the bottoms of the deepest oceans, have lived at the North and South poles with hot and cold running water, helicopters to take them out when they get sick, and nuclear power. You can't put numbers on it, but the jump is enormous; and then since 1969, there has been the jump to the moon. That is, again, many orders of magnitude. In our understanding of infant mortality and bacterial and virus diseases, we probably know and are able to apply ten to thirty times the knowledge we had a hundred years ago. We haven't cured all diseases, the degenerative diseases, cancer, and heart attacks. We will always have some cause of death, even if we live a thousand years. Nevertheless, we have made enormous strides in this area, which ought to be remembered. In our biology in general, plants and animals, it is now humans who are responsible for the numbers and the densities of plants and animals all over the earth's surface. In earlier centuries, we were a minor perturbation on the great fluctuations of nature. Now we certainly are not minor. It is our DDT that is in the Antarctic penguins. It is our ships that are hunting down the last of the great whales. It is our Santa Gertrudi cattle which are in South America and Texas. It is our "green revolution" in southeast Asia. It is our penicillin bacteria that fill the flasks. The result is that it is now human activities, and their consequences, that determine the numbers of plants and animals everywhere.

These are not changes by a few per cent; they are not changes by a few hundred per cent, as in previous generations; they are changes by orders of magnitude. There is no beginning to an exponential curve of growth; and for centuries people have commented on how fast things were changing. In earlier times, the changes would be by a factor of two or five within a generation. Thoreau commented on the telegraph that was laid past Walden Pond: "They have made a telegraph to communicate from Maine to Texas. But it may be that Maine and Texas have nothing to communicate." (Some of us think that that is still true.) Yet, even if we plot these exponents on a logarithmic scale so that they go up with a steady slope, up until now, one still sees a sudden, almost vertical climb, around the year 1945. I have sometimes regarded 1945 as "World Year 0." That means 1976 is WY 031. Some people think that the most optimistic thing I do is to put in the "zero" at the beginning because that implies that one of these days the number may go past a hundred years. Writing these numbers in this way for our current dates is a way of reminding ourselves of how recent our changes are and what a remarkable new world it is today.

In fact, many of these changes have gone so far and so fast that they are pressing against the limits of what is physically or biologically possible. We are not going on with changes with these high exponents for the next thirty years, or even the next 300 years. In most aspects of human interaction we have neared the limit. For example, when you are talking and seeing around the world by television at the speed of light, that is the fastest you can go. There are a few physicists who have discussed "tachyons" that could go faster than light, but they don't know how to create them. Maybe in a few hundred years, we shall know things like that which are now unknown, but for the foreseeable future, we have reached a limit in speed of communication, and it is apparently a fundamental limit.

Similarly, in our use of power, we now put out so much energy and power in many cities that they are hotter than the surrounding country. Los Angeles is seven or eight degrees hotter than Orange County because of the asphalt, the industry, the automobiles, the air conditioners. If we had gone on at the rate we were going a few years ago, by the year 2000 Los Angeles would be 20° hotter than Orange County. Nobody is going to live there under those circumstances. They would move out, and the same is true for all the big cities all over the world. We are beginning to be within sight of limits because of thermal pollution.

In weapons, our overkill is now so vast that it can kill all humanity ten times over. You can't be deader than dead. Our problems are problems of the instability of this situation, not of the absolute size of weapons. We wouldn't be in any more danger if we had a million times this power of weapons than we are now. We are now within three hours of being wiped out, if the instability leads to a breakdown.

In travel, you can't travel faster than orbital speed over the earth's surface, and we are there already. You can't really travel faster than orbital speed through the solar system, and our rockets are already going at that speed.

In data processing, there may be some more opportunities ahead, but in general we are facing the fact that life is finite. The day only has twenty-four hours. You cannot watch television sixty hours a day. In many areas, we are within sight of our limits. Some find this a source of discouragement, but I find it a source of some encouragement. What it means is that if we can solve the problems that these technical developments have brought, we might be able to create societies which would last for a long time. The problem is now to solve these problems quickly so that they do not destroy us before we get there.

What is happening now is that these new technologies are reshaping every social institution. One can now draw a curve of social change, twenty-five or thirty years down the road since 1945, in dozens of social areas. When you change speeds of communication, population densities, energy, modes of biological concepts, diseases, contraceptives, television, or communication, all institutions have to change, because there are no human institutions designed to deal with new problems and powers on such a scale. We can already see our institutions changing around us, into new forms because of the problems they are encountering — if they have not changed in advance in order to cope with them. There are changes in the bank, in the farm, in the factory, in the family, in the school, in the church, in the army, in the police, in the cities, in the nation-state. All of our institutions of past centuries are being dissolved and remade before our very eyes.

These statements are unusual and extreme enough that it may be worth making a list of some of the areas where in the last few years we have turned around our attitudes and our laws of decades or centuries past. Such turn-arounds have been described by Jonas Salk in an interesting book called *The Survival of the Wisest*. When I first saw the title, I thought Jonas Salk was talking about himself, but later I decided that he was talking about all of us. In that book, he compares these S-curves of change in the human race to the curve of growth of bacteria in a colony. The bacteria go on doubling every twenty minutes until they have reached the limits of the flask. Then their poisons wipe them out or else they come to some sort of steady state with the sunlight or the nutrient that is dripping in. He calls the first section the growth part, the A section of the curve — the section of positive feedback. The more the bacteria grow, the more rapidly they grow. The second section of the curve, where it begins to bend over, is the B section — the section with negative feedback. Here the more the bacteria grow, the more they are inhibited. The curvature has turned around and the result is that between these two sections of curve there is a "watershed," as in coming over a mountain ridge where the water has been going one way and then is going the other way. It is like taking your foot off the gas and putting it on the brakes. Salk goes on, then, with the rather interesting observation that in human affairs, this becomes not merely a technical watershed, but an ethical, or legal watershed, in which there is a reversal of the attitudes and behaviour of times past.

We can actually look at some of these social reversals happening today. For example, in the field of population, the A section, when population is small, is the era when you must "go forth and be fruitful and multiply and replenish the earth." That is what God told Adam, and then six chapters later, told Noah, in almost the same words. That is the only way to survive when there are only two of every species. On the other hand, when you get into this second era, the B section, when you have approached the limits of the flask, you have to think about zero population growth as your ethics — two children, or one child, or none, at least for a while. It is not that your long-range goal is any different from what it was before. Maybe your long-range goal is "to maximize the human potential," or some other uplifting phrase of that sort. But your tactics have to change in the limiting situation because the external reality has changed. In the beginning you maximize the human potential by having more humans but in the end you do it by developing the potential of each one. So what we need to do at our present stage on the earth is to increase everyone's human potential rather than increase the number of children.

The same sort of reversal of values happens with consumption of non-renewable resources or energy consumption. In the first part of the curve, it is good to have more consumption of resources, more consumer goods. They get rid of slavery, they give us leisure, they give us diversity of possibilities for human potential. But if you go on consuming resources at a higher and higher rate in the second part of the curve, you are consuming resources your children and grandchildren will need to have a decent life for themselves. It is the same with the growth of power consumption. At first, it is good to have increased power usage, for the reasons just given, but in the end, increased usage overheats the cities and causes thermal pollution.

Once you have seen this principle of reversals, you don't have to look in the *New York Times* to see what the numbers are — 8 per cent up, or 16 per cent down. It is not the numbers that are important, it is the reversal. So what I have been doing, with some of my friends at the University of Michigan, is to look for the reversals that are happening in the world today in our attitudes and laws.

Let us make a list to see how many of these social reversals there have been in the last few years. You can't say exactly when these reversals started. Our exponentials of growth and step-changes go back to the ancient Greeks, or to the invention of speech or fire. We came out of the trees and walked around on the plains and hunted — that was a reversal! But in looking at present changes, we select a recent date, and I have been looking at social reversals from about 1968, the beginning of the Nixon administration, to 1976.

In these eight years, for one thing, there has been a reversal in the new policy of *détente*. Don't misunderstand. *Détente* is not a peace-keeping system. It is not permanent. Nevertheless, it is a very different situation from the Cold War. My mother was a good Methodist in the South, and whenever she had to praise somebody that she didn't like very much, she would say, "We must give the Devil his due." So I have to give Mr. Nixon his due. In 1969, he did indeed in a formal way end the Cold War with Russia and with China. Since that time, we have seen peace and trade agreements between India and Pakistan, East Germany and West Germany, France and Poland, even a sort of unstable truce in the Middle East. This is a recognition that we have reached some limits of the flask, that we are all in one world together, and we had better remember that this is so.

With respect to international money, in 1964, Special Drawing Rights, or "SDRs," were a wild idea; in 1969 they were adopted. That is the first time in human history that we have had money which is neither a national currency, such as the dollar, nor a primitive currency, such as gold. It represents an agreement by many nations — even if it is an unstable agreement — that we are in one world economically.

Our ecology consciousness is another reversal of the old ways. You all know the disputes in the U.S. as we blocked the supersonic transport, and tried to clean up the Alaska pipeline and so on. We have developed an ecological consciousness we did not have ten years ago. The blocking of the SST in the United States was a watershed, even if it gets unblocked one of these days. It was the first time in Western technical history that a billion dollar juggernaut was stopped in advance, on grounds of human or environmental concern. It represents an awareness that the environment is something that we have to put in the mix from now on. Even though we also have to have economic concerns and energy concerns and have to solve multiple problems, the environment nevertheless has come to be a major component in our thinking about the whole system and the flask we live in.

Sex laws are always a source of merriment with undergraduates, but are not really a funny subject. For many people, our recent changes may be a very threatening subject. I don't know if changes in Canada have been exactly like those in the U.S., but there since 1968 we have had reversals in our laws on homosexuality, on pornography, on abortion, and on contraception, reversing centuries of Puritan attitudes expressed in laws, and expressing today the attitude that sex acts between consenting adults are not the business of the state. It was Prime Minister Trudeau who said that the state must stop at the bedroom door. I don't know whether you agree with him or not on that, but I think it does represent a watershed in our Western puritan attitudes towards sex. The reasons for the changes at this time are many, but they include birth control, improved contraceptives, various changes in the nature of work, the nature of household appliances, the women's rights movement, and so on, and these are the things that have caused a turnaround in so many laws of previous centuries. I am not sure the practices have turned around as much as the laws have, but we have come to a moment of conscious-raising on some of these issues that we did not have ten years ago.

Our recent turnaround in birth control deserves special mention. In 1969, it looked as though the population problem was almost unsolvable. Maybe it is still. But it certainly is more solvable now than it was a mere six or eight years ago. For one thing, the United States has had its birth rate below "replacement level" for four years. Last year it had its lowest birth rate ever. England and Wales had fewer births than deaths in 1975 and are actually declining in population, except for immigration. Both West Germany and East Germany are below replacement level. The list goes on. In Lester Brown's book, *In the Human Interest*, he mentions some twelve countries that are at or below replacement level. A few years ago we could not have believed that this could happen so fast. China is one of the dramatic examples, if recent reports are correct. I find it hard to judge reports from Westerners visiting China. One always has a problem about which statistics to believe. Nevertheless, people with diverse points of view and reporters who have tried to look at the numbers of babies and young children, in hospital records, in nursery schools, come away saying that China may be embarking on the biggest and most effective birth control programme in history. The birth rate in Shanghai last year appears to have been nine per thousand per year. It is the lowest birth rate in history, even for a young and urban population. The United States, by comparison, had a birth rate of fifteen per thousand per year. In the agricultural communes in China, it is said that there are women's committees which decide at the beginning of each year how many children the commune is going to have. This is family planning, but with a "family" of twenty to fifty thousand people. We shall see, I think, in three to five years, whether this pressure to reduce births works as dramatically as some of the other changes in China seem to have worked.

I will mention a few more areas of recent dramatic reversals. There are enormous legal changes in the U.S. now in the areas of no-fault divorce, no-fault auto insurance, and the abolition of drunkenness as a crime. Drunkenness represented one-third of U.S. arrests until a couple of years ago, and when you saw police statistics on changes in crime, either up or down (frequently manipulated either by opposition parties or by people in office trying to make their administration look better) you always had to look to see how much of this was drunkenness. But now a number of states have abolished this as a crime. Similarly, the legal changes in the rights of prisoners, the accountability of federal officials, election finance laws, all are enormous changes, the greatest in this century.

About universities, it is commonly said that American students are now apathetic after the exciting years 1968-70. I want to claim that it is the apathy of a well-fed lion. The students won about 80 per cent of the things that they demanded in the student riots. Look at the list, at least at a university such as the one where I am, the University of Michigan: the end of the draft, the end of the Vietnam War, the end of military recruiting on campus, the eighteen-year-old vote, open dormitories so that males and females are both in the same dormitory, pass-fail grading, students on boards of trustees, students grading teachers, the end of old landlord contracts in which the students had to pay twelve months' rent for eight months' residence in a room. The result is that students no longer have the daily hassles that they once had. Students are now treated as participating adults in a way they formerly were not; as late as 1970, the university was legally and effectively *in loco parentis*, in the place of a parent to the student. Now the student is an adult who can talk back to the university and can take part in shaping and designing his own education in a way we never had before. It is the greatest change in the university since the revolutions of John Dewey in the 1900's, when he threw out the classical education of the 1800's and began to replace it by what he called "education for living."

I'll list two more reversal areas: one is "limits of growth," the other is our attitudes toward the future. It was in 1972 that *The Limits to Growth* was published by Donella and Dennis Meadows and the M.I.T. team under the sponsorship of the Club of Rome. Since that time, not only because of the book but for many reasons — money, selfishness, prejudice, city problems — hundreds of American communities have limited their growth in some way. They have limited the heights of buildings, or the use of automobiles in the centre of town, or extension of sewer or water supplies, or developers building new housing. This happens all the way from Petaluma, California, where they still have a suit in court against new developers, to St. Petersburg, Florida. Last year, city council there actually voted "to send back where they came from" the last 25,000 immigrants into St. Petersburg! Impossible, of course. They were going to buy them airline tickets! Two days later it was laughed out of court. Nevertheless, for St. Petersburg to think of it! — in Florida, the great growth state! There is a change of consciousness; people are beginning to think of the quality of their lives rather than of continual expansion in the former American way.

In futures, in 1967 Herman Kahn and Anthony J. Wiener published *The Year 2000*. There was also a study by the Daedalus group on the year 2000. It startled us. Nobody had thought thirty-three years into the future in terms of real extrapolation. How big would growth be? How big would population be? How much food would there be? It's all wrong. Go back and look at these books today and they look as dated as William Jennings Bryan. There is nothing in them about ecology; there is nothing in them about energy; there is nothing in them about oil; there is nothing in them about the women's movement; there is nothing in them about the Third World in revolt and the rich-poor gap. Nevertheless, it has become terribly important to look into the future. There are now dozens of states, and many Canadian provinces, too, that have commissions on the year 2000. We are now making plans for the year 2000 all over the world in a way we were not doing even six to eight years ago. This includes billions of dollars in research and development, on solar energy, on fusion power, on non-polluting cars, on mass transit, on food supplies, on population and habitation. The result is that all over the world, we begin to have a belief in the future, a belief in the possibility of shaping a common human future we did not have before.

I think this is an impressive list, and I think it suggests that we are passing through one of the great evolutionary jumps in all of history. It is like ten industrial revolutions and Protestant Reformations all happening in a single generation. It is, from an evolutionary point of view, a move toward a more global, integrated society than we have had before, a more aware society than we have had before. It is as dramatic on the global scale in terms of its implications for the human future as the invention of speech. Or to say it more strongly, it is as dramatic as the coming ashore of the land animals. It is as dramatic as the invention of wings. Suddenly you make a new evolutionary possibility; a new combination of ways of living, energy, food, communication, habitation, human interaction. Nothing is ever the same after that. That is the situation we are passing through. We are not so aware of it as a revolution, as a great revolutionary step, partly because it has been relatively peaceful. There has not been much blood in the streets. It has not affected our personal ways of living as much as it has affected our global interactions. The changes have not been at the personal level, in what we eat or what we wear. They have been changes in world communication, in what we see on television. A billion and a half people saw the Olympic Games at Munich by re-broadcasts the same day, some thirty-eight per cent of the world's population. Television has grown very rapidly since that time, and I think that in another two or three years, the figure will surpass fifty per cent. The world's population is linked together emotionally by sharing the same events, even under censorship. We all were at Kennedy's funeral. We all walked on the moon together. These events will bind the human race together in a way which is different from any past civilization. This will make us a global society if we can survive the stresses of the next few years.

There are stresses. So let us talk about the next twenty years. There will be disasters, but there will also be integrative steps. In short, it will be a time very much like the present. As Dickens said, "it was the best of times, it was the worst of times; it was a time of hope, it was a time of despair." The disasters will probably include nuclear terrorism, if not the nuclear holocaust. I expect within two or three years that there will be a nuclear bomb of the Hiroshima type exploded by some terrorist group, perhaps in New York City, perhaps in Tel Aviv, perhaps in Cairo. The morning after that happens, we will wake up to a new world. It will be like a Pearl Harbour in terms of turning around all of the attitudes we have had until now. We have drifted into the nuclear age of these enormous weapons. Suddenly we will have a new attitude towards nuclear proliferation, towards plutonium, towards controls, towards surveillance.

If we are unlucky, there may be backlash: dictators, men on horseback who come to power saying, "we will protect you," with inspection of bags in every building, police at every road junction. If we are lucky, there will have been some thought about this in advance, and there might be, let us say, a consortium of two or three great powers, perhaps a cluster of them, saying, "we must control nuclear energy, we will impose a pax consortium on the world, until we can manage nuclear energy." I don't know what the scenario will be, but it will all be different the morning after that nuclear explosion.

Megafamine: the pain of starvation for the individual is the same whether he starves as one person or whether he starves as one of fifty million. But I fear we will see in the world, starvation of ten to fifty million in a single year. This will not be because there is not enough food. At the present time, George Borgstrom, at Michigan State University, has estimated that animals eat three times as much food as human beings do in the world, mostly cattle and hogs. Even in India, there are something like 600 million people and 300 million cattle. One can hardly help but believe that these cattle, given their relative difference in size, may eat as much or more than the people do. I am not going to talk about the Indian social system and why the cattle are there. In the United States, the situation is far more dramatic than that. Our cattle number roughly 100 million, according to one estimate, and eat something like four times as much as the people do.

There is not a shortage of food, or food potential; there is a shortage of social mechanisms to distribute the food there — the planes, the ships, the roads, the trucks, the storage depots which are weather-proof and insect-proof, the methods of distribution, even the governments which are willing to report their own famines when it is still early enough to help.

The reaction of Canada and the United States, the great food exporters in the world, will depend on whether we see the deaths on television, as we saw the deaths in the Vietnam War or as we saw the starvation in Bangladesh and Biafra a few years back. It is possible we might have a great outpouring of conscience, and it is possible we might respond to Third World demands with a certain amount of conscience. On the other hand it is also possible that we might, under bad guidance, succumb to a "lifeboat ethic" of the sort Garrett Hardin talks about, in which we say, "these people are starving. They shouldn't weigh down our lifeboat, we should clobber them over the head so that we can survive." It is a poor analogy. We are more like people eating at the captain's table on a well-stocked ship, while there are people down in steerage who are starving. I think we have to share for a good many years, as well as stop population growth, before we can begin to talk about "lifeboat ethics."

There are many other problems and disasters ahead — economic problems, energy problems, problems of development in the Third and Fourth worlds, problems of possible collapse of world systems, problems of local wars. We all know about them. But let me put against them some of the integrative actions that may also be part of the next few years. I have spoken of television. Television is terrible until you consider not having television. In the long run, the linking together of the world by sharing common programmes and common emotional responses, especially if we improve our programmes and improve our educational quality, is going to be like the linking together of cells in the brain. It is these linkings, emotionally, intellectually, simultaneously, all over the world which are going to do as much as anything else to make us a single family, a family that is responsive to the cries of "help" from anywhere, and responsive to the global planning of the future. We see it happening already. These sudden changes and reversals have not come by stagecoach. They have come because there were television programmes in each of these areas. There were a hundred thousand telegrams to Congress the next morning. There were consciousness-raising groups every Tuesday night in each little town, in each little university community that argued about women's rights, or about ecology, or about sex laws, and changed their representatives and bullied them into doing something.

The result is that television has speeded up our rates of change. Margaret Mead has talked about methods of evolution and methods of education. She calls it "pre-figurative education" when the grandmother taught the grandchild how to talk to the mayor, and what happened in history, and how to be a good person. "Post-figurative education" is when people come as immigrants to the country and suddenly the grandmother can't speak the language, and it is the kids who do, who are out in the street, learning the slang and the way of life and bringing back the jobs. "Co-figurative education" is when all learn together, and move into a new future simultaneously because they are simultaneously moving into a new crisis or a new problem. This is what television is doing. Television brings us the news of ecological problems from age seven to eighty-seven. There is something there for every one of us to pick up and respond to and to mobilize around. Television has been the greatest deadening medium, in one sense, and the greatest activating medium in another sense. It moves all activists simultaneously to man the barricades over ecology, birth control, university problems, in a thousand different centres. I think this is the reason why these new movements are spreading so fast to other countries, especially countries which have television. In Italy, the change of the abortion law, the change of the divorce law, startled the church. "Where did this come from?" It came from television. In France, the change in the sale of contraceptives, the change in the rights of women, is the same sort of reversal. In Japan, the fall of Tanaka: it was a minor financial question about his dealings, but the Japanese people had seen the Nixon Watergate trial. They said, "if the Americans can pull one down, we can too." At least some Japanese have told me that the parallel to our Watergate affair was certainly an important component. I think we are rushing everywhere into the future in large measure because of the activating effects of television, one of the greatest revolutionary forces in the world, for good or for bad.

Another integrating force is multinational corporations. They are awesome and dangerous. They can buy and sell small countries. The biggest of them, like General Motors, or Exxon, are as big as Belgium or Mexico, if you equate their gross incomes with national GNP. On the other hand, they are linking together the world with trade networks which we need. People with bauxite need oranges. People with oranges need bauxite. The result is that if we had abolished the multinational corporations by tonight, and were to have a perfect world government by tomorrow morning, by tomorrow night many of these trade networks would begin to be re-established.

They are fulfilling a necessary function in linking the world together economically and in terms of sharing resources. What we need is some checks and balances to keep them from exerting their power in a destructive way. We need multinational ecology movements. We need multinational labour movements. Detroit autoworkers should see that they have common interests with German autoworkers and Japanese autoworkers, and not scab on one another, just as there are common interests for a labour movement within a country. We need multinational consumer movements, so you can't move around pesticides or products that are unsafe from one country to another. We need multinational anti-trust acts to prevent cartels. I think we will begin to get these in the next ten years and begin to control the excessive power of the multinational corporations.

Finally, I would emphasize that some of these disasters may be the necessary catalytic crises which force us to change our attitudes towards the world and to begin to plan for a better type of future. I say "may be," because it will depend on acts of leadership, on commitment, on revolutionary groups meeting on Tuesday nights in a consciousness-raising movement. Nevertheless, one can imagine that out of nuclear terrorism there might come a better peace-keeping system. One can imagine that out of megafamine, there might come a world food stockpile and delivery system. It has been called for many times, and it may be that it is only the will that is lacking. There might come a population covenant, in which the nations of the world agree with each other to try to level population in the name of getting a more just and longer-range anticipated food supply. One can imagine ocean and world resources boards. These are matters which are too big for a single nation to try to manage by itself; they are too big even for a consortium of a few nations. It is no good for nine nations to agree not to pollute the ocean, if a tenth one is polluting all over the place. You have got to have a total world agreement that goes beyond the sovereignty of individual nations. The same is true of world resources, world food supply, world energy supply, world pollution. We now have a few problems which cannot be solved at the individual or village level. The individual level is terribly important. We have to change our consciousness. I am not denying that. That has to go on simultaneously. But the dangers of the next twenty years for total survival are principally dangers on the global scale, and these are the ones where we need to build new institutions by acts of leadership and commitment such as we built, in the case of the United States, two hundred years ago.

I see the world today, therefore, as being in a pre-revolutionary era. It is hard to say when some of these further reversals and new forms of global organization might come to pass. But consider the speed of some of those which we have experienced already, the speed at which television is moving around the world, and the speed of multinational changes. Consider the speed of the U.N. consciousness-raising conferences on food, population, women's rights, habitat; even though they may not do much more than emit propaganda and make people acquainted with each other the first time around. When you consider the number and speed of these changes, it is possible that 1989 might be the magic date. McGeorge Bundy suggested this possibility in an amusing article in *Saturday Review* about two years ago. The year 1989 would of course be the 200th anniversary of the democracies, but let us allow plus or minus five years, so as not to be too dogmatic about it. I think that by about that time we will have passed the point of no return. We will either have wiped ourselves out by some of these disasters and our response to some of them; or the terrible backlash will have wiped out the democratic possiblity, at least, for a long time to come; or else by then we will have begun to create the needed global institutions to manage some of these problems so that nations and peoples can live and develop in peace and dignity, in their full human potential and without this enormous military threat over us.

As a result, today I see the year 2000 as being essentially unpredictable; as the year 1800 would have been unpredictable in the spring of 1776, with the American and the French democratic revolutions ahead. Or seventy years ago, 1930 would have been unpredictable in 1906, with the greatest war in history still ahead, the Russian Revolution and one-fifth of the world going communist, the fall of the aristocracies of Europe, the "flapper" era. I see us as in that same sort of situation, where everything may hinge on some accident like the intersection of two crises, or conversely on active leadership, or on some university group's new economic strategy, a new pattern of the family, or a more stable new pattern of global institutions. We are in a great historical epoch, a time of enormous danger but also enormous opportunity. The year 2000 is not to be predicted, but to be created.

EXCERPTS FROM DISCUSSION

Question: The theme that underlies your very intriguing arguments is the notion that we have to move from competition to co-operation. But I cannot see how this goal will be achieved. Take television, for example. The national networks in the United States are spreading out more and more, with the Westerns, the sex movies, the crime movies in Europe and around the world. And they have to keep that programming, I think, because this is what attracts most of their viewers. They have to do this because they are in competition with one another and also in competition with European companies. The same is true of the multinationals; they are spreading out more and more. Your very intriguing arguments do not convince me that we will be able to achieve a short-term change from competition to co-operation, and I think this is what has to be done.

Dr. Platt: It will not be easy. It will not be any easier than at any other crucial moment in history. When we got rid of the aristocracies at the end of the 1700's and moved toward democratic mechanisms, the aristocrats said: "These people don't have the education to run a city; these people don't have the education to run an army; they don't know how to do anything."

And from the aristocrats' point of view, it was true. I think the same thing is true today. New movements of integration, of co-operation, are here in the world, and we don't know how to do anything. We are going to have to have acts of leadership, commitment, self-sacrifice in order to do it. It is perfectly true that television often has terrible programmes that can be very damaging. But there are two messages in television. If that first message, the message of the government propaganda, or the big corporation message, advertising, were the only message that was getting through, we would never have undergone these changes in the past six or eight years. We would still have big cars with tail fins. We would still be in the Vietnam War. We would still have the Nixon administration. We would still have cigarette advertising on television in the United States. The fact is that along with the first message there is a second message. The second message begins to have its effects 3 years, 5 years later, and the child says, "I don't like that cereal, no matter how much it's advertised." Or the parents say, "My son came home from Vietnam, and it wasn't anything like what we saw." The result is that you talk back to the medium by getting out in the streets. The students taught us this. If you see your friends picketing city hall — or your enemies — over bussing, abortion, or anything else, the only way to talk back to the box is to get out and picket yourself, or counterpicket. The result is that television generates resistances that were undreamed of by the advertisers and the government. We have seen these managers and manipulators who thought they could boss everything, the ones who were at the top. We have seen them go down now, again and again, before the power of the new movements of consciousness. They were pro-male, pro-birth, pro-growth, pro-Nixon, pro-war, pro-pollution, pro-tail fins, pro-SST; where are they now? Something happened to them. I think television happened to them.

Question: It struck me as interesting that you saw the rise of multinational agreements concerning all these issues as being an integrative action. I don't think your description of the rise of multinational agreements is a move toward a centring of power such as you were just describing. The reversals that you enumerated are the reactions of large-scale legal bodies to already accomplished facts in the minds of people, without power being exerted on them in those ways. They are the recognition of established facts. There will not be universal agreements stated and written down concerning these issues. They will simply be matters of mind with the people, with everyone who is concerned about those issues. There will not be grand, multinational, or even large groups. I think you are wrong.

Dr. Platt: It may be so. I did not mention the U.N., because the U.N. has so many instabilities in its financial and other make-ups. I mentioned instead networks — economic networks, tourism, trade, television, networks of global interdependence. These are functional networks, as in the case of the human body, where you have a blood system, a lymph system; there isn't just a single U.N. cell in the brain that tells all the agency cells around it what to do, so that they in turn tell the sub-agency cells what to do. Instead, you have a functional network which is self-stabilizing by feedback mechanisms. I think we are moving into an era of functional networks around the world, long before we have any world government. You are quite right that it may rise from changes of consciousness, much more than by replacement of officials by other officials.

Question: One of the trends which seems to be apparent is for segments of national interest to want to go on their own for economic or protective reasons. I would judge that we now have infinitely more national states in the world than we had thirty years ago, often for local, protective reasons. How would you explain this, and what would the effect of that be, in terms of global thinking? In Canada, for instance, we want to break up from time to time into three or four little groups.

Dr. Platt: All over western Europe, there is a movement of minorities. The Basques and others are seeking what they call self-determination of subgroups. The same thing is happening in the United States. One sees the homosexuals uniting; women uniting; Indians uniting; one has black power movements, and Irish movements, and Greek movements, and so on. Television becomes a mechanism of diversification. People see their friends and compatriots somewhere else on the screen and they find a common identity and a common interest that they don't find in their own neighbourhoods. I think, therefore, that the world will be more diverse if we survive, in spite of having more unity in terms of global communication. Teilhard de Chardin, the Catholic philosopher and mystic, said, "unity differentiates." If you try to interpret what he said and meant, it is something like the unity of the brain. I made an analogy to the brain a minute ago. The unity of the brain differentiates its cells so that each of them can do a different job from any of the other cells around it. As a result, it becomes an integrated unity because they're co-operating in their differentiation. I think the same thing may happen with the world's people, that we will be differentiated. In many ways, the old nation states are too big to tell us all what to do. At the same time, they will be unified in other ways, because they are too small to deal with the global problems that touch everyone.

Question: It is refreshing to meet somebody as vibrant as yourself who has clearly come through the 1960's, and still, in 1976, believes that we achieved something. Because while there are optimists like you around, there are others who were hurt very badly through their commitments and efforts in the social movement of the sixties, and felt, around 1968 or 1969, that we were on the threshold of the kinds of things that you are suggesting. And yet, despite the analysis that you give us about reversals, it is possible to interpret your data in exactly the opposite way. For example, look at *détente*; here we have the possibility of Ronald Reagan becoming president, with his views on that; international inflation, with the erosion of people's psychological security in total chaos; the British pound disappearing into nowhere. Ecology — we are in a dangerous state of global disequilibrium. It is very refreshing to hear you talk like this, but how do you answer the gross pessimist, like myself, who put out a lot of energy but who feels incredibly depressed, because we seem now to be right back where we were twenty years ago. It seems to me that all the gains of the social movement of the sixties have been lost, and those activists of the sixties haven't disappeared because they had a lion's share, they disappeared because they just got tired out, or gave up the ghost, because of the impossibility of bringing about change. It is no good saying "ah, but the people brought down Nixon." Nixon very nearly got away with it. It was only because of a couple of very skilled journalists and the coming together of a lot of good things that that occurred. There are many other more dangerous things over which we have no control.

Dr. Platt: The world can be seen from the point of view of either the pessimist or the optimist. "I am neither a pessimist nor an optimist; I am a possibilist." This is a quote from Vannevar Bush, who directed the United States's research and development in World War II. A similar viewpoint is that of Harvey Cox, the Protestant theologian who wrote *On Not Leaving It to the Snake*. This title refers to the Garden of Eden, where he said Adam and Eve had dominion over the plants and animals, the fish of the sea, and the fowls of the air, and then, at the moment of truth, they let the snake decide. Cox's book is a plea for human responsibility. He says that there are three attitudes towards history. One is that we are doomed, the "apocalyptic attitude." The second is that some of us are destined to a glorious future. Both of these are contrasted with the third attitude, the "prophetic attitude" of the prophets of the Old and New Testaments, which was always a *conditional* attitude, not determinist. The prophets said, "*If* you lie and kill, you will create hell. But *if* you love God with all your heart, *then* you can create the kingdom of Heaven around you." I believe in this kind of conditional prophecy today. We might wipe ourselves out. It is all too probable. But on the other hand, it is acts of human initiative, and human courage, and humans digging in during the crises that can lead us through. It was the acts of a few humans which brought down Nixon, whether you approve of it or not. I think that these next twenty years are going to be moments when the act of the individual will perhaps count for more than it has for many generations in terms of determining the shape of the future ahead.

Question: I have heard you talk about all these nice things that might happen. From my point of view right now, I don't know what I could do to bring any of those things about. You can't tell me that. But I would like to ask you what you as one person think you can do to bring some part of those about. What are you doing?

Dr. Platt: I know what I am doing. I am travelling about eighty thousand miles a year. I gave up half of my job at the University of Michigan so I could do what I call "raising consciousness." I try to go mainly to science groups, young graduate students, or people with science skills, saying, "work on the research for the crises ahead, whatever in your field bears on human survival." Is it the energy crisis, is it something to do with chemistry and photosynthesis, is it something to do with labour relations, is it something to do with designing a new constitution, or a more stable economic system? Whatever it is, do your homework. This is what Rachel Carson did when she wrote *Silent Spring*. She went off for a year in a Cape Cod house and produced a book which was an analysis of a situation. Because of that analysis, we understood oil spills better, DDT better. We shared the book, got a new constituency of concerned people, built up the Sierra Club, elected legislators, got new federal agencies on the environment. The same thing happened with Ralph Nader. The same thing happened with Paul Ehrlich and the people concerned about population growth. They did their homework, their analyses, and raised consciousness. The same thing happened with *Limits to Growth*. A small group of people got together and did their homework on a problem and raised our consciousness, and the result is that people responded.

I think there are 10,000 problems. Society is at least as complicated as an automobile. A General Motors car has 15,000 parts. Every one of those parts had to be designed by a research and development team. In fact, some of them had to be designed many times over, because the first ones didn't work or they cost too much, or they belonged to a rival manufacturer. We have to design, and sometimes redesign, and redesign, experimentally, new patterns of society which will give us the humane and democratic structure that we need for the world ahead, and will prevent some of these disasters. Whether your concern is the women's movement, neighbourhood structures, or political structures, whatever it is, if you make a little Tuesday night consciousness-raising group of three to four people and talk about what you can do in the spot where you are, you'll find things to do in analysis or action.

I think there are already millions of people working in this way, all over the world. It is already beginning to be a survival moment. We need to realize that there are a lot of people working together everywhere. What I am doing now is going from one group to another saying, "Yes, there are some people in Vancouver who are interested in this thing. And there are people in Stanford, in Illinois, in Hot Springs, and in all the other places I have been in the last month." I go from one place to another saying, "There is hope; there are people working side by side with you; you are not alone." I hope this helps to give us all a feeling of mutual feeling and support, so that when the crunch comes, or the time comes for action, you don't give up right away because you do have friends and we are all working together to build this new world ahead.

12

The Inner and the Outer Limits*

Barbara Ward

What is perhaps the most serious problem facing human settlements today?
— the possibility of a sort of collision course between the outer and inner
limits of planetary existence. It is clear that, in a whole variety of ways, the
rising pressure of people and of their aspirations may be confronting an increasingly serious risk of society being unable to satisfy those aspirations
without doing irreparable damage to the natural resources and eco-systems
of planet Earth. And if this is indeed our future course, the collisions will,
above all, occur in the cities where the largest numbers and desires will be
concentrated and the greatest human impacts — and insults — on resources,
on the life-support systems of soil, air and water resources will be delivered.
For the Habitat conference, therefore, and for man's continued living in
urban areas (which will contain over half the world's people only three
decades from now) the likelihood of this "collision course" and the means
of getting off it — should it prove to be a likely fatality — are the central issues
of our day.

But how likely *is* the collision? At once we encounter a passionate dispute.
Those who believe that population will outstrip resources are passionately
attacked as "doomsayers" who have lost faith in the incredible fertility and
inventiveness of *homo scientificus* and the technological order he has created
for "the use and betterment of man's estate," to use Francis Bacon's prophetic
words. It is as though pessimists in the 1880's were adding up the growth in
the carriage trade and prophesying London streets knee-deep in horse dung
by 1910. What they overlooked was the invention of the automobile. So,
today, if prophets proclaim this or that date in the twenty-first century as the
decade in which population, resource use and pollution will overwhelm
human society (the condition in *Limits to Growth* known as "overrun and
collapse" they simply display loss of nerve and a disquieting underestimate of

*Barbara Ward's Habitat lecture was delivered to the Alumni Association of the University of
British Columbia. A formal version is here reprinted from The W. Clifford Clark Memorial Lectures, 1976, in *Canadian Public Administration* 19 (1976): 385-416.

what science and technology will continue to do to keep human society prosperous and expansive.

But, argue the doomsayers, can you safely draw analogies from a planet of less than two billion inhabitants — the position in the 1880's — and apply them to one which may be rising to fifteen billion? Can any conceivable "technofix" reverse processes which, like a eutrophicated lake or an extinct species, have already passed the threshold of no return? You cannot, for instance, increase the world's sea catch from twenty to seventy million tons in twenty years and then repeat the increase if meanwhile your fishing methods — the equivalent of giant vacuum cleaners — have sucked out the spawn and the young fish. Diminishing returns can be a fact of life in any particular context. Crops per acre may double with the application of the first eighty bushels of fertilizer and go up by another quarter with the next eighty. But you soon reach another kind of threshold: the point at which further applications produce no further output. Then the technofixing has to stop.

However, this is not an argument that can be pursued by way of abstractions. The sensible course is probably to see what particular extrapolations look like and whether they suggest doom or a reasonable "fix."

It is perfectly true that, as René Dubos has put it, "Trend is not destiny." Indeed, the whole purpose of consultations such as all the recent U.N. conferences — on the Environment, on Population, on Food, on the Status of Women, and now on Human Settlements — is to look at trends and, if necessary, redirect them. But we must begin with extrapolations because, paradoxically, there is a vast momentum of inertia in any society, and it is easier to go on doing the same thing because habit, conventional wisdom, and a lot of vested interests are usually ranged behind existing trends. To measure this inertia, we have only to read that one of the first American reactions to a modest let-up in recession is to return to large automobiles. Yet every 1,000 pounds taken off the weight of a 4,000-pound car saves 27 per cent of the fuel costs and conserves a corresponding amount of a critical and wasting resource. Add the fuel drain of automatic gears and air-conditioning in cars. Add that in urban traffic congestion, a motorist may easily secure actual movement from only 6 per cent of each gallon of gasoline. Add that the rest leaks away in polluting exhausts and fumes. Add all this together and it is easy indeed to judge that habit, not rationality, determines a lot of our motoring decisions.

So, let us begin by supposing that we shall go on as we have done for the last quarter of a century.

If we begin with the fundamental resources — water and food — the possible constraints inevitably vary from climate to climate and zone to zone. Although, as M. Jacques Cousteau has graphically pointed out, if all the water in the world were put together, it would be only like a droplet on the side of an egg, the usable part of water, the global run-off of fresh water into the oceans (which cover nearly three quarters of the earth's surface) is about 41,100 cubic kilometres a year. This sounds a lot, but fresh water in lakes and rivers and aquifers is only one per cent of all water. Of course, the sun, the airs and the seas carry on their steady cycle of distillation, the sun's heat evaporating salt water, leaving salts and minerals behind, drawing up pure vapour, cooling it and releasing it as rain over the land. Living vegetation uses the sun's radiance to break up the water molecule, releasing oxygen and using hydrogen to build up carbohydrates — or sugar — for energy which is then passed along the food chains, directly or through animals, to man. In global terms, the scale of water and the reliability of the natural exchanges between sun, water, and vegetation would seem capable of a large increase.

But the *distribution* of the fresh water and the vegetation is another matter. It is obvious that the large desert areas are almost entirely without water and many of them — the Sahara, for instance — are expanding as overgrazing and overuse break down the protection of plant cover on the fringes and erosion spreads. Worse still, cultivation on the densely populated northern plains of the Indian sub-continent is also threatened by overuse. The search for fire-wood and for cultivable land is taking the peasants further and further into the foothills of the Himalayas, and as the trees come down, the exposed soil begins to wash away. The monsoon rains are not mopped up. They come in floods, leaving drought behind. A monsoon régime always has unstable tendencies, and today meteorologists fear that a general increase in instability is observable in all planetary weather systems. What is certain is that defor-estation increases the extremes of drought and flood.

A rather different problem occurs in tropical rain forests — in Amazonia, in central Africa. The whole cycle of vegetation depends upon the fall of the leaves. There is no other source of top soil. Clear the forests and the earth is brick-like laterite within a decade. Again the deserts spread.

Not all desert soil is so unpromising. As the experience of Egypt or the Indus Valley or the western United States has shown, desert soil, well-irrigated, can be very fertile. There are traps, of course. An insufficient flow of irrigation water creates salinity. Sufficient volume can demand high and steady energy costs in pumping. (So, too, can any ambitious plan for desalin-izing salt water.) There is also a problem of diminishing returns. Since 1950, land under permanent irrigation has been increasing at the unprecedented rate of 3 per cent a year. Very many of the most productive dam sites and irrigation areas are in use now. Here we encounter a real constraint on water in the more arid areas. The number of places where successful dams can be built is beginning to diminish and unless each dam's catchment area is scrupu-lously protected from tree-slashing cultivators, the dams themselves silt up.

It may easily be thought that in temperate lands — most of North America, Europe, part of Russia and the Antipodes, southern Latin America — water is no problem. This is not the case, however. It is simply a different problem: not water as such, but water clean enough for human use. The needs of industry have vastly increased. Runoff from factories with an increasing variety of toxic chemicals is just one more factor in the increasing pollution of temperate rivers. Take the Rhine, for instance. Its chloride content has increased five times over in the last fifty years. Wastes from food industries and brewing, from feedlots, and from untreated municipal sewage put the equivalent of the sewage from seventy million people in the river every year. Between fifty thousand and seventy-five thousand tons of oil seep in annually from ships and barges. It receives ninety thousand tons of various metals and phosphates from detergents. This unholy broth is warmed up by waste heat from the power stations which line the river, and it has killed off all fish life save the indestructible eel. If humans try to swim, it is almost as true of the Rhine as of the Hudson, that "you do not drown, you dissolve." By the time the wretched river flows out into Holland, it is virtually beyond any treatment plant's capacity to renew it. But twenty million people still rely on the Rhine for tap water.

Nor are the seas themselves immune to this scale of pollution. The sewage dumped into enclosed waters like those of the Baltic or the Adriatic has removed all the dissolved oxygen in some areas and left behind water too lifeless and polluted for human use. So we have to conclude that simple extrapolations of water use, relying on global availability, may in fact tell us all too little about usable water available at particular places for particular purposes. We cannot be sure how soon or on what scale real constraints may begin to appear.

There are similar anxieties about food supplies. Over the last twenty-five years, food production has kept pace with the annual increase in population — about 2.8 per cent a year. This global figure is, as usual, misleading. It suggests a comfortable trend. But perhaps a billion people (over three hundred million of them children) are malnourished now. At the other end of the dietary scale, North Americans, Russians and most Europeans are eating more than ever before. And the way in which they are eating plays a big part in determining whether or not future shortages occur. If food is measured in terms of the equivalent in grain, most citizens in developed lands, including North America, have nearly doubled their consumption. This is not because they are stuffing themselves with bread and muffins and doughnuts. They are eating far more grain already processed through hens and pigs and cattle. (One should add that some of the processing is also carried on in whisky and vodka distilleries.) In fact, North Americans only eat about 150 pounds of actual grain a year. But their total (grain plus the grain equivalent of eggs and pork and chicken and beef and lamb and whisky) is just under a ton per person. By contrast, the average Indian eats about 400 pounds of grain in the form of — grain.

There has undoubtedly been a general expansion in food consumption and production in the last twenty-five years. But the largest increases have occurred in North America, and there, virtually alone, are all the reserves for export. American grain exports have increased from about five million metric tons to over ninety million in the last three decades. Australia has kept a small surplus for export. Southern Latin America has virtually lost its grain exports. Europe's import demand is steady, at about twenty million tons. The deficit areas are, among developed nations, parts of eastern Europe and the Soviet Union, once exporters and now, in a bad year, requiring imports of over twenty million tons. Among the developing nations the crisis areas are in parts of Asia and Africa where the deficit has soared in some years to over fifty million tons of grain. Thus every area in the world, save North America and Australasia, has become or remained a food deficit area since the 1930's. True, given European's steady imports, and given the near-doubling in high protein meat-based diets among Europeans, they have very greatly increased their own output. (Indeed, western Europe can produce milk and butter and beef mountains — and wine lakes — with apparently very little difficulty.) It is also true that the so-called Green Revolution of new hybrid seeds, fertilizer, assured water and increasing mechanization has produced some startling increases in developing countries. India became self-sufficient in wheat between 1967 and 1971. The Philippines began exporting rice. But both are returning to precarious deficits. China, by different means, has managed to combine an increase in its population of several hundred millions with a continued balance of grain imports and exports. The two great reversals of productivity are in the Soviet Union and temperate Latin America and comparing figures for productivity in the U.S.S.R. and Argentina with other (western) countries helps to explain the gap. It is a remarkable fact that in virtually every category — grain per acre, eggs per hen, milk per cow, meat per head of cattle, sheep and pigs — North American output is *twice* as high. True, Argentina's sorry tale is one of simple negligence. The Soviet Union's is more complicated. It had to survive the erasing of all past farming experience and institutions during collectivization; it had to get through a terrible invasion and then rebuild industry at the speed felt to be necessary to "catch up" with the United States. Only recently has agriculture received any priority in attention and investment. Unhappily, two agricultural ministers later, the patient is still failing to respond. But this is not the only problem. Even the nature of possible success presents difficulties. What the Russians are attempting and the North Americans have achieved is, basically, a vast increase in output per acre by an almost total substitution of energy for manpower and the development of a whole series of scientific discoveries in the breeding and feeding of plants and animals. And these, too, can be subject to diminishing returns.

Between 1940 and 1970, the man-hours in American agriculture fell from just over twenty billion to about three billion. During the same three decades, the energy invested in American farms in terms of kilocalories increased nearly four times over. It has been pointed out that a New York farmer who spent 150 minutes producing a bushel of corn in 1905, can do it now in three.* The difference lies in a massive substitution of mechanical for human energy.

On the face of it, this is not an unpromising picture. Improve the Soviet Union's farming. Get the bull of its sudden massive grain purchases out of the china shop of the grain trade. Speed up the Green Revolution. Improve Latin American temperate farming and surely supplies are secure. But again, the prospects are not so straightforward. Leave aside the present scale of human malnutrition. Leave aside the difficulty that countries without export incomes cannot enter the world grain trade at all. These are old, if tragic, problems. Uncertainty rests over two new ones: our old friend, diminishing returns, and a new difficulty, the quintupling of energy costs. The clearest illustration of diminishing returns has already been cited — the use of fertilizer. Much of the added productivity in North America has come from more fertilizer. Today, however, all the acres are back under the plough and fully fertilized. The increase from five to ninety-nine million metric tons of grain for export cannot be repeated by that route. Even if world population does double, North America cannot redouble its export surplus.

There are other examples. We can leave aside the pesticides and herbicides which began concentrating dangerously in food chains, killing off other organic life, and producing "silent springs." They gave not so much diminishing as dangerous returns. Where the real margins are shrinking is in the simple fact already mentioned. So much of the best sites for irrigation — essential to the Green Revolution in monsoon Asia — have been already brought into use. So have the rich prairies of North America. Untilled areas which may still prove arable (tropical lands, the tsetse belt) are likely to be much less productive. In the 1950's and 1960's, land which was withheld from production in the United States (in order to keep up food prices) could usually grow not less than the equivalent of two hundred days of world grain consumption. Last winter, world reserves were equal to less than twenty days. The once unploughed lands are now in use; we cannot count on them twice over. The food must be found elsewhere.

Nor can we safely assume the old price levels. Here, admittedly, we enter a debate in which extrapolations tell us very little. It is no use basing your trend on petroleum at a dollar a barrel if it now costs eleven. Everything turns on the question whether the higher price will do what, in classical market theory, it is supposed to do — and often does. Will greater costs lead on the one hand to the invention of innumerable substitutes, and on the other hand will it discourage overuse?

*These and other examples of energy use are reproduced from Mr. Denis Hayes' indispensable pamphlet "Energy: The Case for Conservation," published by the World Watch Institute, Washington, D.C.

On the old trend, fossil fuels are on the way out. First natural gas will be finished by the end of the century, petroleum not too long after. Coal could last another century or so, but the southern hemisphere has very little of it. So shortages will be a fact. Yet if energy substitutes appear quickly, there is no reason why prices should not fall and use continue to rise as steadily as in the fifties and sixties. Then the trend would go on being a trend, as the return to big cars in the United States suggests people prefer. But equally they could decide to use less — with very different results and a complete rewriting of the extrapolations.

The outlook for energy substitutes is, of course, dominated by the nuclear issue. Admittedly, the present generation of reactors can only use the very small percentage of uranium which is fissile — the so-called uranium 235. It makes up a minute percentage of the world's uranium stocks. Fission reactors could be in trouble for supplies by the 1990's. This is why interest is concentrated on the breeder reactor which can break down the much more abundant uranium 238 into plutonium and, using plutonium as a fuel, actually "breed" more fuel than goes into it in the first place. It can also use up the plutonium which present reactors spin off as a useless by-product — except for bombs. With the further possibility of fusion energy, using unlimited fuel from the oceans' deuterium, already in the research stage, energy-gobbling man looks quite safe for the next quarter millennium. The old rates of growth, powered by cheap abundant energy, can continue, and this fact also clears up a lot of subsidiary worries about shrinking supplies of raw materials.

Provided enough energy is available, more inferior ores can be used, mixed in with abundant scrap, and more and more high-energy resources can be made from virtually universal materials like silicon (which is only sand) or even granite. At the same time renewable resources from vegetable matter can be chemically bonded and welded into new and useful materials. In the last cupboard of the Sorcerer's Apprentice is the fusion torch which can break everything down into its basic molecules for reassembling into useful goods.

The overwhelming problem raised by this nuclear vision of unlimited energy is the possible by-products: the risk of reactor melt-downs, the steady accumulation of totally lethal, cancer-causing wastes, indestructible over fifty thousand years, the possibility that the kind of men who kidnapped every OPEC oil minister with hand weapons could threaten whole countries with atomic devices which, once the needed bit of nuclear waste had been secured (and never doubt there would be a black market in it as there is now in heroin), would require no more than the handbooks of the U.S. Atomic Energy Commission to cobble together an effective nuclear weapon — a student at the Massachusetts Institute of Technology has already done so.

These risks lie at the centre of the familiar bitter debate between the optimists who dismiss the fears as a lack of confidence in technofixing, including the disposal of millennial wastes, and those who believe the risks to both present and future generations horrifying enough to warrant a much longer, slower approach to the nuclear option and possibly a phasing out of everything except fusion research, since fusion may have no environmental dangers of accumulating lethal and indestructible by-products. The critics are now reinforced in their views by such events as the single candle flame at Brown's Ferry, Alabama, in 1975 which, used to test air flows, started a fire which led to the sudden closing down of the whole 1,000-megawatt complex. The most disturbing feature of the disaster was the failure of the "automatic" safety mechanisms to prevent the spread of the fire or to safeguard the core of the reactors. In 1976 came the resignation of senior nuclear engineers in California and New York on the moral grounds that they could no longer honestly guarantee the safety of the reactor programmes on which they had been working.

But such events only reinforce a deeper questioning. Never before has mankind had to deal with totally lethal wastes whose "half life" is twenty-five thousand years. That these radioactive materials are entirely hostile to organic life is proved by our planet's millennial history. So long as the undiluted radiance of the sun poured down upon the earth in seering radioactivity, no life was possible; for perhaps seven billion of our planet's ten billion years, the earth held nothing but exploding, contracting, cooling, irradiated rock. Only as the steaming earth cooled and the vapour turned to rain, pouring down for thousands upon thousands of years and filling up the deeps, did a first oceanic shield for life appear. Later, the invasion of the rock by breathing plants from the oceans built up the further shield of our planet's atmosphere.

Behind these defences, the sun's radiance has become benign, sustaining all organic life and ripening every harvest entirely free of charge. But what we are doing with atomic energy is to bring that pitiless radiation back behind the protecting shields and to expose ourselves directly to a force which is, in the last analysis, incompatible with life. It has been called a Faustian bargain. Perhaps it is nearer to a Promethean curse; for the "fire of the gods," the sun, is nuclear fire, and the penalty imposed on Prometheus, the archetypal man, for stealing it, was to be chained to the rock, perhaps the lifeless rock of an irradiated planet.

No one doubts the sincerity and honesty of the scientists who say that safeguards will be found — that plutonium and other wastes can be safely embedded in clay and glass, that the breeder reactors will, in any case, use up most of the plutonium as a fuel, and that the kind of safeguards required for reactors, reprocessing plants, and wastes in transit will be no more insecure than the present guard set on nuclear armaments, none of which, so far, have been removed by stealth. But the doubts persist. The first is the sheer length of time. How can anyone be sure of any process over twenty-five thousand years? What simulation techniques can be really the equivalent of the long wearing away of the implacable years. The second is the kind of safeguards.

Will we have full military protection on a growing network of power plants — from Anatolia to Zanzibar by way of Ulster and Uganda? It hardly presages an increasingly open and confident civil society. The third concerns greed. What will people pay for the ultimate blackmail? Can we really guarantee a race of guardians so uncorrupt for at least twenty-five thousand years that no one will approach their price?

The last concerns stability. No social order in human history has lasted more than five hundred years without violent civil disturbance. The world is menaced enough, heaven knows, by its military nuclear arsenal which is adequate to blow it up at least twenty times over — one would have thought once would suffice. If we add all the installations of nuclear industry and then postulate civic breakdown, the terrorists of the twenty-first century will carry plutonium devices; yet a piece of plutonium no larger than an orange can threaten the whole of humanity with lung cancer. If these are not real risks, then language has no meaning. It is not doomsaying or Cassandra-type prophecy or any ignoble loss of nerve that suggest a cautious approach to the nuclear option. It is sober common sense.

Must we then conclude that the collision course is unavoidable? Certain key resources (water regionally, food more generally, energy everywhere) will come under strain. The critical alternatives, above all in energy, present environmental dangers and possibilities of literally death-dealing pollution too lethal to contemplate. Yet numbers are rising. So are aspirations. What gives? What *can* give? Do we, as so many times in past history, enter "a time of troubles" in which, to all the other more traditional troubles, is added the risk of nuclear destruction?

There are, of course, those who strongly deny any irresistible force to rising aspirations, especially to those in the Third World where military weakness and a certain political "incoherence" offer no pressure and no threat. But this assumption reckons without the world's ideological divide. After Vietnam and Angola, there is no reason to suppose that poor people demonstrating their desire for a larger share in the world's benefits will receive no outside support. This is not, incidentally, to see the world neatly divided into ideological blocks with democracies steadily shrinking. I cannot say I have noticed much spread or contraction of democracy since the end of that totally undemocratic system known as western colonialism. Germany has, almost miraculously, been regained for the open society. Italy is not certain to return to authoritarianism. Spain, Portugal, and Greece are stirring. For the rest, democracy is alive and reasonably well and living in its old haunts. Where communism has taken over, I do not observe that there is any change in political forms — from one dictatorship to another and, certainly in China, to a very much more socially desirable one.

Nor do I suspect that communist "takeovers" in Africa and Southeast Asia will cut these areas off from western contacts. Oil and minerals still have to be sold and technical assistance secured. What I do mean is that the world's peoples are not ready to return to the colonial epoch that was so remarkably convenient for the Atlantic world. (It may even be that Russia's subject peoples will finally resent their old nineteenth-century bonds.) There will be pressure. There will be demands for more sharing. Moreover, this kind of pressure will not be confined to ex-colonials. The unions, the workers, the farmers inside western society may be as wealthy as any "bourgeois" in terms of the homeless family in Calcutta. But they are not looking at the *bustees*. They are looking at Lockheed and the French patronat and Mr. Getty and the Rockefellers, and, like Oliver Twist, they want more. No, the pressures are certain. So is there no hope?

I believe there is, *provided* we are prepared to accept three vital but not totally radical changes in our methods of running our affairs. The first is to take a new objective and constructive look at our productive processes and realize how profoundly, over the last century and especially in the last twenty-five years, waste has become a way of life among us. The second is to realize (it is not very difficult, we do it all the time) that however valuable market mechanisms and signals may be as rational, unbiased, automatic and decentralized methods of distributing goods, there are certain circumstances in which they do not work well or work at all. The third is to extend to the interdependent market we have made of the whole world some of the moral disciplines and ideals we try, however faultily, to observe within our domestic societies. If at the planetary level we institutionalize nothing but our greeds and fears, how can we hope to survive in the age of space flight and instant communication? No community can endure without some sense of a Sacred Order, of moral imperatives men cannot manipulate for their own use. This small home of man is no exception. If we run it as no more than a huckster's stand and a slaughterhouse, then "the bright day is done and we are for the dark."

Happily, all three conditions of survival are not beyond our reach. Let us begin by looking at the chances for a more conserving, a more thrifty and careful economy. They are surprisingly large just because we are so surprisingly wasteful. Possibly the most reliable clue to follow is the use of energy. Since it can only be defined as "that which makes work possible," it enters into everything. In the shape of petroleum at fifteen cents a barrel at the wellhead, and less than two dollars to the consumer, it has also been fantastically cheap. If anything were ever designed to encourage careless use, it has been our fuel bonanza. Let us begin from there.

In the last quarter-century, energy has virtually been substituted for nearly everything else. The farming example has already been cited. So has the comparative weight of cars. But these are simply specific examples of a whole economy based upon energy waste which, in North America, has reached the astonishing outcome that literally 50 per cent of the energy put to use does no work at all. It simply streams off into the biosphere, sometimes harmfully — as when thermal discharges into rivers kill off fish life or idling car engines help to build up photochemical smog — sometimes harmlessly — as when the heat leaks out of poorly fitting doors and windows, yet makes no impact on the homes' surroundings; but it is waste nonetheless in that it could have done useful work (keeping the house warm, for instance) and does not do so.

It is almost inconceivably stupid to waste 50 per cent of man's most useful auxiliary, the "energy slave" which heats and cools him, brings his news and music, clothes his family and furnishes his house, cooks and cleans for him, lights his way, and, above all, moves him about. Yet, in North America, this is the figure. (It is not quite so lunatic in Europe. Sweden, France, and Germany, all countries with comparable living standards, use about a third less energy per head of population.)

How does all this indispensable and increasingly expensive resource simply get wasted? First of all, there is the production of electricity itself. One-third of the energy generated in traditional power stations leaks off in waste heat. The further the generators are from the points of use, the longer the transmission lines, the more certain is this steady wastage. The tendency to waste is increased if power companies give lower rates to larger users. Here is a direct incentive to be profligate. If you leave the lights on all night in the office, the bill may go down, not up.

Then there is the side of investment to consider — the possible waste of capital. The average nuclear reactor provides electricity at a cost of $3,000 for each kilowatt delivered. If steam in industry is used for electrical generation, the cost is only $190 to $250 a kilowatt. Recapturing waste heat from factory chimneys need cost no more than $70. Experimental future technologies (for instance, using the sun's radiance directly by means of fuel cells) are already in the $500 per kilowatt range. It is obvious common sense to produce the same amount of energy from a smaller input of capital. It frees resources for other uses, including, incidentally, all the energy indirectly used up in the building of mammoth power plants and gigantic grid systems for transmission — not to speak of the guards and defences round future fast breeder reactors and processing plants that could make medieval walled fortresses look like open cities.

When we go from the actual production of power to its uses, the same vast possibilities for saving appear. If we begin with the productive system itself, the contrasts in efficiency in the use of energy and resources are startling. As a percentage of value added in dollar terms, Sweden uses 25 per cent less in food processing than North America and as much as 80 per cent less in its chemical industry. Europe and the Soviet Union cool their coke with recycled inert gas and reuse the heat as it is given off. In America, water is sloshed on and all the heat goes to waste. Continuous casting in steel mills saves a million British Thermal Units of energy per ton when compared with pouring ingots. In concrete mixing, European plants use heat captured from cement kilns to decompose limestone and only use 550,000 Btu's for each barrel of cement. In North America, twice as much energy goes into each barrel because waste heat is disregarded. Some of the largest savings can come from recycling. Recycled steel, for instance, requires only 25 per cent of the energy used for the original processing. For copper scrap, the figure is between 5 and 10 per cent, for aluminum (the basic component of so many containers), only 5 per cent.

A lot of the saving in industry does not even require new processes or heroic changes in production. One large British commercial firm reduced its energy use by 15 per cent simply by consulting with the staff and switching off lights and heaters. An American corporation managed the same economy by asking for energy reports from each department. What such enquiries can show up is well illustrated by the firm which discovered that the heating devices for de-icing its yards were still going full blast at midsummer. All such reductions in industry have a double advantage. They not only save energy now, but they reduce extrapolations of future use which would, if acted on, tie up more energy in ever larger numbers of future generators.

Defence is another energy-gobbler. Estimates in the United States put the armed forces' share, both direct and indirect, at some 6 per cent of all America's energy budget. It is safe to assume, given the very modest internal disciplines on military spending, that the defence establishment does not depart much from the national average of 50 per cent wastage. In any case, an essential part of military duty is to hang about in a state of preparedness. How carefully is all this monitored? One B 1 bomber in a year uses anything from 300 million to one billion gallons of fuel. Estimates suggest that in 1974 *all* America's buses used only 320 million gallons of fuel.* In the literal sense, the bomber certainly takes the economy for a ride. Since the Soviet Union spends an even higher proportion of a lower GNP on arms (and is not noted for the most sophisticated forms of cost-benefit analysis) Russian waste is certainly higher still and also more damaging to civilian needs. The fuel used up in Angola might have been better employed on Soviet farms.

Nor should we forget that the defence issue covers more than carelessly used resources. With or without carelessness, defence spending is essentially inflationary. It is strange to remember how carefully we were taught that lesson during the Second World War. All the efforts of public education were directed to the task of making us understand that the production of arms generates wages but does not provide the goods required to mop up those wages

*The calculation is that of James Comoy and Paul d'Eustachio in "Boom and Bust: the B 1 Bomber and the Environment" (Environmental Action Foundation, 1975).

when people go out to spend them. We are still unable, thank heavens, to order machine guns and howitzers at the friendly neighbourhood corner store, although in some countries, hand guns are another matter. We are not offered the latest line in tanks. So the wages of the workers and the profits of the arms manufacturers (not to speak of their "commissions") spill out into the economy in the shape of purchasing power unmatched by goods that can be purchased. Thus, by definition, there is more money than supplies. Equally, by definition, this puts up the price of goods as more money competes for them. The result? Inflation. All this was drummed into our heads by our leaders in wartime. I have not heard a murmur of it from any banker or politician or business leader (manager or unionist) during these latest years of inflation. Yet the world spends $300 billion a year on "defence."

Now I do not mean that defence expenditure is unnecessary. Only when the Soviet Union gives up the dream of empire, combined with worldwide ideological uniformity, can we hope for serious, supervised disarmament and the substitution of international police forces for the lethal anarchy of competing national and very unsacred egoisms. But I do say that, for all the world's peoples, it is a con game to suggest that the haemorrhage of energy, materials, and skills into weapons systems which can blow up the earth twenty times over, is anything but appalling, inflationary waste and qualifies our planet for designation as the lunatic asylum for the entire cosmos. I also believe that, even now, in spite of our insecurities, we could have some cutbacks in defence spending, earmarking the saving for development and conservation among the poorer groups. This is a point to which we will return.

There are other areas which actually waste more energy than the defence sector and often with no less lethal risks. Here transport is the prime example. Either directly or indirectly, it is responsible for over 40 per cent of North America's energy costs. The archetype of wasted energy is the single driver in the 150 horsepower station wagon, sitting in the middle of a commuter log jam. Yet in the United States 56 per cent of all commuters drive to work alone in their cars. The comparative figures speak for themselves. According to Wilfred Owen, the outstanding expert in transport at Brookings Institution, the relative efficiencies of various forms of transport can vary from the helicopter using one U.S. gallon of fuel for 7 passenger miles to the 1,000 passenger miles per gallon of the bicycle. In between, an average-size car with one passenger does just over 20 miles to the gallon, a city bus (in the rush hour) 95 miles, a city subway (rush hour again) 120 miles, a broad-gauge train 390 miles. If a small car carries four passengers, it does as well as the rush hour bus. But a microbus with seven passengers is nearly as economical as a train.

We find the same pattern on the side of freight. Pipelines move things least wastefully at 450 Btu's for each ton mile. Railways and canals are in the 670-680 Btu range. But trucks jump to 2,800 Btu's. (Aeroplanes are harder to cal-

culate since freight and passengers are often carried together but one estimate*
puts the figure at 42,000 Btu's.) These figures explain why, in the United
States, trucks use up one-half of all the fuel used for freight while carrying
only one-fifth of it.

And if I may at this point interject another factor of "waste" into the automobile figures, please do not convict me of undue emotion and sensational-
ism. The longer I live, the more incomprehensible it becomes to me that
western man seems entirely and callously indifferent to the daily massacre on
the roads. We kill, maim and injure some four million people a year; the death
figure alone for North America and Europe is over 150,000. Early in 1970,
the two millionth car victim perished in the United States. At that point, road
deaths exceeded all the deaths in all America's wars. We glibly say that the
cost is covered by insurance. Dear God, what is insurance to the spouse deprived of a beloved companion, to parents called in to identify the bloody,
mangled body of an only child, to the family of young couples killed on their
honeymoons? For sheer horror, let me give you a recent incident. Five young
people in Britain had drawn off the road onto the hard verge to eat a picnic
lunch. Along came a juggernaut truck driven by a rather tired French driver,
so tired that he could no longer remember which side of the road he was supposed to drive on or even what was verge and what was road. So he drove his
thirty tons of metal into the stationary car, killing all the young people and
smashing the car 270 yards along the road before coming to a halt. (In paren-
thesis may I say his knuckles were knocked with a small feather in punishment
— a $500 fine and three months without a licence, clearly a perfectly adequate
reminder that killing off five young lives in a stationary car off the road on the
wrong side is really rather naughty.)

Among all the "externalities," among all the uncounted costs and wastages
we do not pay or even recognize for our use of energy in transport, death and
mayhem are the worst. And western man, who has smugly congratulated himself on his "respect for life," does not give a damn. The proof is all the array of
precautions, most of them conserving precautions, which could be taken and,
in equivalent terms, would be screamed for if the killer was cholera or plague.
Smaller safer cars, tougher speed limits, public transport in cities, more
freight and passengers on railways, segregated roads for giant trucks — all
these are conserving both of energy and life. Transport is, after all, along with
war, the most desperate user and waster of life itself. Some hint of this creeps
into the names often given to cars — Avengers, Thunderbirds, Jaguars — an
ugly predatory image which, all too often, is not far from the truth. But do
we care? No.

---

*Hirst and Herendeen, *Total Energy Demand for Automobiles* (Society of Automobile
Engineers, 1973).

Now let us look at a rather less depressing area of waste: the buildings we construct and live in. They are not killers, but they are formidable energy-sinks. Most building codes in developed societies lay down standards for constructional safety. Some include environmental safeguards such as minimum availability of space and light. But it is surprising how few really look at the use of energy in heating and cooling dwellings and buildings and how much waste occurs as a result. If we look first at the beginning of construction, we should notice an example already given — North America's wasteful methods of producing concrete. Nearly 50 per cent of the energy could be saved if kiln-heat were recycled. Steel is part of the equation, too, substituting continuous casting for ingot-pouring. Stainless steel is also much less energy-intensive than aluminum, although in the last eighteen months (Allah bless the Arabs?) one aluminum company has cut the amount of energy used in processing by a third. Then we should remember that of all building materials, glass, however flashy the result (almost literally) is the worst of all insulators, and exacerbates both heat and cold. Thus we observe the ludicrous outcome of hermetically sealed highrise ziggurats which have to be heated and cooled simultaneously, and this often in climates so temperate that opening a window and facing the breeze are all that is needed for comfort throughout a large part of the year.

This brings us to the second failure: building codes. They rarely specify well-fitting doors and windows, orientation towards breezes, defences against summer sunshine, and, above all, proper insulation. This may cost more at the time of construction, and so it is skimped. But all building codes should include an energy calculus for the expected life of the building. It would then be found that, in quite a short span, the original capital costs of insulation would have been amply covered and the annual energy cost — and waste — drastically reduced. The American Institute of Architects estimates that different, energy-efficient building codes could be saving the United States 12.5 million barrels of petroleum a day by 1990. And this may err on the side of pessimism. The energy savings can be cumulative. Better insulated buildings require smaller furnaces to begin with (including the saving of energy in *their* materials). Nor does this level of insulation take into account all the supplements to energy which are beginning to be adopted with the installation of solar technology in individual buildings and their use to increase and store energy and at the same time to reduce the load on the power stations. Some sensible southwestern states in America are beginning to give subsidies to people who install solar energy devices and the Ford Foundation's Energy Study has suggested that a graduated energy tax, introduced over a decade to allow people to readjust to the end of the slosh-it-on, all-electric heat sink, would help to bring about a whole new conserving technology in which all the possible supplements to high cost, high wastage forms of energy (supplements such as solar energy, wind power, environmental siting for breeze and shade) would be brought into play and contribute to that 50 per cent cut in annual energy use which many experts believe possible in North America.

Conservation is the key to these new building methods. But it covers a much wider field of community services and conveniences, particularly in the recycling and reuse of all kinds of waste. In the last three decades, we must remember, the amount of solid wastes simply discarded by citizens in developed countries has become astronomical. The litany of waste in the United States as the seventies began made Don Giovanni's list of conquests pale in comparison. The discards included sixty-five billion metal caps, sixty billion metal cans, thirty-six billion bottles and over a million junked cars. Now, we have already seen how much less energy is used in recycling. How then can we afford to burn, sink, or bury this treasure trove? Why do we pollute the air and waters with it? Why do we run out of areas for landfill and repeatedly find that some of the more noxious dumps have allowed poisons to seep into surrounding rivers and aquifers? One reason, which we will examine later, is that pricing policies exclude pollution costs. Another lies in our civic attitudes to waste. The chief expense of waste is collecting it and sanitation officials are not precisely the workers of highest repute. (In some European cities, every one of them is a foreign worker, almost a new breed of untouchable.) At the same time, little is done to enlist the help (or the self-interest) of citizens in sorting out their own wastes and thus making it easier for the cities to recycle metals and glass and all the organic materials (paper, food, cloth, plastics) which can be recycled as fuel or as fertilizer in the form of compost. The result is that every year in developed societies billions of tons of wastes are simply pollutants when, if they were conserved and reused, they could create real wealth in factories and farms.

To give only one example, but a critical one. If there were a sizable tax on non-returnable containers, it would encourage citizens to separate their tins and bottles for recycling. But here we encounter another problem: attitudes to employment. In the present structure of employment, the men who work in the highly mechanized, high-energy factories which produce cans and bottles from virgin materials are reckoned to be skilled mechanics and receive high wages. The garbage-collectors, on the contrary, are in low-prestige and relatively lower wage occupations. Unions tend to see in extensive recycling a threat to their highly paid skills which, they believe, depend on a high use of energy. To switch to the more labour-intensive methods of collection and recovery would save massive amounts of energy. But it could seem to reduce high-energy jobs and substitute for them supposedly "untouchable" forms of employment. There is, of course, a possible solution — to pay the sanitation corps the balance saved by using less energy and to shift the "elite jobs" into the collecting and recycling sector. But the illustration shows the kind of changes in our perception of economic and social values the conserving economy will come to demand.

In fact, one can argue that in a variety of ways the kind of settlements we have slipped into in the nineteenth and twentieth centuries, in this first tentative fumbling phase in man's use of high science and high technology, are from most points of view exactly the kind of "habitat" which a sane, stable and conserving society ought to reform if they have them, and avoid if they have not. No one really intended the kind of megalopolitan sprawls typical of our age; indeed, it is a sobering thought that many of them have come into being as a result of people wanting to get away from the city they found. The latest urban statistics in the United States tend to confirm this. There is a vast move going on not simply from cities to suburbs but from the whole of the old northeast to the new southwest. As early as the 1790's, anyone who could afford to get out of Manchester's increasingly crowded, factory-packed, smoke-ridden centre was moving away to Wilmslow and Alderly Edge. (Later on, that forerunner of all effective town planners, Patrick Geddes, suggested another route. "Getting drunk," he said, "is the quickest way out of Manchester.") Manhattan passed its maximum density in the 1860's. The coming of the motor car spun out the spread until Greater London and Greater New York and Greater Tokyo began to reach towards the twenty million mark, in dense, built-up urban regions which, in numbers, in spread, in complexity, were utterly unlike anything hitherto produced in the history of man.

At first, these new centres sucked people in, for employment, for gain, for adventure. Then they spewed a large number of the more successful out again to the spreading rings of suburbia. Later on, profound transformations of employment began to take place. After the Second World War, more and more activities began to take place in the tertiary sector of services — shops, beauty parlours, art dealers, entertainment — and in the quaternary sector of transactions and the knowledge-industry — banking, finance, data banks, planetary communications by satellite and computer. In New York, in the late 1960's, manufacturing jobs — the secondary sector — fell by nearly a quarter, and the number is still falling. In the country at large, the primary sector — farms and mines — shrank to less than 10 per cent. (The U.S. farmer with his bushel of wheat in three minutes is the archetype here.) But this shift of employment did extraordinary things to the cities. It emptied the black workers from the southern United States into the northern cities (and pulled in the Puerto Rican, just as "guestworkers" have been drawn into Rotterdam and Birmingham and Munich and Marseilles). But in the cities the migrants moving into rundown buildings that had already housed all the earlier migrations found a disadvantage the others had missed. The sniggering joke of the 1850's — that "God invented the wheelbarrow to teach Paddy to walk on his hindlegs" — reminds us of how many migrants could find their feet in the city because manual work and manufacturing jobs were available. But the new quaternary sector does not want hands; it wants brains. To give the example once again of New York, services and the transactional sector have grown by over 30 per cent. But the deprived child of a Mississippi farm worker cannot cope with "transactions." The people who can are precisely the children of the people who earlier moved out to suburbia and pulled a lot of light industry and commerce out after them. So we get the entirely unintended and even ridiculous situation in which the urban poor live all too often unemployed and in decaying homes alongside the shining skyscrapers of the transactional world. The employees in this sector have homes and services and pay their taxes outside the city centre — sometimes up to twenty miles outside — and commute to work in the kind of avalanche that brings the equivalent of the whole inner city of Paris in and out of Manhattan every day. At the same time, the fall in farming and the suburbanization of light industry has drained vitality from many country regions. The conurbation enmeshed in a spinning cocoon of movement, throwing out its wastes, using up its energy, and producing an ever-widening risk of tension between the underprivileged core and a more fortunate suburbia and exurbia — this, all too often, is the pattern of the modern human habitat, straining both the inner limits of civic tolerance and respect and the outer limits of a sustainable biosphere.

And if this is the pattern in wealthy developed countries, how much more dire are the prospects in developing lands. Here the mismatch between human needs and capabilities and the form of human settlements is even more precarious. In the first place, the cities often come first as mere adjuncts of western trade. Rio, Lagos, Bombay, Shanghai were all racing to and beyond the two million mark before even 5 per cent of the local people were engaged in industry. At the same time, the agricultural revolution based on machines and energy arrived to drive peasants and landless men off the land before there were alternative jobs in the cities. It is broadly true to say that in the nineteenth century, the lure of city work pulled the labourers in. In the twentieth, it is lack of jobs on the land that pushes them out. And there are so many millions more to push. Once again, the timing has aggravated the mismatch. In Europe, the industrial revolution came first; the sanitary revolution, second. The work force grew by less than 0.5 per cent a year. But in the developing world, it now probably equals 2 to 3 per cent, as seventy-five to eighty million people are added to the planet's population every year. Nor is this the last of history's tricks and ironies. The Green Revolution of productivity based on energy and machines, not manpower, is simply a reflection, in farming, of the wider trend — to automation, to energy-intensive technology, to the highly skilled transactional society. The last thing this society needs is "hands." Yet these are what are steadily and remorsely increasing, and their owners have little choice in their own eyes but to leave their small, overworked, often eroding mini-farms and make for the great cities (established under the old imperial and commercial system) and seek a fortune which all too often consists of little more than barely keeping alive. The crowded shanty towns round every developing city — the *calampas* of Santiago, the *bustees* of Calcutta, the *bidonvilles* of Algiers — these are symbols of a profound disequilibrium in the entire economy and one which, if trend is destiny, is carrying us to catastrophe.

Thus in our settlements we find some of the most wasteful and inhuman patterns of living and working into which the human race has ever stumbled. There is the waste of human beings without work. There is the waste of energy in careless building and endless movement. There is the fantastic waste of smog-filled skies, accumulating garbage dumps, polluted water — over 40 per cent of the human race lack assured access to clean water. And if trend *is* destiny, then all these monster cities are destined to continue to grow, in developing lands, by anything from 4 to 8 per cent a year and, in many developed societies, to continue in the present energy-wasting, time-consuming, polluting, degrading and socially divisive patterns of which perhaps New York City, commercial capital of the world's most powerful economy, is the near-bankrupt symbol. For, if in so superlatively well-endowed and skilled a society, a major city can be seen to be almost visibly disintegrating, one must surely surmise that something, somehow, somewhere along the line has gone *very* badly wrong.

But while we can sense the decay, can we grasp the possible means of revival? At this point, we turn to the second theme of possible reform and renewal: a reconsideration of the strengths and weaknesses of pure market mechanisms. We did not really intend to have the kind of large urban settlements that we live in today. They were called into being by the needs of industry which, for the first time, took the bulk of man's heavy work out of the fields and into the towns. And within this new industrial order, the patterns were largely set, until the middle of the twentieth century, by market signals, in particular by the private market in land. And this fact has had a number of profoundly distorting effects. The first affects costs and rewards, the second side-effects and "externalities." Let us take first the question of price and profit in the urban land market. The proponents of the market mechanisms as the sole, benign, reliable, impersonal, and decentralized arbiters of peoples' wants and satisfactions will, of course, protest that any curtailment of the freedom to buy and sell land will "distort the market" because those who need the land most urgently will no longer be able to bid for it, thus risking its use for less valuable purposes.

But does the market always function as the instrument of optimal use? We need not deny that, all other things being equal, it is the best and deftest and fairest and least bureaucratic way of distributing goods. Even the most hardened collectivist has had to come round to some form of price mechanism. (Indeed, in societies where the overalls of workers in vodka distilleries positively clank with bottles as they leave after the day shift, one can argue that the distribution and sale of this particularly sought-after consumer good (or bad) take place through the most "private" system of enterprise known to man.) But the trouble is that in markets, all other things are often very far from equal. Neither on the side of demand nor of supply can the market cope in an "optimum" way with absolute shortage. Let us look first at the side of demand. The market cannot cope with demand — even demand for such basic instruments of human dignity as food, water, shelter, skills — if income is too low to admit the citizen into the market at all. Nearly half of humanity, especially the subsistence farming communities, lives on less than $100 a year. How can they register their demands, however fundamental? And as their numbers increase, the margins of income fall further. In the nineteenth century, such people (dispossessed cottagers, displaced weavers) simply starved to death. A large part of the reforms in developed societies in the later nineteenth and twentieth centuries have been concerned with putting some floor of income and opportunity under the lives of the mass of the people. We have no such planetary institutions, and if supplies go short, the majority may be pushed beyond the "inner limits" of survival itself.

On the side of supply, the great value and flexibility of market signals lie in the fact that when, given constant or increasing demand, supply declines and prices rise, more producers are induced to increase their output, and as supply increases, prices fall and come back into balance. Demand and supply in the open market operating impersonally and irresistibly, restore equilibrium with the reliability of universal law. But suppose supply cannot be increased? Suppose the limits have been reached? The market's answer then is to go on pushing prices up and up and up until only the fullest purse is still in the bidding. The clearest example of this can be seen during a time of food shortage. As harvests begin to fail under a market system, hoarders buy up the shrinking supplies, prices rise more rapidly as a result, the rich alone can eat, the poor starve. The market cannot expand supplies until next harvest. But families cannot last so long. The same pressures operate when soil and water are scarce. The poor farmers have to push out into poorer and poorer land. Then cultivation erodes the soil. This in turn increases the risks of alternate drought and inundation. As we have noted, these terrible pressures are at work along the Himalayan foothills and the Sahel. Market mechanisms will not reverse the fatality. Absolute shortage is in sight.

Distortions of a similar kind can begin to operate when other forms of land are scarce. Land in cities, particularly in central cities, is precisely in this category. Nothing will make Manhattan Island bigger — which was lucky for the Astors who once owned a lot of it. If more and more people want to do more and more different things with an absolutely unexpandable stock, its price goes through the roof. The happy original owners of the latter-day "assemblers" of property lots cream off vast fortunes for which, in a creative sense, they have done precisely nothing. And only the richest demanders stay in the ring. Thereafter, to pay off the fantastic prices they have had to give, they must sweat every dollar out of their tract of land. This can mean the intolerable repetition of skyscrapers, each staring into the next and down on the pitiful human ants below. It can mean overcrowded rack-renting in private houses. It can mean antisocial behemoths of public housing. It is bound to mean a total insufficiency of parks and playgrounds and vistas and monuments since what, in heaven's name, do *they* earn?

But notice the paradox. If a public-spirited citizen like Frederic Olmstead manages to impress the necessity of a city park on unwilling city fathers ("the rich do not need it, the poor will abuse it") every landowner on the edge of Manhattan's Central Park enjoys quintupling of private property values as a result of the "worthless" community decision.

Once sky-rocketing land prices deprive the city of even minimum amenities, the revulsion of wealthier citizens, first sparked by industrial squalor, increases still further the expansion of the suburban belt. And out there, a similar inflation of land values goes on occurring. Brisk selling swallows up acre after acre over an ever wider area of expanding sprawl. So instead of the "fresh fields and pastures new" the citizens hoped for, they are caught up in square miles of "slurb" across which, along with millions of others, they drearily commute, wasting hours of their brief and fleeting existence breathing in their neighbours' exhausts or crowded against them in bus and train. And the "vote with the feet" goes on — first to suburbia, then to second homes and now, as we have seen, away from the old cities altogether. Thus the operations of the private land market have played a direct part in distorting the patterns of living and working in the modern urban order. And some of the indirect effects are no less antisocial. It makes sane land-use planning virtually impossible, and it directly encourages inflation. The figures speak for themselves. Urban values went up by 10 per cent a year in the fifties and sixties in Paris and Madrid. Tokyo experienced a 40-fold increase between 1945 and 1970. British land prices went up 220 per cent between 1970 and 1975.

Let us look at the planning problem first. Uncontrolled speculation undermines better spatial planning in cities because, for whatever area the new or renewed construction is projected, the property developers move in in search of a killing. The French have tried to control this risk by designating certain areas as "zones for development" and freezing the land price at the date of designation. But the developers have bought up the land alongside the zone, prompting the cynical comment that public plans for settlements are "the speculators' guide." It is significant that some Swedish cities have largely checked these distortions by wisely buying up land for their own development long in advance — Stockholm, for instance, at the beginning of the twentieth century. Many Dutch cities have taken the same precautions. The developer cares little about the "optimum" use of the land. It may be indispensable agricultural land threatened, as in Ontario and the Niagara peninsula, with the proliferation of suburbia and second homes. But in a world growing yearly more hungry, it is *not* the best use of prime farm land to cover it with communities' tracts or the homes of people who have homes already. The unfettered market gives the wrong long-term answer simply because rising prices do not fulfill their classical function of making more of what is needed available. On the contrary, in the case of land, again and again they sacrifice the lesser to the deeper need. Only full soil and resource surveys, with "development rights" vested in the community and land speculation excluded, offer reasonable hope of rational and balanced development.

The other consequence of uncontrolled land markets is inflationary pressure. All justifications of private property, particularly in land, rest on the argument that the owner has a right to it because he has improved it from its virgin state. But, we must repeat, land values can be created not by what a man invests in his land but simply because, as a city grows, other people want it. The supply is fixed, so up goes the price. This is in itself inflationary; mortgages, the cost of houses, goods containing an element of urban land purchase or rent in them, all go up. But what is sometimes forgotten is that the utter lack of justification for the fortunes thus secured becomes an overriding difficulty in persuading the communities in general to check inflation by restraining demand and spiralling wages.

Take a recent example from Britain. Mr. Smith of Bewbush happened to own a few hundred acres of land in an area into which the town of Crawley wanted to expand. He was able to sell the land for $6 million simply because he was there. Three months later, the land was resold for $12 million to a pension fund because meanwhile it had been designated "for development." Thus our Mr. Smith received over $6 million because he happened to live near Crawley. That is the full extent of his contribution to the development and well-being of the British economy. The various agents, pension funds and business directors who pocketed the next $6 million did not even make this modest contribution. They simply resold development values created by the town of Crawley to which their contribution was zero. So some $18 million changed hands in various amounts in return for virtually nothing in the way of work, input and investment.

It is this aspect of buying and selling land that makes it so sharp an instrument on inflation. It makes absolute nonsense of any attempt to persuade people, in order to counter inflation, to accept restraints on their wages and salaries. If a Mr. Smith of Bewbush can clean $6 million simply by sitting about near Crawley, why, in heaven's name, should a miner, doing a hard, difficult, and dangerous job at the coalface, restrain his demands to, say, an extra $12 a week? He would have to live and work a very long time to get the equivalent of the $6 million earned by doing nothing. It is, above all, for this social reason that an end to land speculation and a regulated land market have become preconditions not only of better settlement planning but of any sustained policies for countering inflation.

But there is no reason why societies should not combine the values of the market as a flexible tool of relative abundance with planning policies designed to secure that abundance and deal with absolute shortage. In the critical area of water, pollution controls, and regulations in developed societies can prevent clean water in the Rhine or the Mediterranean from becoming a scarce resource. One part of this policy is to make prices cover the environmental costs of pollution and land degradation and to see that the "polluter pays." This engages their technical skill in reducing avoidable costs. The alternative, "licences to pollute" — in other words, fines or permitted levels of pollution at a price — simply favour big firms and leave water, air, and soil at risk. The sure way is to compel companies to carry the full cost. Even providing municipal treatment plants can be ruinous to the taxpayer unless the biggest polluters pay for their use. American policy is weak here. Too often, firms do not contribute anything save their pollutions.

At the international level, the investment by the international community of only about $3 billion a year for ten years could bring clean water to all settlements by 1986 and incidentally, by lessening infantile mortality, give parents the hope of keeping their first-born alive — the greatest incentive that can be given them to stabilize family size. Larger schemes for tapping the vast waters stored under the Sahara and storing the equally vast waters pouring from the Himalayas also offer the best hopes of stabilizing soil and increasing land reserves in the places of greatest pressure. And this type of capital investment could be part of the larger strategy outlined at the World Food Conference in Rome in November 1974: first, to create an immediate emergency reserve of ten million tons of grain, and secondly, to build up a world reserve system internationally financed and distributed, equal to about two hundred days of world consumption (as a safeguard against a failed monsoon and yet another poor Russian harvest coinciding with North American drought.)

But the third element of the Rome strategy is the most vital — massive investment in Third World agriculture. Sole reliance on the market will not bring it about for the reason already mentioned; the mass of the farmers are subsistence men, not in the market at all and wholly lacking the capital to secure more water, fertilizer, better seeds, and small machines which can triple and quadruple their output. (Nor have they the knowledge, resources, and political clout to form cooperatives and begin to gain some of the middlemen profits in agriculture.) But with extra investment — say, $25 billion from the developing world itself and $5 to $6 billion extra from wealthy lands — and with the kind of labour-intensive, soil-conserving, waste-avoiding communal or cooperative techniques of mainland China or Taiwan — an India or a Brazil could multiply fivefold the output per acre and begin to reverse the deadly drive in developing lands towards absolute food shortage. This investment strategy naturally includes land-use surveys and the preservation of the best farming land. It also implies a new approach to the distribution of population. To check the lemming-like movement to the biggest cities, the strategy demands the building up and reinforcement of intermediate market centres with schools, clinics, cooperative headquarters, banks, light industry and cultural opportunities. The farmers' work is supported and developed, their children cured and educated, the young people employed and entertained. If by the year 2000 India had a hundred new cities of a million instead of a hundred million in Bombay, New Delhi, and Calcutta, agriculture would be in a better condition and social disintegration much further off. But this kind of spatial planning for a better, more conserving, and more productive distribution of population and a more rational and workable system of settlements brings us slap up against the "shortage" and inadequacy already outlined: the inability of the market to deal with the problem of urban land use and planning.

Yet there is no reason to accept this obstacle as final. In fact, a number of communities are already experimenting with new approaches to land-use planning, and there are a whole range of new models which can be examined for better strategies and better results.

We can begin with the new concept of "development rights" in land. To own land in much of Europe no longer implies exclusive rights to the underlying minerals. There is no reason why development rights should not equally be reserved to the community. The Mr. Smiths or Joneses or Robinsons of the world's Bewbushes would own their land privately. But they could only *sell* it at a price fixed by an independent, public and responsible land commission. This separation of development rights from ownership would end the socially disrupting "something-for-nothing" aspect of uncontrolled land markets. Thereafter, the community could resell or lease the land for real development (drainage, lighting, laying out streets, building up houses and commercial premises and factories) and the gains from these sales would accrue to the community, as they do, for instance, to the Development Corporations of Britain's New Towns. Then the people who create the value by their needs get it back through their municipal government. Most New Towns actually show a profit. So do Swedish municipalities who rely mainly on leasing.

At the same time a policy of securing development rights for the community would not destroy the individual citizen's right to private ownership which remains an invaluable curb on arbitrary state power. And where, as in all communities, land has sometimes to be taken over for public purposes under such ancient laws as that of "eminent domain," the procedures could be hedged round with all the safeguards (such as agreed compensation and "due process of law") which prevail in most developed democracies.

When the land market is thus properly regulated, the process of planning for less disordered urban systems becomes possible. And there is some sign of an emerging pattern which can be both more conserving of the outer limits of resource use and more respectful of the inner limits of human dignity and self-respect. We can see one example of it in the thorough and careful replanning of the urban patterns in France. Another pattern, this time in the developing world, is provided by some of the strategies pursued in China.

Let us first look at France. The national plan is basically an elaborate effort to prevent the kind of convergence of population and economic activity which has brought together one-third of Japan's peoples and most of its industry in the single Tokkaido complex along Tokyo Bay. Paris had been heading in that direction for over a century. Now, however, eight other metropolitan areas* have been established with all forms of economic and social activity, including the growing tertiary and quaternary sectors. Round Paris itself the attempt is being made to take the pressure off the city by establishing new communities in which work and dwelling and services are grouped together in what has threatened to become undifferentiated "slurb." Cergy-Pontoise, St. Quentin-en-Yvelines, Evry, Melun-Sénart, and Marne La Vallée are the new, more compact communities in the basin of the Seine. At the same time, a ring of cities about 100 to 150 kilometers from Paris (Amiens, Rouen, Caen, Le Mans, Tours, Orleans, Rheims, and Troyes) will be expanded and revivified. All these communities will be linked to Paris by new forms of rapid transit. Meanwhile, parts of Paris itself are being rebuilt and jobs restored in order to prevent the tragedy of New York City in which, as the centre decays, the poor remain but the jobs — now even the high-income quaternary jobs — are moving out, taking their resources and the city's tax base with them.

In China, the policy of the last thirty years has been, on the whole, to push development back to the provincial centres, to decant a certain percentage of the population, particularly the young, into the countryside and the intermediate towns and, making agriculture the prime base of development, to give each province the range of agro-industries and light industries necessary for a measure of self-sufficiency. Where, as in Shanghai, the monster city had already been built in the semi-colonial era, the effort has been made to transform the various city quarters into communes with their own social services and patterns of work. The whole city has been surrounded by a belt of market gardens for intensive food production in order to cut down on the costs of long-distance supply. At the same time, in this first phase of modernization, the basic input of energy has been China's vast reserves of manpower. Only now, as industrial jobs are beginning to multiply, is mechanization and a larger use of artificial fertilizer advancing on the farms. Even so, the old conserving strategies (small-scale water schemes, massive tree planting, the use of all human and animal wastes, the pond-duck-fish cycle) are being carried on as steadily as ever.

Thus in both the French and the Chinese patterns, unlike as they are in scale

*The *metropoles d'équilibre* are Nancy and Metz (as twinned quaternary cities), Nantes and St. Nazaire (also twinned), Lille, Strasbourg, Lyon, Bordeaux, Toulouse, and Marseilles.

and degrees of development, an element of decentralization and concentration underlies the new urban structure. And one of the consequences is a far greater possibility of conserving energy and scarce resources. Another is to decrease the social barriers within the community. In China's radical revolution it is, of course, a fundamental aim to end the contrasts between town and country, peasant and worker, hand and brain. But in the much more complex position in France, the effort is also being made to safeguard or build up mixed communities, to end the ghetto-like segregation of peoples according to income (and sometimes, as with "guest workers," of colour), and to restore that mixture of classes and occupations and housing and entertainment which can still be found in smaller cities (many of which are to be enhanced and revivified under the French plan) and in the old urban "villages" like Montmartre — or London's Chelsea or Rome's Trastevere.

At the same time, this new approach can be, potentially, far more sparing of resources, far more respectful of the environment. The first and most obvious saving lies in transport. The incoherence of jobs and living in modern megalopolises virtually builds the private car into the system. People may not want so much mobility. But how otherwise will they gain access to the employment or the services or the homes or the culture that underpin their lives? But the new grouping of communities with quick, clean, and, if necessary, subsidized public transport can enable governments to push up the cost of the private car until it covers all its costs of pollution, killing, and mindless mobility; and, if necessary, they can prohibit its use altogether in areas which will be preserved for the pedestrian. As the mayor of Toronto remarked, everyone has a right to come to downtown Toronto but not to bring a ton of metal with him. Taking pressure off the roads makes it easier to do generally what is done in parts of Europe: that is, separate heavy trucks in their own traffic lanes and get the juggernauts away from travellers. Better siting of marshalling yards on the fringes of urban communities and greater flexibility in the assembly of freight trains would help to get bulky goods back to the railway and reverse the waste we have already noted; for example, 20 per cent of America's freight is being hauled with the use of 50 per cent of the energy. Since transport accounts for over 40 per cent of North America's energy budget, such savings would be a giant step towards cutting out the region's spendthrift waste and, with it, the compulsion towards a premature plunge to the nuclear economy.

A new, more compact settlement pattern would also contribute to another whole range of conserving strategies. In a number of European cities, energy is being saved by doing away with individual boilers in homes, workshops, and commercial buildings and replacing them by larger district units. But greater savings are possible if these units receive the waste heat from electricity generators and even more if municipal trash is used to supplement coal in the boilers. Here, indeed, a whole new range of conserving possibilities opens up. A new invention, the "fluidized bed combustor," blows hot air upwards through an inert bed of ash and coal and the temperature keeps the bed in a liquid state. The combustion process is so efficient that organic wastes can be added, thereby saving coal and virtually no pollutants are given off to the air.

But this is only one possible use of city wastes. Three-quarters of all waste is likely to be organic — wool, paper, wood, food (a recent estimate in the United States suggests that 15 per cent of all food is thrown away.) If this organic part is separated from the rest, it can, as in Leningrad or Holland, be used as compost for the fields. Or, as in Düsseldorf, it can become fuel for district heating. The other quarter — metals, glass — can be retrieved by a variety of technical means such as shredding, "air-classification," electrolysis, and so on. Then it can be resold as scrap. The state of Connecticut has set up its own Resources Recovery Authority, and nearly $30 million have been spent on a plant at Bridgeport to recover glass and metals and produce fuel supplements. Thus the energy saving is twofold. Old wastes take the place of new fuel; and glass and metal wastes require, as we have seen, up to 80 per cent less energy for their reprocessing. It is these new techniques and the whole range of efficient conservation that they open that has led American experts to argue that if $500 billion were invested in *saving* fuel, the result would be to make twice as much energy available as the investment of the same amount of dollars in conventional energy systems.

These techniques of turning wastes into valuable materials also affect directly the availability of food and water. Careful composting can enrich land and sustain yields on soils threatened with erosion. To keep all metals and organic substances out of the water courses means that the dilemmas now confronted by municipalities along the Rhine will no longer occur. Indeed, if one of the new techniques of reprocessing — the production of single-cell protein from organic wastes — proves successful, town councils may find themselves producing an animal feed which relieves the strain on the world's grain harvests but turns in a handsome profit as well. The Thames Water Authority is testing a method of using electrolysis to take metals and chemicals out of wastes and sterilize the remaining organic material. The resulting stew, which is 60 per cent pure protein and fat, is then mixed with chopped straw to make cattle feed which, sold at sixty dollars a ton (half the present price of feedstuffs) could earn a million dollars a year from a municipal plant serving, say, 250,000 people. Once again, we see the double gain: the sewage is kept out of the water, and the organic materials are reused in the earth's cycle of nutrition. It is these perspectives that can give us hope that the outer limits of our planetary inheritance need not constrain us, provided we turn from our wasteful, careless, and demanding ways of life and practise instead the thrift and good husbandry which, traditionally, have been the hallmarks of genuine civilization.

Can we go further and see in these new possibilities some hope for man's inner limits as well, the need for dignity and respect, the longing for a more equal sharing in the benefits of existence? Here we come to the third of our three issues of reform: the kinds of personal and communal commitment that can make possible ways of life that are at the same time more generous and more conserving. It is, at least, clear that our present pattern of settlements (with the tendency to segregate the poor and unskilled in the decaying cores of developed cities or the desperate shanty towns of the developing world) tends to accentuate differences, underline fear and resentment, and reinforce barriers by physically separating groups and classes from each other. The strategy of restoring city centres, building up more close-knit communities for living and working, lessening the strain of unwanted mobility, and, within these communities, using every means of policy to encourage thrift and conservation, could have the effect of producing calmer and wiser ways of life. There is surely something of the same kind of mindless egoism behind the readiness on the one hand to foul a stream and chuck away rubbish and, on the other, indifference and contempt for strangers or the less fortunate or those from different cultures or those handicapped by age and ignorance. If we are greedy in one thing, the chances are we shall be greedy in others. "More for me" at all costs can underlie both environmental degradations and social tensions. It is at least certain that without some commitment to wider loyalties — to the neighbourhood, to the city, to the planet itself — the present risk of a collision course between needs and numbers does not seem to fend off.

It is here, surely, that Canada has a special role to play. It is, on a per capita basis, one of the richest nations in the world. It will be richer still when two hundred miles of exclusive economic control over oceanic resources are added to all its shores. At the same time, it is not big enough to scare anyone or to risk the criticism that it is throwing its weight about. If it could form a coalition of wise and progressive middle-sized states to work for a better balance in the distribution of world resources, for agreed strategies for development and investment, for a minimum standard — of food, of water, of literacy, of health, shelter and work — for all mankind, it could achieve the same role in planetary society as was played in the early days of the technological order by such giant figures of reform as Lord Shaftesbury, Edwin Chadwick, and Benjamin Disraeli. The evils of nineteenth-century Britian, divided between "the nation of the rich and the nation of the poor," were not much less acute than those of our contemporary world. But two forces made for creative change; the conscience of the fortunate to whom the reformers appealed, and the growing strength of the poor themselves — the union, the voters — who began to realize the effectiveness of common action. Is it inconceivable that such a coincidence of forces should begin to nudge the world today away from collision and towards a more rational course?

The revolt of the dispossessed is a fact. But is there a conscience to which enlightened governments can appeal? History does not give us a wholly negative answer. All the great ethical traditions of mankind had their origin in the millennium before the birth of Christ when the first efforts of civilization — in the world's great river valleys of Egypt and Mesopotamia, North India and China — were collapsing in a welter of war and imperialism, of civil war with bestial cruelty and corruption. These times of questioning were well summed up in the fourth century BC by a Chinese nobleman exiled from the court during China's long feudal wars. He cried out in grief and frustration:

> The times are upside down. The wing of a cicada weighs a thousand pounds. The jewelled cup is used as a cooking pot. *How* can I distinguish right from wrong?

But the answer given in all the world's religions is the same: greed and power are not the ultimate answer to our drives and desires, and we ourselves, for happiness, for survival itself, must learn to recognize and accept in our own hearts the inner and the outer limits — the respect for other selves and their needs, restraint and modesty in our own. Once again, a Chinese voice gives us perhaps the most complete summary of an answer that is everywhere the same. The great sage Lao Tse said:

> These are my three treasures. Guard them well. The first is compassion, the second is frugality, the third is the desire *not* to be foremost under heaven.

If the earlier times of trouble could cause such reassessments, may we not hope for a similar enlightenment in our even more troubled age? We have gone from the candle to the atom, from the village to the moon in not much more than a century. And now we have the power to destroy ourselves, our cities, and our planet and to wipe out human existence itself. The very extremity of our peril is, perhaps, our greatest hope that we shall begin "to guard our treasures" and to learn all over again "to distinguish right from wrong."

Notes on Contributors

HUMPHREY CARVER was educated at Oxford and the Architectural Association in London, and has taught and practised in Toronto. He joined CMHC in 1948 and served for twenty years. Carver is a former president of the Canadian Institute of Planners, is honorary vice-president of the Canadian Council of Social Development and is an honorary member of the Canadian Society of Landscape Architects. He is the author of *Housing for Canadians* and *Cities in the Suburbs* and has just completed a widely acclaimed autobiographical work, *Compassionate Landscape*.

JEAN GOTTMANN, an internationally renowned geographer and teacher, has written more than a dozen books since 1942, including *Megalopolis* in 1961. A study of the urbanized northeastern seaboard of the United States, *Megalopolis* is credited with changing the entire concept of city development and planning. He is professor of geography and head of the School of Geography, University of Oxford and Directeur d'Etudes (en détachement), Ecole des Hautes Etudes en Sciences Sociales (Sorbonne), Paris.

LOUIS-EDMOND HAMELIN, professor of geography at Université Laval, was the founder and former director of the Centre d'Etudes Nordique at Laval. He has served on the Northwest Territories Council.

LORD LLEWELYN-DAVIES was educated in Trinity College, Cambridge, and Beaux Arts in Paris and the Architectural Association in London. Active in many professional organizations, he was created a life peer in 1963 for his professional and academic work. During the past ten years he has been associated with the University of London as head of the Bartlett School of Architecture, professor of town planning and ultimately dean of its new School of Environmental Studies. He has pioneered development plans for "new towns" in Britain, the United States and elsewhere.

TREVOR LLOYD, professor of geography at McGill and a former chairman of that department, has travelled widely in northern lands, particularly in Canada, Scandinavia, and Greenland, and has visited the Soviet Union seven times, most recently in 1973 when he crossed Siberia and studied new settlements in the Lena Valley.

GEORGE MUHOHO. Representing his native Kenya at the United Nations for the forthcoming United Nations Conference on Human Settlements, he was elected by the participating countries to chair the preparatory committee responsible for developing agenda and procedures for the Habitat 1976 conference.

ENRIQUE PENALOSA. After a distinguished career in the public service of his native Colombia, he served with the International Development Bank and was appointed secretary-general of the United Nations Conference on Human Settlements: Habitat 1976, in 1973.

JOHN PLATT, a physicist by training, had a long teaching career at the University of Chicago before going to the University of Michigan where he is now with the Mental Health Research Institute. At Michigan he began to work on general systems theory as applied to the problems of science and society. The author of numerous articles on great social changes, he is presently completing a book *On Social Transformation*.

JOAN ROBINSON, professor emerita of economics, Cambridge University, is well-known for her extensive publications and forceful views on Marxian economics and the recent developmental progress of China. Her dozen books include *Economics of Imperfect Competition*, *Theory of Employment*, *The Accumulation of Capital*, and *Theory of Economic Growth*.

K. C. SIVARAMAKRISHNAN. After two degrees at Madras University, he joined the Indian Administrative Service in 1958 and began a career which led to specialization in urban planning and administration. He has been instrumental in the development of "new towns" in India and upon creation of the Calcutta Metropolitan Development Authority in 1970, became its chief executive officer. He has served in advisory capacities on the management of urban growth to the United Nations and to the World Bank.

AUSTIN TETTEH is dean of the Faculty of Architecture and Planning at the Kumasi Institute of Science and Technology in Ghana, a graduate of the Universities of Ghana and Cornell in sociology and Pennsylvania in planning. He headed Ghana's first demographic census in 1960 and since then has had a distinguished career as teacher and professional in his country's public service.

BARBARA WARD, LADY JACKSON is well known for her many publications dealing with international ecnomic development and other Third World issues. With René Dubos, she co-authored *Only One Earth*, which served as the unofficial background paper for the U.N. Conference on the Environment held in Stockholm in 1972. Her most recent volume, *The Home of Man*, served a similar purpose for the U.N. Habitat Conference in Vancouver. She was created a life peer in 1976 and was awarded an honorary doctorate at U.B.C. in the same year.